Swimm ... ching

This book ha ... te Course.

The content illustrate ... ding will inevitably

This publication h ... nd Coaching –
Level One – first pu ... of the text of the

The 'ASA' Teache ... to teach/coach

Published by ASA Swimming Times Ltd

Swimming Teaching and Coaching

Level One

Author:
Lynn Hogarth

The author wishes to acknowledge contributions from ASA Teaching and Coaching – Level 1 (1991):

Anne Craddock	Rick Cross
Cliff Dedynski	Alan Donlan
Bill Furniss	Colin Hardy
Joan Harrison	Tony Holmyard
Colin Lee	Mike Seddon
Nick Sellwood	David Sparkes

and the help given by:

Phil Mynott	Photographer
Empire Leisure	Use of facilities
Champion Coaching – Cambridge	Provision of swimmers
City of Cambridge Swimming Club	Provision of swimmers

The Amateur Swimming Association, Harold Fern House, Derby Square, Loughborough, Leicestershire LE11 5AL
Tel: 01509 618700 Fax: 01509 618701

First published 1998

ISBN 0-900052-48-1

Printed by Echo Press Limited, Loughborough

Published by: Swimming Times Limited 1998

Wherever the pronoun "he" has been used it should be interpreted as applying equally to men and women as appropriate.

Contents

CHAPTER 1

HEALTH, SAFETY AND HYGIENE

Introduction

The importance of a healthy lifestyle has been much emphasised by the medical profession and various health education groups, particularly in more recent years. One of the areas which contributes to healthy lifestyle is exercise, and swimming is particularly appropriate as it is known as an activity which gives all round benefit.

Concerns for safety should never take anything but first priority for the teacher/coach. This chapter will assist the teacher/coach in ascertaining good safe practices as well as addressing a number of safety issues related to the swimming pool environment.

Health

It is now firmly established that anyone wanting a healthy lifestyle should take part in some form of regular physical activity. The type and level of this activity must take into account the age, general fitness and medical condition of the individual. One form of exercise which might be appropriate to one person in an age-group may be quite inappropriate for another of the same age. Not least among the benefits of swimming is the development and maintenance of good health for everyone, regardless of age, type and physical condition, including those with some disability. These benefits include:

- improvements in the condition of the heart and cardiovascular system in general
- increased physical capacity
- improvement in the control of the individual's body composition by helping to burn up some of the fat stores
- contribution to helping control stress
- the promotion of a feeling of physical well being
- a long term reduction in the risk of developing coronary heart disease

The advantages of swimming arise from the following two factors:

- the body is supported by the upthrust of the water
- the push and pull forces created by the muscles are directed against water rather than a solid medium, thereby reducing the risk of injury to ligaments and joints

Regular exercise benefits the strength, stamina and suppleness of the body (often known as the three S's. Table 1.1 shows the comparison with swimming and other sports. It is clear to see that swimming rates highly in every area.

Table 1-1

Swimming - The Only Four Star Exercise

Look at the guide below to see which activities give you the three S's. If you want all round fitness look for the activities with the most stars.

Activities	Stamina	Suppleness	Strength
Badminton	★★	★★★	★★
Canoeing	★★★	★★	★★★
Climbing stairs	★★★	★	★★
Cricket	★	★★	★
Cycling (hard)	★★★★	★★	★★★
Dancing (ballroom)	★	★★★	★
Dancing (disco)	★★★	★★★★	★
Digging (garden)	★★★	★★	★★★★
Football	★★★	★★★	★★★
Golf	★	★★	★
Gymnastics	★★	★★★★	★★★
Hill walking	★★★	★	★★
Housework (moderate)	★	★★	★
Jogging	★★★★	★★	★★
Judo	★★	★★★★	★★
Mowing the lawn by hand	★★	★	★★★
Rowing	★★★★	★★★	★★★★
Sailing	★★	★★	★★
Squash	★★★	★★★	★★
Swimming (hard)	★★★★	★★★★	★★★★
Tennis	★★	★★★	★★
Walking (briskly)	★★	★	★
Weightlifting	★	★	★★★★
Yoga	★	★★★★	★

★ no real effect ★★ beneficial effect
★★★ very good effect ★★★★ excellent effect

This table should only be used as a rough guide. A great deal will depend on how much effort is put into the activity.

(Table taken from the Health Education Council 'Look after yourself' pamphlet)

Strength

Muscles which are not used tend to deteriorate and waste away., i.e. "use it or lose it" theory. Regular exercise reduces the likelihood of this happening and maintains or improves the size, strength and efficiency of muscles and muscle groups.

Stamina

People who take little or no exercise usually become breathless quickly when involved in any sudden exertion; they experience a rapid pulse rate which takes a considerable time to recover to its norm and they tire easily, requiring frequent rests. Regular exercise increases the efficiency of the heart, blood and circulation and breathing which lead to improved stamina. A further effect of this improved efficiency is the reduction in the risk of heart disease.

Suppleness

Joints which do not experience their full range of movement regularly tend to stiffen - a condition which normally becomes worse with age and may lead to greatly reduced mobility and problems with posture. Regular exercise considerably delays the onset of these conditions.

When considering a healthy lifestyle there are additional factors other than the three S's which help individuals to remain healthy:

Rest

The swimming teacher/coach should be mindful of the appropriate amount and quality of rest and sleep. The requirements for rest differ in individual people and, therefore, it is not possible to set hard and fast rules which apply in all cases. How much rest somebody requires within a swimming lesson situation will be affected by the general levels of fitness of each individual. The swimming teacher/coach should watch individuals closely within the lesson to ascertain the need to provide any additional rest that may be required. This is particularly important with groups of adults attending swimming lessons who may have done little exercise previously, or pupils who suffer with conditions which affect their breathing (e.g. asthma). It may also be necessary for the teacher/coach to enquire about the pupil's sleeping habits when trying to ascertain why the swimmer is displaying signs of lethargy which are not normally observed in this particular individual.

Diet

A balanced diet is important to everyone whether they take an active part in a sporting activity or not. Much of the energy used by individuals comes indirectly from the food eaten. Therefore it is particularly important that the high level competitive swimmer keeps a close check on their diet as they will be using large energy stores during each training session. For people learning to swim close scrutiny of diet is less important and a good balanced diet should suffice.

To achieve this balance it is important to control within reasonable limits the intake of the three main food types, carbohydrate proteins and fats.

- Carbohydrates - the main source of energy for the body is obtained from carbohydrates which are found in starchy and sugary foods such as potatoes, pasta, bread and rice.

- Proteins - the body requires protein for replacement of tissues worn out by normal body processes. In addition children need a significant amount of protein to foster healthy growth. Foods such as meat, fish and dairy products are high in protein.

- Fats - The body stores energy in the form of fat, but it will only be utilised when exercising at very low levels or when all other stores have been utilised. It is the least essential of the three main food types and its intake should be kept under strict control.

A good balanced diet would contain the percentage of carbohydrate, protein and fat shown in the first pie chart, whilst the diet of an high level competitive swimmer who is training frequently (every day) should have the balance shown in the second pie chart.

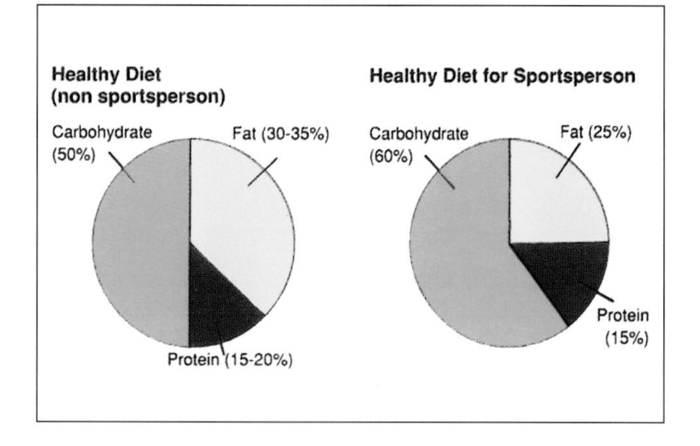

It is now very easy for any individual to monitor their intake as many food products purchased from leading supermarket chains include nutritional information on the packaging.

The other consideration when participating in exercise is the appropriate time to eat. Ideally a period of at least one hour should be allowed between eating and exercise. This allows food to be partially or wholly digested prior to beginning physical activity. It is also beneficial to top up energy stores as soon after the completion of exercise as possible. A snack or meal which is high in carbohydrate will replenish the energy stores most effectively.

Safety Working Environment

In 1988 a document called *'Safety in Swimming Pools'* was published jointly by the *Sports Council* and the *Health and Safety Commission.* This report set out guidelines for the safe use of pools. It has since been followed by two other reports *'Diving into Swimming Pools'* (ISRM 1990) and *'Safe Supervision for Teaching and Coaching Swimming' (ASA/ISRM/ISTC/RLSS 1996).* All of these documents seek to make the swimming pool a safer place and the teacher/coach should ensure he is familiar with the general content and have a good working knowledge of the areas related to the activities of teaching and coaching.

'Safety in Swimming Pools' recommends that all of those involved in the teaching/coaching of swimming are strongly advised to hold a life saving qualification appropriate to their level of responsibility. The *'RLSS Rescue Test for Teachers'* is designed specifically for those involved in teaching/coaching. The ASA recommends all swimming teachers/coaches, involved in any facet of the sport, gain and keep up to date

some form of lifesaving qualification. Swimming clubs are advised to monitor continuously the level of life saving expertise of their teachers, coaches and helpers.

The *'Safety in Swimming Pools'* report considered all aspects of pool operation and recommended all pools should produce a Normal Operating Procedure (NOP) and an Emergency Action Plan (EAP). The teacher/coach should obtain a copy of these plans from the pool and develop a good working knowledge of them.

Every pool should have a written Normal Operating Procedure which sets out the way in which the pool will operate on a day to day basis. The list below is a helpful check list of key areas which should be included:

(a) details of the pool, including for example pool dimensions, and a plan of the building
(b) potential risk factors
(c) dealing with the public (safety education: controlling access; etc.)
(d) maximum bather loads
(e) first aid supplies and training
(f) conditions of hire to outside organisations
(g) details of alarm systems and any emergency equipment; maintenance arrangements
(h) lifeguard duties as well as any special supervision requirements for equipment etc.
(i) systems of work, including
    (i) lines of supervision
    (ii) call out procedures
    (iii) work rotation (if applicable);
    (iv) maximum poolside work times;
(j) lifeguard training
(k) number of lifeguards during particular activities

('Safety in Swimming Pools' - Sports Council 1988)

In contrast to the Normal Operating Procedures the Emergency Action Plan specifies, in detail, the actions to be taken in the event of every type of foreseeable emergency. It should show clearly the role of every member of staff, including teachers/coaches during an organised swimming tuition session. The list below gives some examples of the foreseeable emergencies the plan may cover:

(a) overcrowding
(b) disorderly behaviour
(c) lack of water clarity
(d) outbreak of fire (or sounding of alarm to evacuate buildings)
(e) bomb threat
(f) lighting failure
(g) structural failure
(h) emission of toxic gases
(i) serious injury of a bather
(j) discovery of casualty in the water

('Safety in Swimming Pools' - Sports Council 1988)

Whilst it is desirable for every teacher/coach to have a copy of the NOP and EAP, this is not always possible. If these documents are not available, the teacher/coach should ensure they know the following information:

- location of emergency signalling equipment, e.g. alarm, klaxon
- location of rescue equipment, e.g. pole, ropes, throw bags
- location of first aid, including resuscitation equipment where appropriate
- location of any duty supervisor
- location of nearest telephone outside line
- telephone number of accident/emergency services
- procedure for reporting/recording accidents

Use of Electrical Equipment – increasingly the teacher/coach may find himself utilising electrical equipment around the poolside. Portable public address equipment is becoming increasingly popular within swimming lessons and aquafit sessions.

Water and electricity are known not to mix well and for this reason extra care is needed when using electrical equipment. Some key points include:

- all mains electrical equipment, including portable, should

be kept in a dry area at least 3.5 metres from the poolside
- all mains electrical equipment should be protected by a residual current device
- trailing cables, etc., must be specifically designed for the purpose
- all electrical equipment should be properly supported
- pool managers should be consulted before any electrical equipment is used on/near pool surrounds
- **under no circumstances should swimmers in the water touch electrical equipment**

Rescue Techniques

As a matter of principle, the teacher/coach should avoid going into the water in an emergency. This will reduce the risk of the teacher/coach getting into difficulties and permits a measure of control to be maintained over the rest of the class. However, where essential for the saving of life, the teacher/coach must be prepared to go into the water and effect a rescue. It is useful for the teacher/coach to be familiar with common dry rescue techniques, the following are just two examples of methods which can be effected in a swimming pool environment.

Reaching rescue – a reaching rescue is both safe for the rescuer and effective for the casualty. It is particularly effective for weak or non swimmers who are in difficulties close to the pool side. The rescue aids used may be rigid e.g. a pole or non rigid e.g. a towel. To perform a reaching rescue a few simple rules should be followed.

The rescuer should:

- attract the attention of the casualty and give reassurance
- keep his centre of gravity as low as possible (lying down or kneeling)
- keep the casualty under close observation
- attain a comfortable secure position
- reach out with the aid and tell the casualty to grab hold of it
- pull the casualty to safety with a steady movement

Throwing rescue – ideally a throwing rescue would be performed with a rope. If this is also weighted by a floating object (Torpedo buoy) it can generally be thrown with greater accuracy. In order to perform successfully the rescuer should:

- attract the attention of the casualty and give reassurance
- tell the casualty to expect something to be thrown
- avoid standing to close to the edge of the pool
- coil and throw the rope
- instruct the casualty to hold the rope with both hands
- pull the casualty to safety with a steady movement

Safety Code

It is important to establish a clear safety code of practices with the pupils in each of the swimming classes. This code should not only set a standard for the lesson but also reinforce good practice whenever they visit the pool.

In some cases, for example schools swimming lessons, safety considerations may have been discussed as a classroom activity prior to arriving for the first lesson, it is still important for the teacher/coach to outline procedures again as some pupils may have missed the initial lesson or forgotten elements of it.

Some of the areas a teacher/coach should be addressing in a code of practice are:

- pupils not to enter water without direct permission
- pupils not to leave the class without permission
- any whistle code which may be used for signalling
- the importance of wearing appropriate swimwear
- procedures relating to the wearing of jewellery
- safe methods of entry and exit
- respect for other pupils in the class
- checking their path is clear before beginning to swim (particularly on their back)

Swimming Ability

When meeting pupils for the first time it is important that the teacher/coach makes a personal check on their ability. Information from other sources can be misleading (e.g. badges on costumes, parents/guardians opinion)

Illness & Accidents

Opinions of whether pupils should swim while suffering from certain common medical conditions vary, and therefore, where there is any doubt, professional advice should be sought from a family doctor or school nurse. It is preferable to exclude the pupil from swimming until medical advice has been obtained rather than risk additional complications. There are, however, some generally accepted conditions which should lead to exclusion, these include:

- infectious diseases
- open wounds
- coughs, colds and related infections such as catarrh, sinusitis
- sore eyes
- ear infections

Veruccas and Athletes foot are two conditions which give rise to differing opinions. Modern views on verruccas indicate that the infectious warts can only be transmitted from the poolside and not in the water. Therefore, the pupil could wear a poolside shoe or an appropriate verruca sock whilst walking around the poolside but this could be removed once in the water. However it may be easier for the verucca sock to remain on the infected foot throughout the lesson. With regard to athlete's foot there are still differing views to the effect of swimming with this condition. Although the spread of infection can be stopped by the wearing of a rubber sock, the chemicals in the swimming pool water may have an irritating effect on the condition.

There are a number of medical conditions which do not prohibit a pupil from taking part in a lesson but which the teacher/coach should be aware of prior to taking the swimmer for the first time. Awareness of these conditions will allow the teacher/coach to plan the lesson accordingly taking into account individual circumstances. Some examples of such conditions are:

- epilepsy
- diabetes
- asthma
- arthritis
- immediate post operative conditions
- shoulder injury
- knee injury

Ideally a pupil attending swimming lessons should be given an opportunity to notify the facility of these conditions (perhaps on the lesson enrolment form). This information should then be relayed to the teacher/coach prior to the first lesson. In the case of schools swimming lessons it is likely that the class teacher will be able to provide the necessary information on each pupil.

Accidents

In most cases there will be pool procedures to deal with accidents in the pool environment, and the teacher/coach may only need to ascertain that the casualty is brought to safety and appropriate help called.

The teacher/coach constant awareness of safe working procedures helps to avoid accidents, e.g., running on poolside, correct water depth for activities, maintenance of class control throughout the session, particular care on entries and class well spaced.

The list below includes some examples of accidents which may occur:

- hitting head on hard surface
- suspected fracture
- deep cut - glass in shower
- grazes
- bruising

All accidents which occur in and around the swimming pool should be recorded. Most pools will have some form of accident book or accident form which will need to be completed by either the teacher/coach or an appropriate member of staff.

Child Protection

Child abuse is a very emotive and difficult subject. As many of the swimming lessons taught involve children it may be possible that a teacher/coach could come into contact with a child who they think is being harmed.

Many sporting governing bodies are now aware that they have a role to play in protecting children from abuse and there are a number of information leaflets and booklets available to assist the teacher/coach in understanding their role.

Child abuse can take many forms:

Physical abuse, where adults:

– physically hurt or injure children (e.g. by hitting, shaking, squeezing, biting or burning)
– give children alcohol, inappropriate drugs or poison
– attempt to suffocate or drown children

In sport situations, physical abuse might occur when the nature and intensity of training exceeds the capacity of the child's immature and growing body.

Neglect includes situations in which adults:

- fail to meet a child's basic physical needs (e.g. for food, warm clothing)
- consistently leave children alone and unsupervised
- fail or refuse to give children love, affection or attention

Neglect in a sports situation might also occur if a teacher/coach fails to ensure children are safe or exposes them to undue cold or risk of injury.

Sexual abuse. Boys and girls are sexually abused when adults (male or female) use them to meet their own sexual needs. This could include:

- full sexual intercourse, masturbation, oral sex, fondling
- showing children pornographic books, photographs or videos, or taking pictures for pornographic purposes.

Sports situations which involve physical contact (e.g. supporting or guiding children) could potentially create situations where sexual abuse may go unnoticed. Abusive situations may also occur if adults misuse their power over young people.

Emotional abuse can occur in a number of ways. For example, where:

- there is persistent lack of love or affection
- there is constant overprotection which prevents children socialising
- children are frequently being shouted at or taunted
- there is neglect, physical or sexual abuse

Emotional abuse in sport might also include situations where parents or the teacher/coach subjects children to constant criticism, bullying or unrealistic pressure to perform to high expectations.

There are currently two publications which consider the role of the teacher/coach in protecting children. Every teacher/coach should ensure they are familiar with the information contained in these texts before taking any action in this area: The publications are:

Protecting Children From Abuse - (Sports Council/Childline/NCF/ASFG B/NSPCC - 1996)

Child Protection Procedures in swimming - (ASFGB/Sports Council/NCF/NSPCC - 1996)

The ASA Teacher Certificate Log Book also includes a policy document related to this area.

Code of Ethics

The ASA now publishes a Code of Ethics for the swimming teacher/coach. It is expected that ASA qualified teachers/coaches will work to these standards.

The purpose of the Code of Ethics is to establish and maintain standards for teachers/coaches and to inform and protect members of the public using their services. The code of ethics comprise such values as:

- integrity
- responsibility
- competence
- confidentiality

Copies of the code of ethics are available from the ASA or ISTC. A copy is included in the ASA Teacher Certificate Log Book.

CHAPTER 2

PERSONAL SURVIVAL SKILLS

Introduction

Swimming is a life skill, and as part of any comprehensive swimming programme it is important for the skills of personal survival to be taught. The Amateur Swimming Association has recognised the importance of the development of these skills by including two awards (Personal Survival 1 & 2) within its awards scheme. The teacher/coach should include the skills of personal survival in progressive stages of the learners' development to assist pupils in being safe, both in and out of the swimming pool environment. The competence level of the pupil can then be rewarded through the appropriate ASA Awards.

Survival in Cold Water

In recent years there has been a considerable amount of research in the subject of survival in cold water and it has been firmly established that the main consideration for the casualty should be the conservation of body heat. When the water temperature is below 25° Celsius any movement carried out by a human being in that water will lead to a drop in the body temperature. It should be noted that the water temperature around the British Isles rarely reaches 15° Celsius.

Body Cooling System

Exercise increases the blood flow to the body surface, the heat in this blood is then removed by the cold water and the cooled blood is subsequently left to complete its circulation through the body. The more movement generated the more heat lost, causing a gradual decrease in the core temperature.

Assessing the Situation

Clearly each individual incident needs to be assessed and the appropriate action taken. If the casualty slips into a river or lake and is still close to land, in the vast majority of cases, would be able to swim the short distance to safety. However if an accident were to occur at a reasonable distance from land the casualty would need to consider their actions in relation to their knowledge of water safety.

Personal Survival Knowledge

The teacher/coach plays an important role in developing the pupils' understanding of:

- the dangers of cold water
- their ability to assess the situation
- the application of their knowledge of principles of personal survival.

When teaching personal survival skills it is not sufficient for the teacher/coach just to teach the techniques involved in survival. The teacher/coach should also develop the pupils' knowledge and awareness of the effects of cold water, thus allowing them to apply this to real situations effectively.

Hypothermia

Hypothermia is a cooling of the body's core temperature. This begins to occur in water temperatures of below 25° celsius. Pupils should be made aware that the ambient temperature in swimming pools is far different from the reality of falling into cold water and it should be strongly emphasised that survival practices carried out in a swimming pool are designed to mirror the real situation.

There are a number of recognised factors which lead to heat loss:

- lack of subcutaneous fat
  The fat around the body provides an insulating layer. Most teachers/coaches will be familiar with the pupil who is very thin and gets cold very quickly in a swimming lesson of 30 minutes duration held in the comfort of a swimming pool.
- lack of suitable clothing
  Clothing maintains a warm layer of air between its inner surface and the skin. Whilst it is important for the swimmer to retain clothing careful consideration must also be given to the nature of the clothing retained.
- low water temperature
  Heat is conducted from the person to the water.

- physical exertion
  Increasing blood flow to outer parts of the body where it is more easily cooled.
- movement in the water
  Causing the loss of the warm layer of air and allowing cold water to circulate between body and clothing.

When the teacher/coach is conducting personal survival lessons, and advising pupils of the effects of hypothermia, the following points should also be remembered:

- children cool more rapidly than adults (because they are generally thinner)
- girls cool more slowly than boys (because normally they have more fat).

The teacher/coach and pupils should also be aware of the progressive symptoms of hypothermia:

- shivering
- change in behaviour
- slurring speech
- lack of co-ordination/balance
- persistent muscular rigidity
- unconsciousness

If the teacher/coach or pupil begin to witness these progressive symptoms in a swimmer the following action should be taken:

- send for help
- ensure own safety
- remove casualty from water
- cover casualty including head
- create shelter if in open conditions
- carefully move to warm environment
- if conscious – warm, sweet drink, warm bath
- dry clothing
- unconscious casualty – warm cover – recovery position

The skills of Personal Survival

There are a number of basic skills and techniques related to survival in cold water. All of these skills relate in some way to the retention of body heat. The core skills, to maximise the retention of body heat, are:

- Treading water
- HELP
- HUDDLE

The techniques involved in effectively conducting these skills should be the backbone of any Personal Survival Lesson.

Entering the Water – in many cases, the skills of entering the water will not be necessary as the casualty will find themselves in the water as a result of the accident. However, in some situations it may be necessary to enter the water voluntarily.

Climb or Slide in – the safest method of entry is to climb or slide into the water. When executing this action the casualty should be continuously aware of hidden dangers below the surface.

Straddle Jump – if it is necessary to jump in to the water a straddle jump should be performed. The straddle jump is intended to keep the casualties head above the water and give the shallowest method of entry from a jump.

Rather than being a jump it is much more of a step from the side. The following key points of technique should be taught.

- standing with chest leaning forward, chin pushed forward
- one foot on the pool edge the other approximately 0.5m behind

- arms bent at elbow and held at shoulder height
- step off poolside with back foot
- maintain the leaning forward position
- keep the legs apart
- on entry press the arms down on the water
- look forwards and upwards

The technique can be considered to have been mastered successfully if the points above have been achieved, and the pupil's head remains out of the water.

Tuck Jump – where it is not possible to slide into the water, the entry should be made from the lowest possible height, by jumping using a tuck jump. The following points of technique should be taught:

- step away from the starting point
- draw up knees to the chest until seat and feet are at same level
- wrap the hands around the legs to hold position securely

Treading Water – the prime aim of treading water should be to keep the swimmer in one place, in an upright position with the head above the water. The action of the limbs should be minimal with no more effort than that required to prevent sinking.

A number of variations of leg action can be adopted and each pupil should find the kick most suited to their needs. The recognised actions are:

- breaststroke type leg action
- cycling type action
- flutter kick
- eggbeater kick

The arm action should offer additional support to the leg action. The hands should perform a sculling action just under the surface of the water.

A number of practices which can be used to teach/coach treading water are:

- standing in shallow water and sculling
- leg actions holding rail
- leg actions within depth resting on two floats
- leg actions holding rail with one hand and sculling with other
- leg actions holding float in one hand and sculling with other
- complete action

Heat Escape Lessening Posture (HELP) – this posture is recognised as being the most effective way to prevent heat loss. The principle involved is that those parts of the body which lose heat most easily should be protected as effectively as possible, whilst keeping the head out of the water. The posture is most easily and effectively achieved when a good quality life jacket is being worn, however the HELP position can be adopted whenever floating objects are available.

The key points of the HELP position are given below:

- head clear of the water

- lower limbs pressed together tightly
- upper arms held close to the sides of the body
- body suspended straight downwards or leaning slightly backwards

When teaching/coaching the skills of HELP it is important for the teacher/coach to stress the need to retain heat in cold water. The teacher/coach should also relate this to hypothermia.

Huddle – where several people are involved simultaneously in an emergency they may assist each other in conserving heat by huddling together as closely as possible. The effectiveness of the Huddle will depend upon the type of floating support available.

If casualties are wearing life jackets a tight circle will probably be most effective. Other items such as lifebelts or large blocks of timber can be used.

Swimming in Clothes – the technique of swimming in clothes needs to be taught as it may differ considerably from other swimming styles or techniques used within an ordinary swimming lesson. First and foremost the pupils must understand the need to conserve energy, and consequently body heat. Actions used should involve gentle swimming movements, for example it would be more acceptable for the pupil to use a breaststroke type arm action than an overwater recovery, as it would involve a greater effort to get the clothed arms out of the water and as a result of lifting the arms out of the water the body is more likely to sink underwater. For safety reasons it is much better for the swimmer to swim on their front, this allows them to see where they are going and enables them to keep their head out of the water more easily.

Climbing Out – the technique of climbing out is an important one as many accidents in water occur in situations where the water level is below the land. The following technique points need to be taught to the pupil:

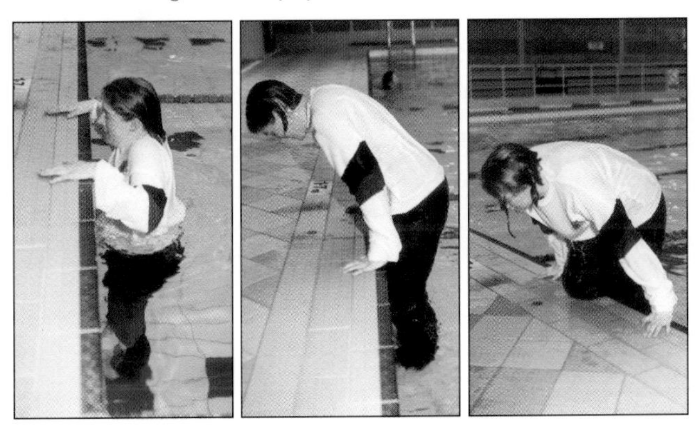

- place palms of hands on top of wall
- give a strong breaststroke leg kick downwards
- whilst kicking press with hands and allow elbows to bend
- straighten and lock elbows
- lift one leg and put knee on wall
- lean slightly forwards and lift other leg on to wall

Teaching Personal Survival

Many of the skills used in personal survival will be learnt as part of a normal swimming programme, the ability to float and swim with minimum energy expenditure, the techniques of sliding in and climbing out and the ability to tread water and scull. Progress to swimming longer distances can be done through stroke development lessons. HELP & HUDDLE practices can be done with a variety of different floating objects with the teacher/coach guiding pupils to discover the best floats.

Occasionally a whole lesson or a course of lessons may be devoted to survival skills. The Scheme of Work for courses such as this is often planned around one of the ASA Personal Survival Awards. Before attempting a comprehensive programme of personal survival pupils should be competent in a variety of strokes and able to swim a distance of at least 400m.

In the early lessons skills should be practised in swimwear with a gradual introduction of clothing. Once the basic survival skills have been learned, and the pupils are fully aware of the reality of survival in cold water, a series of realistic simulations should be used to develop understanding and application of the real life situation. A course of four personal survival session plans are included at the end of this chapter *(Session plans taken from "The Competent Swimmer – An Illustrated Guide To Teaching Further Practices" courtesy of Anne Eakin, ASA Principal Tutor).*

Summary

It is essential for the teacher to remember that:

- the skills must be thoroughly developed in the swimming pool environment in order for them to be carried over in to a real situation effectively.
- the pupil must understand the principles behind survival in cold water, and should be able to confirm their understanding through decision making exercises in simulated situations, and through responses to questions related to safety.

Personal survival lessons can be great fun but the teacher/coach must be constantly aware of the real dangers in and around water.

Prevention is always better than cure and the following safety guidelines will help to prevent unnecessary accidents:

Do not:

- swim alone unless competent help is at hand
- bathe in areas where red flags or other warnings are displayed
- fool about at the sides of rivers, lakes, canals or quay sides
- venture on frozen ponds without making sure that they are safe
- float out to sea on airbeds
- go out in small boats without wearing a life jacket

Personal Survival

First Lesson.........

Setting The Scene: Explain that for the next four weeks they should imagine that the pool is the sea or a lake, and the water is so cold they would quickly get a headache if they swam in it.

"Imagine you are on a boat trip, and one of the passengers is an Olympic swimmer. The boat hits a submerged log, turns over, and everyone is thrown into the water."

"It may seem strange, but the Olympic swimmer would probably not survive much longer than an average swimmer like yourself. Why? The COLD WATER!"

The "Core" temperature.

"Think of the winter, when people can't start their cars because the engines are too cold. Well, we have an engine too, made up of our heart, lungs and liver, and it will stop too if it gets too cold.

The freezing water takes away the heat from our skin, and our engine gets colder and colder until it stops. The Olympic swimmer has just the same engine as you, and his will stop too!

It is very important to keep your head out of this very cold water. Why? Place your finger on top of your head and press hard. There's no fat there. It doesn't matter how fat or thin we are, there's no fat on top to keep our heads warm. And most of the heat from our engine escapes from the top of our head. In the olden days before central heating and double glazing, people's bedrooms were very cold, so they wore night caps on their heads!

See if you can keep your head dry throughout the lesson."

(Session plans taken from "The Competent Swimmer – An Illustrated Guide To Further Practices". Reprinted with kind permission of Anne Eakin, ASA Principal Tutor).

Personal Survival

Action

"Imagine the side of the pool is a boat.

Find a way of getting into the water, and then swimming four widths, without getting your head wet.

How would you get in if the boat side was some distance above the water level?"

Ensure the water is at least full reach depth, then teach the straddle entry. Allow them to experiment with this, as well as sitting and swivelling in.

"Choose the entry you're best at, then tread water for two minutes. While you're there, try waving. Do you think you could keep waving for the whole two minutes?"

The selected entry and the ability to wave determine whether Level One or Level Two is appropriate.

"Also, can you think of three reasons why you should stay close to the scene of the accident?"

a. The rescue boat will find you more easily.

b. You'll find more things to support you near to the boat, like wood and plastic containers.

c. You'll save energy and body heat by not swimming.

(Session plans taken from "The Competent Swimmer – An Illustrated Guide To Further Practices". Reprinted with kind permission of Anne Eakin, ASA Principal Tutor).

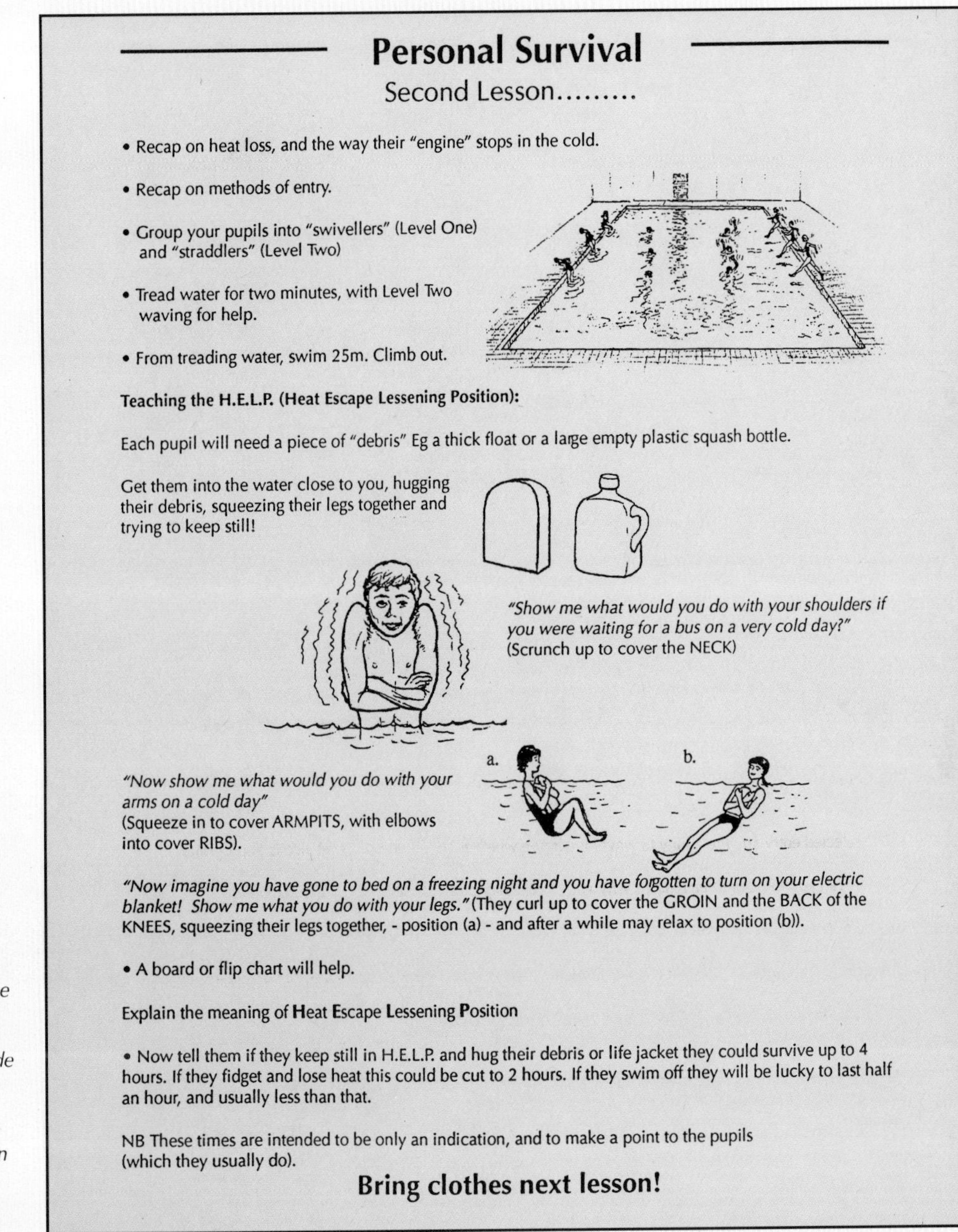

Personal Survival

Second Lesson.........

- Recap on heat loss, and the way their "engine" stops in the cold.
- Recap on methods of entry.
- Group your pupils into "swivellers" (Level One) and "straddlers" (Level Two)
- Tread water for two minutes, with Level Two waving for help.
- From treading water, swim 25m. Climb out.

Teaching the H.E.L.P. (Heat Escape Lessening Position):

Each pupil will need a piece of "debris" Eg a thick float or a large empty plastic squash bottle.

Get them into the water close to you, hugging their debris, squeezing their legs together and trying to keep still!

"Show me what would you do with your shoulders if you were waiting for a bus on a very cold day?" (Scrunch up to cover the NECK)

"Now show me what would you do with your arms on a cold day" (Squeeze in to cover ARMPITS, with elbows into cover RIBS).

"Now imagine you have gone to bed on a freezing night and you have forgotten to turn on your electric blanket! Show me what you do with your legs." (They curl up to cover the GROIN and the BACK of the KNEES, squeezing their legs together, - position (a) - and after a while may relax to position (b)).

- A board or flip chart will help.

Explain the meaning of **H**eat **E**scape **L**essening **P**osition

- Now tell them if they keep still in H.E.L.P. and hug their debris or life jacket they could survive up to 4 hours. If they fidget and lose heat this could be cut to 2 hours. If they swim off they will be lucky to last half an hour, and usually less than that.

NB These times are intended to be only an indication, and to make a point to the pupils (which they usually do).

Bring clothes next lesson!

(Session plans taken from "The Competent Swimmer – An Illustrated Guide To Further Practices". Reprinted with kind permission of Anne Eakin, ASA Principal Tutor).

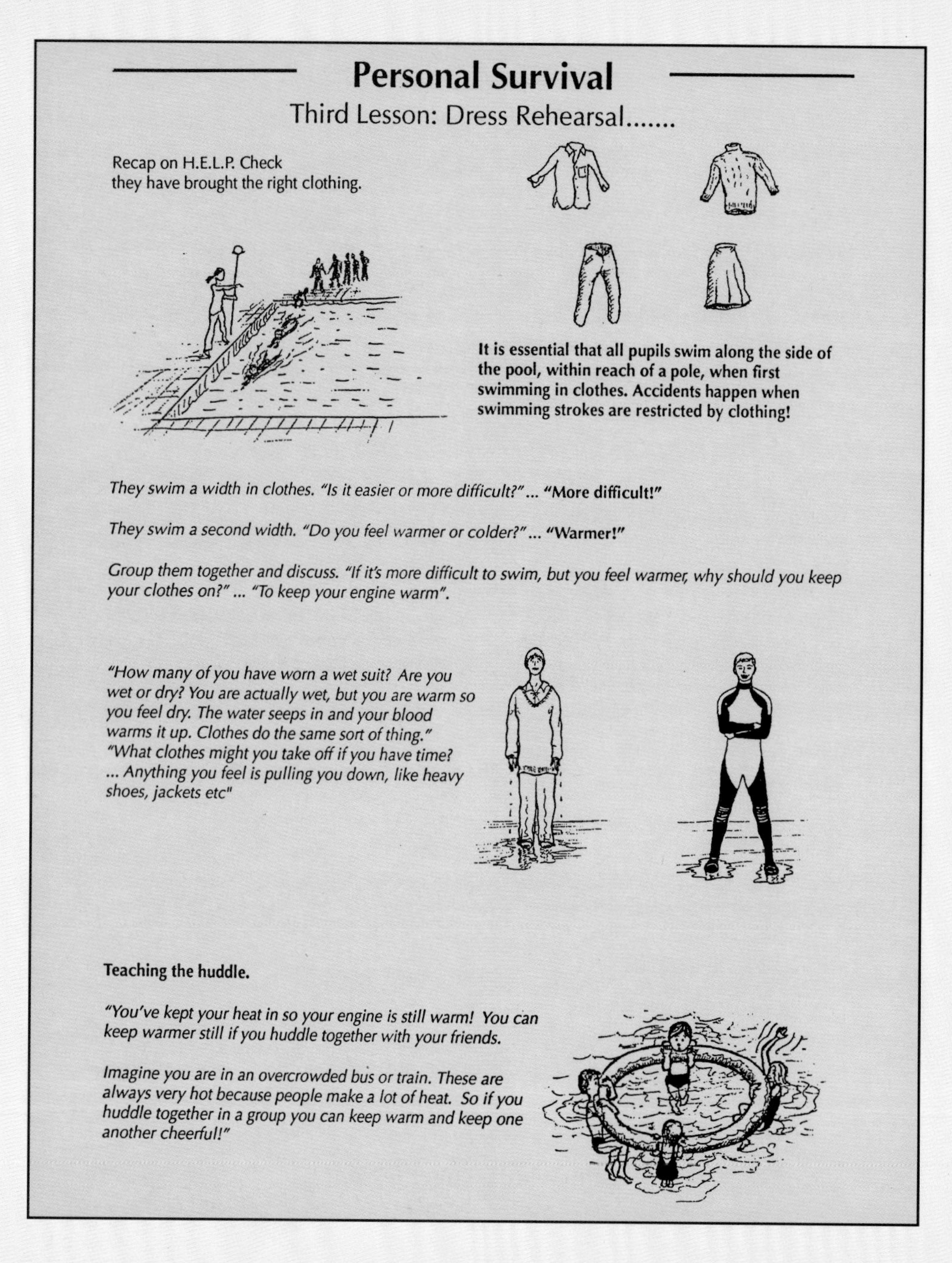

Personal Survival

Third Lesson: Dress Rehearsal.......

Recap on H.E.L.P. Check they have brought the right clothing.

It is essential that all pupils swim along the side of the pool, within reach of a pole, when first swimming in clothes. Accidents happen when swimming strokes are restricted by clothing!

They swim a width in clothes. "Is it easier or more difficult?" ... **"More difficult!"**

They swim a second width. "Do you feel warmer or colder?" ... **"Warmer!"**

Group them together and discuss. "If it's more difficult to swim, but you feel warmer, why should you keep your clothes on?" ... "To keep your engine warm".

"How many of you have worn a wet suit? Are you wet or dry? You are actually wet, but you are warm so you feel dry. The water seeps in and your blood warms it up. Clothes do the same sort of thing." "What clothes might you take off if you have time? ... Anything you feel is pulling you down, like heavy shoes, jackets etc"

Teaching the huddle.

"You've kept your heat in so your engine is still warm! You can keep warmer still if you huddle together with your friends.

Imagine you are in an overcrowded bus or train. These are always very hot because people make a lot of heat. So if you huddle together in a group you can keep warm and keep one another cheerful!"

(Session plans taken from "The Competent Swimmer – An Illustrated Guide To Further Practices". Reprinted with kind permission of Anne Eakin, ASA Principal Tutor).

Personal Survival

"Imagine the rescue boat has arrived. Do you throw your piece of debris away, or take it to the boat with you? ... Keep it with you!

The boat may take quite a long time to pick everyone up, or it may be full so you will have to wait for another!"

Waiting to get into the rescue boat.

Have them kick their way to the rescue boat (usually the teacher) hugging their debris, but without reaching for the side when they get there. Resume the H.E.L.P.

"Should you all climb onto the boat at the same time? ... No, it might capsize. So climb out five at a time."

"Is there a rail on the side of a boat? ... No! So climb out without using the rail." (Useful to imagine the rail is electrified!)

REMEMBER! Assessment next week. Bring your clothes!

(Session plans taken from "The Competent Swimmer – An Illustrated Guide To Further Practices". Reprinted with kind permission of Anne Eakin, ASA Principal Tutor).

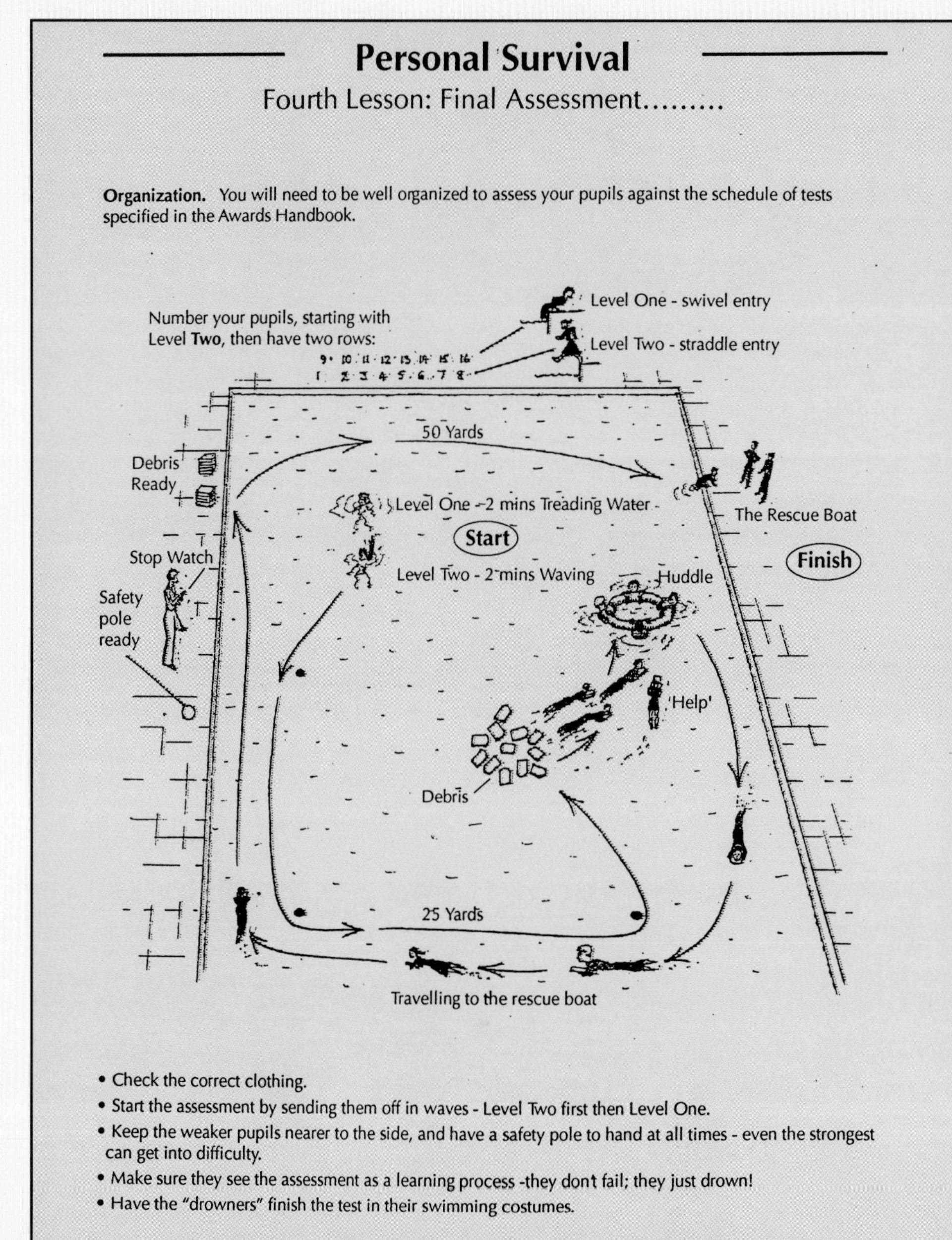

Personal Survival

Fourth Lesson: Final Assessment.........

Organization. You will need to be well organized to assess your pupils against the schedule of tests specified in the Awards Handbook.

- Check the correct clothing.
- Start the assessment by sending them off in waves - Level Two first then Level One.
- Keep the weaker pupils nearer to the side, and have a safety pole to hand at all times - even the strongest can get into difficulty.
- Make sure they see the assessment as a learning process -they don't fail; they just drown!
- Have the "drowners" finish the test in their swimming costumes.

(Session plans taken from "The Competent Swimmer – An Illustrated Guide To Further Practices". Reprinted with kind permission of Anne Eakin, ASA Principal Tutor).

CHAPTER 3

PRINCIPLES OF TEACHING/COACHING

Introduction

The process of teaching in any sphere has a number of common principles which underpin the practical application. A successful teacher/coach will have spent time learning and developing these skills in order to be able to carry out their role to the full. The skills explained in this chapter do not relate to teaching/coaching swimming alone. Many swimming teachers have found that once these skills are developed effectively they can be carried over to other areas of teaching, meaning that only the technical knowledge of the new subject has to be learned in order to be an effective teacher/coach in another discipline. Despite the fact that the information which follows has little direct relation to the technical element of swimming it is of equal importance and individuals will not be proficient teachers without knowledge and ability in both the principles of teaching and the technical knowledge. To illustrate this further the following examples should be read:

Example 1 *– Fred is very knowledgeable with regard to technical knowledge in swimming. He knows the strokes and skills inside out and can tell you exactly how to perform any stroke. Unfortunately he is a poor communicator and organiser and is unable to pass on his vast knowledge effectively.*

Example 2 *– Joan has all the skills of a good teacher, she has learnt the principles well and put them in to practice regularly when teaching other subjects. Unfortunately she has not had an opportunity to learn the technical details of swimming skills. Although she is able to teach well the information she passes on to the pupils is often incorrect.*

Example 3 *– Ian has taken the opportunity to learn the principles of teaching and practices them on a regular basis. He has also recognised the importance of having a sound technical knowledge of the activity he is going to teach and has learnt the technical elements well. He can now combine his knowledge and skills to offer the pupils the best possible lesson.*

The teacher/coach needs to remember the underpinning principles of teaching should be learnt and practised to enhance the teaching of swimming skills.

A teacher/coach who understands the principles is a much more flexible, adaptable teacher/coach as he is able to make sound judgements and decisions in a wider variety of situations based on his underpinning knowledge. In swimming the teacher/coach meets many different situations, it would be impossible to learn from any book how they should react to each situation. This chapter provides the tools to enable the teacher/coach to think his way through many of the situations in which he finds himself and arrive at the most satisfactory solution.

The principles within this chapter are:

Teaching & learning
Organisation methods
Teaching methods
Communication
Motivation
Working with assistants

Teaching/Coaching and Learning

When beginning to consider the process of teaching/coaching the first most important point which should be learnt and remembered is that teachers/coaches work with people. Although this may seem to be an obvious statement it is important that each teacher/coach understands what this means.

Every pupil the teacher/coach comes into contact with is an individual. Individuals learn at different rates and for different reasons. The teacher/coach must take account all of the individuals and their differences. Some of the differences are listed below:

- physical
- social
- gender
- age
- experience
- intellectual
- psychological
- maturation rate
- innate ability
- motivation

The teacher/coach may have other differences he could add to this list. Before reading further the teacher/coach should consider the list above and try to relate it to any swimming teaching/coaching in which he is currently involved. Doing this should help the teacher/coach to understand why they often receive different responses to the same instruction.

The teacher/coach should always remember that he should teach/coach the subject to the individual and make adjustments to allow for each individuals differences rather than just teaching/coaching the subject regardless of the individual's needs.

Organisation Methods

"An organised office is an efficient office"

This quote and other similar quotes are often used to demonstrate the need to be organised. Applying this quote to a swimming session shows how important it is to be organised prior to, during and after a lesson. There are three main organisational areas within a lesson:

- equipment
- activities
- pupils

The first two of these areas will be described in chapters relating to equipment and skills teaching. This chapter will focus on the area of pupil organisation. The following influences will affect organisation:

The teaching area – when teaching/coaching there will normally be an allocated amount of space in the pool. The shape and size of this space will influence the pupil organisation.

The number of pupils – class size can differ considerably from only small numbers to large classes (up to 25 pupils). This will, inevitably influence the organisation.

Ability of pupils – the class may have pupils of similar ability or they may be quite different. This will influence the grouping and activities.

Safety – above all the safety of the pupils needs to be considered and the pupils organised accordingly.

Having considered reasons which influence the organisation it is then important to look at the methods of organisation most commonly used.

Working with a group – *all swimmers carrying out activities at the same time.*
If outside influences permit the group to be worked as a whole this presents little organisational difficulty.

This diagram shows a teacher/coach working with a group as a whole.

Key Points – The pupils can see the teacher/coach
– The pupils have necessary equipment at hand
– The pupils each have their own swimming area

Working with a number of ability groups – *swimmers divided into groups in accordance with their ability.*
If pupils within one class have different ability levels the lesson should be organised in to ability groups to ensure all individuals have an appropriate lesson.

X

XXX XXXX XXXX
XXX XXXX XXXX
1 2 3

This diagram shows a teacher/coach working three ability groups.

Key Points – teacher/coach initially assesses pupils and places in ability groups.
– each group will work on activities appropriate to its ability.
– the teacher/coach will circulate around all groups giving instructions and feedback.

Wave Swimming – *swimmers organised in to ones and twos.*
This is often used when space is limited and working the class or group as a whole would be unsafe and unproductive.

XXXXXXXXX – wave 2
XXXXXXXXX – wave 1
X

This diagram shows a class organised in wave formation.

Key Points – Teacher/coach initially numbers or names each wave.
- Swimmers may be carrying out the same or differing activities.
- 2nd wave follows at a reasonable distance after the 1st.
- 1st wave returns when either all of the 2nd wave have finished or when the other swimmer in their pair has finished.
- Each pupil has their own swimming space.

Cannon Swimming – *each pupil follows on with a reasonable interval.*
This is often used to finish off an activity and allow the pupil space to swim, and the teacher/coach chance to observe in more detail.

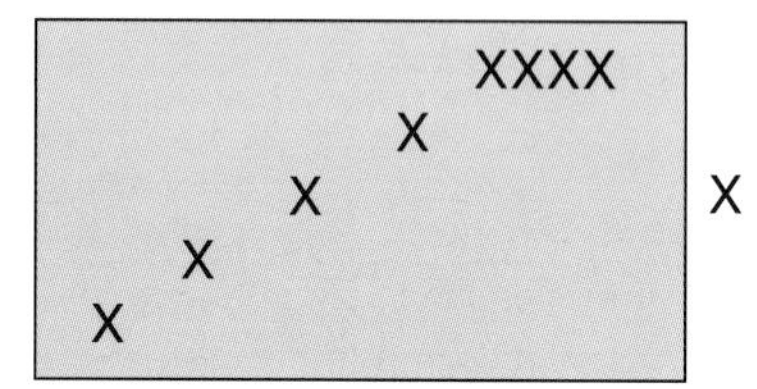

This diagram shows a class organised in cannon formation.

Key Points – the teacher/coach sets pupils off one at a time.
- all swimmers carry out same activity.
- the first pupil can begin again as last finishes.
- each pupil has their own swimming space.

Lane Swimming – *the lesson is conducted over the length of the pool.*
The organisation in lanes is normally either wave or chain formation. Swimmers are set off at approximately 5 sec intervals.

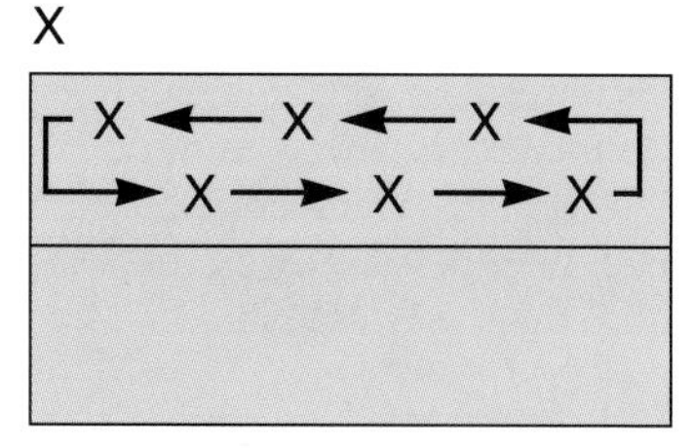

This diagram shows a class organised in a chain formation.

Key Points – teacher/coach sets off pupils one at a time.
- the interval between swimmers is normally 5 seconds.
- lanes are organised in clockwise, anti-clockwise formation.
- lanes are normally organised in ability order.

Teaching Methods

The teacher/coach will develop his own style and method of teaching. The method is normally based around a number of recognised principles for different levels of swimmer. The most common methods of teaching/coaching are described below:

Non-swimmers

Shallow water method – this method of teaching/coaching can be used with non-swimmers in water between 30 - 45 cm in depth. The pupils do not utilise any buoyancy aids but support themselves in a prone or supine position on the pool floor with their hands and arms. From a stationary position pupils can then introduce a leg action and gradually develop an arm action as they gain confidence.

Deep water method – pupils are taught in deep water with the use of buoyancy aids to provide the necessary support. As the swimmer develops the appropriate movement patterns the artificial aids can be removed. In this situation it is normal to have an assistant in the water in addition to the teacher/coach on the pool side.

Teaching with buoyancy aids – most non-swimmers are taught with the use of a range of buoyancy aids ranging from arm bands to floats. This method is described in more detail in the Chapter 6 *'Teaching the Non-Swimmer'.*

Partner Support – pupils are assisted by a partner to gain a prone or supine position and progress through the water. This method is particularly useful when teaching adults.

Multi Stroke Approach – non-swimmers are taught a varied range of movement skills which can be developed at the appropriate time into recognised swimming strokes. Chapter 11 *'Skill Acquisition'* describes how this develops a much wider range of movement skills and patterns.

Improvers

Whole, Part, Whole – once the non-swimmer has developed the skills necessary to progress through the water in a prone and supine position more specific teaching/coaching of the recognised strokes and skills can begin. The main theme of a lesson will normally be structured as whole, part, whole. The teacher/coach begins with a brief explanation of the whole stroke/skill and the pupils make attempts. The stroke/skill is then broken down into a series of progressive part practices which permit development of the stroke/skill at the appropriate level. The teacher/coach may then return to the whole to assess progress before continuing further. The main theme of any lesson conducted in this way should start and finish with the whole stroke/skill.

Early Competitive Swimming

Technique Coaching – when swimmers reach the early competitive level they would be expected to have a sound technique on backcrawl, frontcrawl and breaststroke with the basic fundamentals of butterfly. Techniques now require additional development and refinement and swimmers can now be introduced to stroke drills. These can be defined as variations on the whole technique which provide a specific focus for development. The structure of a set of work to develop technique still normally follows the whole, part, whole theme.

Endurance & Speed Development – it is important for a competitive swimmer to be able to maintain technique whilst swimming for a long duration and whilst swimming at speed. Recognised training principles are utilised to ensure that skill acquisition continues whilst endurance and speed are developed. Chapter 20 *'Principles of Work and Rest'* covers this area in greater detail.

Communication

The ability to communicate knowledge is one of the most important principles of teaching/ coaching.

When communicating on pool side, the teacher/coach should know the different methods which can be used, and how to use them to their fullest. This section will explain the methods, outline the principles of good communication and look at why communication sometimes fails.

Methods: Verbal – what is said by the teacher/coach
Visual – what the pupil sees, demonstration, video etc.
Manual – the teacher/coach assisting the performer to create the correct movement

Usually the teacher/coach combines these methods, e.g. by means of demonstration accompanied by an explanation, or a swimmer's hand is moved through a given path whilst the teacher/coach explains what the swimmer should be feeling and remembering. The latter method is probably the least effective and should be used sparingly.

A good communicator will follow a number of basic principles when using the above methods. The main principles are described below:

Positioning – The teacher/coach and the pupils need to be positioned appropriately for communication to be effective. The size of the group, position in the pool and method of communication chosen will influence the position used.

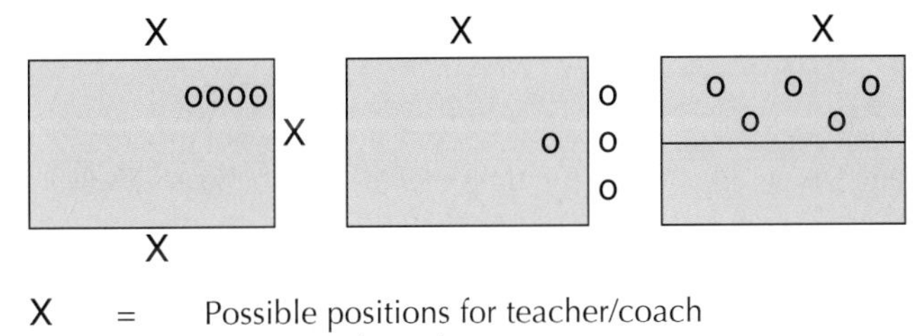

Clarity – voice should be clear, demonstrations should be obvious.

Concise – explanations should be concise and cover only the main points.

Accurate – technical accuracy in all methods of communication is essential when describing a physical skill.

Two Way – communication is a two way process and should offer opportunities for the pupils to communicate how an action feels. Knowledge & understanding can also be checked using two way dialogue in the form of questions and answers.

Enthusiastic – an enthusiastic teacher/coach communicates enthusiasm through his body language as well as his words. Enthusiasm is contagious.

Interesting – the information given via any of the methods needs to be communicated in an interesting way.

Appropriate – communication needs to be at a level which is appropriate to the individuals involved and the activities to be undertaken.

Some teachers/coaches have many or all of these communication skills, but on occasion communication can still break down, There can be a number of reasons which provide obstacles to good communication, some of them are listed below:

Learner saturation – being asked to think about too much in too short a time.

Distractions – noisy or cold environment, spectator (often parent) waving or calling.

Confused delivery – sequencing of activities not progressive and therefore making the learner's task even more difficult.

Wrong assumptions – the teacher/coach may make wrong assumptions about pupils in the group based on what he thinks the pupil has previously done, or on the activities of some of the group.

Poor image – pupils have expectations of the teacher/coach. The general demeanour, appearance, voice, sense of humour of the teacher/coach will indicate to the pupils whether or not they are in the charge of a pleasant, competent, knowledgeable person.

Repetitive ideas – a good teacher/coach will endeavour to reduce learner frustration by providing a variety of ideas in a given theme. However, there are often times within a swimming lesson when repetition is a valuable part of learning.

When communicating with a class the teacher/coach will normally try to achieve a number of objectives. First of all he needs to provide information. This may relate to the organisation of the class or the skills to be performed. Secondly, he needs to check understanding. This can be done by either questioning or observing the pupil. Thirdly, he needs to provide feedback on performance. The teacher/coach is the pupils eyes and the feedback he gives will enable them to understand the movements the body has made and permit the swimmer to make appropriate changes.

Every pupil differs so the information communicated within the lesson will also differ from pupil to pupil. This means that in the process of a lesson the teacher/coach will need to communicate with the group as a whole, part of the group and on a one to one basis. The teacher/coach needs to develop each communication skill accordingly in order to be able to communicate successfully at all levels.

Good communication skills need to be developed, they do not always come automatically. The skills of communicating on the pool side are not unique but similar/the same as those used when teaching/coaching any subject or skill. The swimming pool does, however, add another dimension and the best means of communication in this environment needs to be considered carefully by the teacher/coach

Motivation

One of the many roles a teacher/coach will play is that of a motivator. The teacher/coach needs to encourage the learner to want to learn and maintain motivation to help the pupils to continue to develop and progress. The teacher/coach has a number of motivational tools at his disposal. For example:

Praise – it is important to praise effort as well as success

Feedback – although praise may be a type of feedback it is often quite subjective and does not give the learner a clear indication of how they are improving. Feedback provides more specific information with regard to performance. If feedback is to be motivational it needs to be given constructively and positively. (The chart below gives examples of praise, positive feedback and negative feedback).

Positive Feedback	Negative Feedback	Praise
Pull closer to the centre line.	You didn't pull down the centre line.	That was a good try.
Your legs were kicking from the hips.	Don't bend your legs.	Well done your legs kicked hard.

Incentive Schemes – the ASA has the most comprehensive award scheme in British Sport, it offers awards for progressive stages of development from beginner to advanced level. Awards can provide incentives and motivation to progress, but they should be used sensibly as the failure of an award or too much emphasis on achieving the award can have a demotivational effect.

Goal Setting – the setting of realistic goals for swimmers can provide motivation to progress. Goals can come in many forms:

Badges & Awards

- winning a particular race
- moving up to the next class
- achieving a target time

When setting a goal the teacher/coach needs to ensure it can be measured and is achievable within a realistic time scale for the pupil.

Individuals are motivated when their own perceived competence level increases, the examples above are all methods of increasing perceived competence.

Working with Assistants

There is one more role which a teacher/coach may be required to perform, that of supervising a helper or an assistant teacher. Whilst this may only appear to be a case of providing a series of instructions, in reality it is much more than this. If the helper or assistant teacher is to gain from the experience he also needs to be given the same learning experience as any pupil. This means the principles already discussed in this chapter need to be applied.

This section of the chapter provides information related to working with an assistant teacher under the following headings:

- Preparing sessions
- Allocating tasks
- Providing instruction
- Recording and evaluating
- Providing constructive feedback

Preparing sessions – planning is an important process for any teacher/coach. The work of an assistant needs to be prepared prior to teaching/coaching. This will ensure that they will gain from the experience and the tasks allocated will be at an appropriate level. Preparing for an assistant requires prior knowledge of their experience.

Allocating Tasks – there are numerous tasks which can be allocated to an assistant within a lesson. Some examples are:

- assisting in the water
- setting swimmers off
- looking after a small group
- giving the group instructions
- organising equipment
- observing an individual
- taking times in a coaching session
- demonstrating skills to be taught

When the teacher/coach allocates a task he needs to ensure he still maintains overall responsibility for pupils and provides appropriate supervision to an assistant.

Providing Instruction – the instructions given to an assistant can be provided verbally or in writing on the lesson plan. Once initial instructions have been provided, ongoing support, encouragement and feedback should be given at intervals throughout the lesson.

Evaluation – for the assistant to benefit from the experience, and feel motivated to continue, it is necessary to provide feedback on the effectiveness of the contribution. In the same way that a practice is allocated to a pupil then an evaluation made of his efforts, an evaluation of the assistants efforts needs to be made. This requires observation of the assistant at regular intervals throughout the lesson.

Providing Constructive Feedback – constructive feedback can be provided on an ongoing basis during the lesson or as the lesson is completed. The feedback offered can provide both motivation and assist the assistant's learning process.

If the steps above are followed carefully the experience should be of great benefit to the development of an assistant teacher, The input of the teacher/coach could provide a vital part in the assistant teacher's progression to further qualifications. A meaningless experience at this stage could result in an unwillingness to progress or continue further.

Summary

The role of a teacher/coach is not an easy one but will be enhanced considerably by careful consideration and implementation of the principles outlined in this chapter. Skills in only one area such as technical knowledge are not enough, they only form part of the overall picture of the complete teacher/coach.

CHAPTER 4

PLANNING, RECORDING AND EVALUATING

Introduction

Planning, recording and evaluating are the things a teacher/coach does to promote learning whilst no learners are present. These are the unseen tasks which are of vital importance. The teacher/coach who approaches his work in a professional manner can be seen to be well organised and well prepared. This is usually due to careful planning resulting from previous experience, recorded information and past evaluations. As the teacher/coach becomes more experienced he will find the time spent planning is reduced as he will build on past experiences which will help to give a better knowledge and understanding of the needs of particular individuals, groups and situations.

Stages of Planning

There are a number of stages in the process of planning which should be followed prior to any course of lessons or even one-off teaching sessions.

- gathering information in readiness for planning
- planning the Scheme of Work and Sessions
- executing the plan
- recording appropriate information
- evaluating the actual session - planning and practice

Gathering the Information

Before planning any Scheme of Work/Session the teacher/coach must have a knowledge of the group to be taught and the resources available. It is only the foolish teacher/coach who teaches/coaches without some prior thought.

Gathering this information may be a simple task if the teacher/coach has taken the same group or taught in the same situation previously. However, this should not compromise the planning process.

Listed below are some examples of the information which should be gathered prior to planning:

- size of group
- previous experience
- ability range/age range
- space available
- exclusive/shared use
- water depth
- safety equipment
- equipment available

Planning the Scheme of Work and Sessions

Schemes of Work – a scheme of work is essentially an outline of what is to be covered over a particular period of time, e.g. a ten week course of swimming lessons. It is the teachers/coaches long term plan. A teacher/coach working with competitive swimmers will often refer to this as a training cycle.

Once the initial information has been gathered some thought can be given to the aims and objectives for the group within the period covered by the long term plan. An aim is a general statement about what the teacher/coach intends to do during the course, for example:

- introduce non-swimmers to movement in water

Aims should be realistic for the group within the time frame available but should also provide a challenge. A scheme of work without an aim is like a boat without a rudder, it meanders from one place to the next with no direction.

Objectives indicate what the teacher/coach anticipates the pupils will be able to do at the end of the course. This can be likened to climbing a step ladder, the aim is to get to the top, the objectives are the steps on the way to the top. The following list may be examples of objectives for the aim above:

Participants will be able to:

- enter and leave the water in various ways
- demonstrate the ability to regain standing from prone and supine positions
- demonstrate confidence in submerging and breath control
- demonstrate basic propulsion on the front and back (with or without aids)

The teacher/coach can then consider the content of each individual session in order to meet the objectives and, ultimately, the aim. When deciding on the content areas it is important for the teacher/coach to consider the following:

- are the warm up, main theme and contrast complimentary to one another?

- does each lesson follow on progressively from the one before?
- can examples of positive transfer (see Chapter 11) be seen in each session?
- is time permitted within the lesson to allow for revision of past tasks?
- will the content of the whole scheme be suffice to reach the aim?
- is the content of the whole scheme realistic?

Once all of these steps have been followed the scheme of work is complete. Having done this level of planning before a course starts means that the planning of individual sessions is relatively simple. It is based on two things:

- what has been set down in the scheme of work
- the evaluation of what happened at the last session

The value of long term planning should never be underestimated. Any teacher/coach who works in a professional manner, and desires to offer his participants the best possible learning opportunity will spend time on long term plans, and observation of his lessons over a course would show a structured approach to teaching/coaching.

Session Plans – the objectives which formed part of the long term planning can now be utilised as aims for each individual lesson taught. If a teacher/coach is planning a one off lesson it should still have an aim to work towards.

Although the prime purpose of the lesson is to fulfill the aims, such concepts as balance, pace and variety are important if the interest of the participants is to be maintained. When planning each session some of the following questions should be asked:

Balance – are the pupils spending the right amount of time on one practice?
– is there enough specific work to meet the aim?

Pace – are the pupils spending plenty of time doing?
– are the pupils receiving adequate rest periods to maintain skill?

Variety – are there different ways the same movement could be practiced?
– does the contrast offer a change from the main theme?

In order to assist the teacher/coach with balance, variety and pace it is normal for a swimming session to be divided into phases:

Introductory Activity/Warm Up

The teacher/coach should either relate the activity to work performed in a previous lesson or just select a known activity that will quickly involve the swimmers.

Main Theme/Main Set

This section of the session should occupy the largest proportion of the time, normally about 50% of the session, i.e., 15-20 minutes in a half hour session. This is the main work of the session and the content should help to achieve the main aim of the session. If it is a technique session, it should follow a whole/part practices/whole stroke format. If there are two or three ability groups there should be a series of two or three sets of practices.

Contrasting Activity

The teacher/coach should either relate the activity to an on going subsidiary theme or select a contrasting activity that reinforces previous work or prepares for future activities

Concluding Activity

The teacher/coach should:

- reinforce the points crucial to fulfilling the aim of the lesson
- check whether the aim has been fulfilled
- give swimmers an assessment of their performance and indicate how the work will be developed.

There is a minimum amount of information that any written session plan should include in order for it to be a useful document. The example overleaf shows a possible layout for a session plan.

SESSION PLAN – Swimming

Class: Imps	**Session No.** 1 of 8			**Date**	**Time**	**Duration**
Age Range 5-7 yrs	**No. in class:** Eight	**Male:** Five	**Female:** Three	10th Dec, 96	4.30pm	30 mins
Venue: Parkside Pool	**Type of Pool** – deck level – **conventional**	– leisure – other	**Water depth** 1.5m	**Safety equipment available:** Poles, Throw bags, Ropes		**Working area required:** Middle of Pool

Additional information (if any) provided by: participants, parents, teachers etc. including medical conditions
Non

Aims of session To improve backcrawl & touch turns	**Specific Objectives** To improve arm action To improve approach and turning action
Ability of pupils (include any reference to lack of water confidence) Swim 25m all three strokes with weak technique	**Additional information**
Equipment required 1 float per swimmer	**Assistants available (if any)** Non

Activity/Practices	Teaching Points	Organisation	Time
Warm Up Jump in entry 2 widths choice – on front 2 widths choice – on back	Ensure space is clear Steady pace swimming	All swimming at same time	5 mins
Main Theme 2 widths backcrawl full stroke	Keep tummy up Keep legs moving	The number of widths and number of repeats will depend on the pupil's progress. All at the same time in most cases. Occasionally cannon formation	20 mins
Backcrawl kick – 1 float on chest	Loose floppy ankles Keep knees under the surface		
Backcrawl kick – 1 float over knees	Legs long and loose Kick up to surface with toes		
Backcrawl kick – no floats	Knees and big toes to brush past Make the water boil with toes		
2 widths backcrawl full stroke	One of above teaching points		
Backcrawl single arm – with float	Stretch arms straight in recovery Little finger enters first		
Backcrawl full stroke	Point elbow to pool floor Push through to hip		
Contrast Touch turns on breast & f.crawl – approach at swimming speed – practice touch and throw away – push & glides – throw away and push & glide	Look at wall Touch with both hands Jab elbow back Like an arrow	Swimming to wall from middle of pool. Cannon formation	5 mins

The section relating to activities/practices is self explanatory and reference should be made to any planned schemes of work prior to completing this section.

Teaching/Coaching Points – this column should contain brief points relating to each practice listed. Two or three teaching/coaching points should be included with each practice. The teaching/coaching points should be brief phrases which can be used gradually throughout the practice.

Organisation – this column should show how practices will be organised:

- in chains/waves
- 1's/2's
- random spacing

Time – this column should show, approximately, the amount of time in minutes that you intend to spend on each task.

Executing the Plan

Once the initial planning processes are complete the plans are now ready to be executed. The teacher/coach already knows that the lesson will have a sound structure and appropriate content because plans have been laid. Once on poolside ready to execute the plan the following points should be remembered by the teacher/coach:

- the plan was carefully thought through
- should only be referred to when necessary
- to be flexible in its use
- adjustments can be made for changing circumstances
- adjustments made to be noted

Recording appropriate information

There are a number of areas of consideration with regard to the recording of material about a particular group of participants during a swimming session:

- Keeping a register – this is an essential safety document for the teacher/coach as well as the facility where the lessons are taking place. If an incident occurred and a roll call was necessary the register of the teacher/coach would be used. It may also be used to report any particular medical conditions of which any teacher/coach taking the group should be aware. It is also a useful document for the teacher/coach as it enables him to identify any tasks which a particular pupil may have missed. This can be done by comparing it with the scheme of work, or possibly incorporating the scheme of work into the register as shown in the example below.

- Recording progress – recording progress of participants' can often assist the teacher/coach to make a more accurate assessment of whether the aim for the scheme of work has been achieved. Many teachers/coaches are expected to make a formal assessment towards the end of a course which will determine a participant's class in the future, this assessment may also include a report for the participant or his parent/guardian. The teacher/coach should find a simple method of gathering this information, either a specific space on the register or an additional form specifically for this purpose could be used.

- Recording adjustments to session plans – earlier in the chapter it was stated that there are a number of stages of planning, one of which is evaluation. It is important that any adjustments to sessions are recorded to enable a more accurate evaluation of the session to be made. This easiest way of recording changes is by using a different coloured pen on the original written plan, or writing on the plastic wallet containing the plan with a non permanent marker pen.

Swimming Session Register/Scheme of Work

Aim of Course:	To swim 25m continuously To improve technique on frontcrawl To improve technique on backcrawl To improve technique on breaststroke To tread water out of depth
Length of Course:	10 weeks

Class: Improvers (2A) **Teacher:** Harry Haddock

Day: Monday **Time:** 4.00pm

Week Number Name	1	2	3	4	5	6	7	8
Susan Seal								
Freddy Fish								
Peter Piranha								
Timmy Trout								
Debbie Dolphin								
Michael Minnow								
Stephen Salmon								
Graham Goldfish								
Angel Fish								
Caroline Carp								
Scheme of Work:	Assess swimmers' ability on Back, Front & Breast Main Theme – Frontcrawl Leg & Arm Practices Contrast – Sculling	Warm Up – Backcrawl & Choice Main Theme – Frontcrawl Arm & Breathing Practices Contrast – Surface Dives – Head First	Warm Up – Backcrawl & Choice Main Theme – Backcrawl Leg & Arm Practices Contrast – Treading Water	Warm Up – Breaststroke & Choice Main Theme – Backcrawl Arm & Timing Practices Contrast – Treading Water – Out of Depth – Close to Wall	Warm Up – Breaststroke & Choice Main Theme – Breaststroke Leg Practices Contrast – Straddle Jumps – Out of Depth	Warm Up – Frontcrawl & Choice Main Theme – Breaststroke Leg & Arm Practices Contrast – Early Diving Practices – Rotation	Warm Up – Choice Main Theme – Frontcrawl Arm & Breathing Practices Contrast – Early Diving Practices – Submerging & Surfacing	Warm Up – Frontcrawl

Evaluating the Session - Planning & Practice

When the teacher/coach completes the session it would be very easy to walk away and forget all about it. If this occurs the teacher/coach has omitted a vital stage in the planning process, that of evaluation. It is the evaluation of this session which will determine the content of the next session. There are a number of different areas which can be evaluated :

Objectives – this should be the first consideration of the teacher/coach. It would be easy for the question *"Has the objective been achieved?"* to be answered with merely *"Yes"* or *"No"*. In order for an evaluation to be useful for future planning the teacher/coach needs to be able to identify the reasons for the outcome.

Individual Progress – if the teacher/coach has recorded progress during, or after the session, this information can then be evaluated and acted upon if necessary. Evaluating the progress will help the teacher/coach to determine practices to be used in future lessons, and whether repetition of activities may be necessary.

Teacher/Coach Performance – two teachers/coaches executing the same plan may have different results because of their personal performance. Continued evaluation of their own teaching/coaching permits them to identify any weaknesses and set strategies to improve them. Chapter 3 *'Principles of Teaching/Coaching'* indicates a number of areas which the teacher/coach could evaluate, e.g., his communication during the session.

Adjustments to Plan – if it were necessary to make adjustments to the original plan these should be evaluated to assist with the planning of future sessions.

Once any evaluation of a session is complete it is useful for the teacher/coach to set some action points for future planning and executing of sessions. Action Points could relate to organisational matters, teaching skills or content, for example:

- helper to go into the water with the new non-swimmer
- introduce more advanced practices for the able swimmers
- practice backcrawl arm action demonstration
- check Jane has brought inhaler

For any evaluation to be useful to future planning its content must be objective rather than subjective. Objective evaluation means that each area of the session has been considered, and reasons for its success/failure given. Subjective evaluation considers each area of the session but does not consider the reasons for the outcomes. An example of each is given below:

Objective – "I felt my communication was clear and concise but some of my demonstrations lacked accuracy as I dropped my elbow on the backcrawl arm action"

Subjective – "I felt my verbal communication was good and my demonstrations were poor"

Summary

Planning is the invisible part of swimming teaching/coaching. Planning is essential for any teacher/coach who desires to give participants the best possible session in the time available. Every teacher/coach should remember that there are a number of stages to planning and each has a bearing on the next. The process is cyclical:

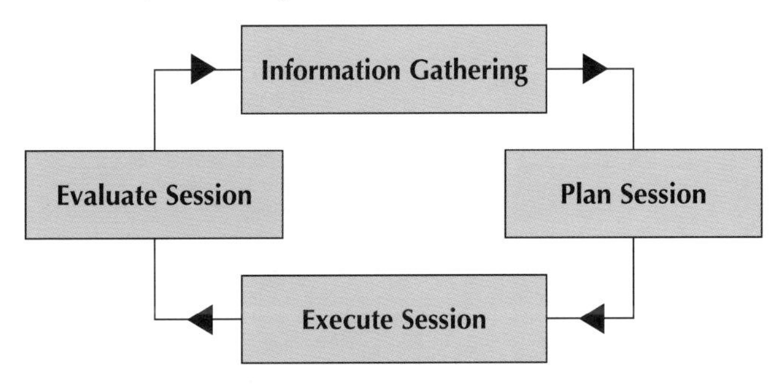

Just because planning, recording and evaluating are the invisible areas of teaching/coaching does not mean they can be omitted or done inadequately. Careful planning, recording and evaluating will result in better sessions.

CHAPTER 5

EQUIPMENT

Introduction

There is always a wide range of equipment available for those engaged in teaching/coaching. Any catalogue of swimming goods will contain a wide range of aids available. Some of the equipment available will have been on the market for many years, is tried and tested and provides excellent service. The teacher/coach will see other equipment appear and disappear fairly rapidly. As in any walk of life there are novelties and gimmicks which arrive on the market but are often found to be impractical when tested.

The Range of Equipment

Equipment has a wide range of uses. Some items are designed specifically for the non-swimmers market whilst others can be utilised across the whole range of abilities from non-swimmer to advanced swimmer. Other types of equipment may be provided to ensure safety of participants in and around the swimming pool.

Since budgets are nearly always limited, well informed selection is essential. This chapter is designed to point out some of the advantages and disadvantages of equipment. It should help the teacher/coach to make a choice related to their budget, but more importantly to the needs of the pupil.

When purchasing or using equipment the teacher/coach should have in mind the following considerations:

- is the equipment safe to the user or those close by?
- does it contribute significantly to learning and development?
- is it durable and with few maintenance problems?
- can it be stored securely and made available when requested?
- is it suitable for general use, or is it limited to special individuals or circumstances?

In an attempt to make this chapter more useful and structured, equipment has been divided into a number of categories, as follows:

- buoyancy aids
- aids which encourage submersion
- competitive training equipment
- teachers equipment
- learning toys

This should enable the teacher/coach to use the information as a reference document when considering different aspects of swimming teaching/coaching.

Buoyancy Aids

The equipment available in this category ranges from buoyancy aids which can be attached to a non-swimmers body, enabling them to float with the feet clear of the pool bottom and head safely above water level, to buoyancy aids which can be used intermittently to provide additional support. Buoyancy aids can also be used to ensure pupils are safe in a more difficult environment. e.g. the non swimmer who cannot stand up at the far side of the teaching station or the improver who is not completely confident to carry out a whole lesson out of their depth.

There is always a concern for the teacher/coach that the pupil can become reliant on the buoyancy aid and be reluctant to take it off. This tendency can be offset by making it clear from the outset that the additional support is only an initial phase of learning and that, once the basic movements are understood, the extra buoyancy should be reduced or removed soon after. Some learners may feel that the buoyancy aid identifies them as a non-swimmer and may be keen to dispense with the aid prematurely. The teacher/coach must be aware of these individuals and handle them sensitively but firmly.

Arm Bands – Probably the most commonly used buoyancy aid for non-swimmers. When fitting arm bands the teacher/coach should check the air chambers are secure and that the arm bands are the appropriate size. If little children use large arm bands their movement will be impeded, whilst adults may not receive enough buoyancy from small arm bands.

Arm bands allow freedom of movement of the legs and a reasonable amount of movement with the arms. They only offer support when submersed so pupils should be taught practices that keep the arms in the water.

The putting on and removal of arm bands can be a time consuming process and pupils should be taught how to do this and be able to assist each other. Arm bands need not be deflated after each lesson, as this only uses additional time.

The teacher/coach should be aware of the additional buoyancy the arm band provides to the upper body and expect the pupils to find it harder to achieve a streamlined position.

Arm bands are a reasonably cheap, very durable buoyancy aid which assist in the early development stages of teaching.

Polystyrene Disks – these are buoyancy aids which are very similar to arm bands. They are more versatile as the number worn on each arm will determine the amount of buoyancy given. When a pupil is wearing only one on each arm he is receiving little assistance and after a short period of time should be able to remove them and swim.

Polystyrene Body Belts and Jet Packs – Another popular and effective buoyancy aid is the polystyrene body belt or the plastic jet pack. These particular aids fit around the pupils abdomen and give an evenly balanced body position in the water. The body belt is not as effective with complete non-swimmers as, unlike armbands, it does not provide the same security of keeping the face above the water. It provides an excellent progression from the arm bands as it permits free movement of the arms and legs. Once the non-swimmer has gained a horizontal body position and travel with arm bands, it is a simple task to change the aid and permit further development of swimming activities.

The polystyrene body belt is also a useful aid for pupils who are able to swim but are now progressing to the deep water. The use of a body belt can give added confidence and also assist the pupil in maintaining a good body position throughout the lesson.

When fitting either body belts or jet pack care must be taken to secure them well. The body belt is made up of a number of polystyrene cylinders, this allows different amounts of buoyancy to be achieved by adjusting the number of cylinders accordingly. This is quite an arduous task and should be completed prior to the lesson beginning.

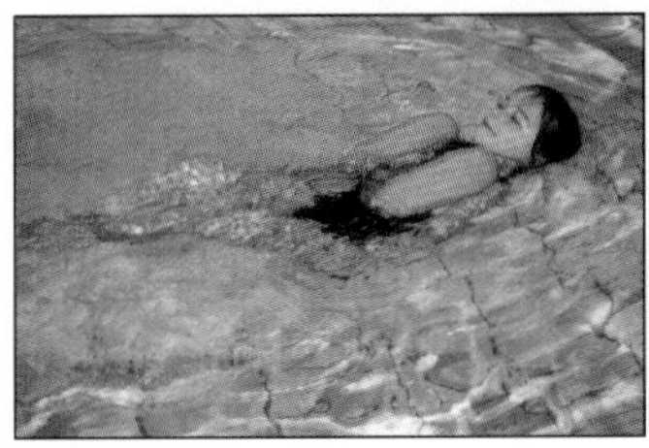

Swimming Floats – Probably the best used buoyancy aid available, it is adaptable and suitable for all levels of ability from non-swimmer to advanced level. Swimming floats are now available in different sizes allowing the teacher/coach to select the size appropriate to the swimmer. Although this may seem trivial it is in fact very important. Always be aware of the length of the pupils arm and look carefully at the task being set to check that the flotation aid will help and not hinder.

Swimming floats can be used in twos, one under each arm, or singly, held out in front with two hands. Some time spent using the equipment appropriately is important, for example, if the swimmer holds the float at the far end there is a risk of the float sinking. If the swimmer holds the float at the sides it is more likely to stay afloat and also offer support. If the swimmer holds the float at the near end it can be difficult to control and offers less support. In different situations any of these positions may be correct. Similar principles can be applied to the use of floats when swimming on the back. The use of two floats one on top of the other is not ideal.

Once again the teacher/coach should consider the effect of the flotation aid on the pupil. Two floats, one under each arm, will offer good balance and support but will have the effect of elevating the top half of the body, so it may be more difficult for the swimmer to obtain a horizontal body position. When attempting a one arm practice on frontcrawl the float should be extended far enough away to permit the swimmer ample room to place the head in the water. At the non-swimmer stage it is very easy for the teacher/coach, in an attempt to provide additional buoyancy, to give the pupil too much support to the upper body, consequently making it increasingly difficult for the pupils to obtain a horizontal position.

A final point with regard to swimming floats is that they are not only available in different sizes but also different shapes. The teddy bear shaped floats provide an interesting distraction to young non-swimmers and can enhance the lesson considerably.

Woggles – currently the newest flotation aid on the market. A woggle is a polyethylene foam cylinder approximately 7 cm in diameter and 1.5m long They were initially used in England as an Aquafit accessory but have gradually and very effectively infiltrated into swimming teaching/coaching.

The big advantage of the woggle is its ability to offer good support and balance whilst allowing the non-swimmer to use both arms and legs. The fact that it is not a fixed aid also allows the pupil to use it and remove it very easily. It can be used in both the prone and supine position in a similar manner. Whilst the length of the woggle is perfect for adults it can often be too long for children making it difficult to cope with, this could be overcome by putting two children on to one woggle. This has the benefit of not only adding fun to the lesson but also giving propulsion from two sets of arms and legs, making activities quicker.

The woggle is mainly a non-swimmers aid , the amount of balance given makes it prohibitive for teaching/coaching alternating strokes effectively and it would not permit an over water recovery on butterfly. However, it can be used during breaststroke practices and is very effective in correcting a swimmer who is pulling too far back.

It also has many functions as a learning through play aid. The photographs demonstrate sea horses, woggle races and speedboats. A vivid imagination should be able to create many more ideas.

Inflatable Rings – these were commonly used in the past, but they have some disadvantages. Adventurous youngsters often dive or plunge forward vigorously and the ring can slip down below the centre of gravity then continue to support the body in an inverted position. If used, rings should be close fitting and incorporate a diagonal shoulder strap to prevent movement down the body.

Aids which Encourage Submersion

Hoops – a variety of hoops is now available, some which completely submerge, others which partially submerge and others which can be held close to the surface and encourage early submersion activities or make a useful addition to an early diving practices lesson. It is important that the teacher/coach selects the appropriate equipment carefully. Ideally a number of hoops should be available to allow plenty of practice even in a large class.

Sinkables – there is a wide range of objects available which sink to the bottom and encourage submerging practice in a variety of different ways. Rubber bricks are often used to practice life saving skills of search and retrieval. Small brightly coloured plastic sticks, rings or shaped objects make useful and interesting additions to non-swimmer or improver lessons. As with the hoops a large selection should be available for each class. Many teachers/coaches now provide their own to ensure they are able to complete their lesson objectives fully.

Competitive Training Equipment

Pull Buoys - a more specialised piece of equipment for arm action practices is the pull buoy, which may be a solid one piece block of buoyant material shaped to fit between the thighs, or made up to two short cylinders loosely linked by cords so that the legs can be closed between them leaving one cylinder at the front and the other at the back of the thighs.

The pull buoy gives a competitive swimmer a chance to isolate the arms. This has two possible benefits, it allows the legs to rest (this may be necessary after a hard set which made considerable use of the legs) or it can assist in improving the muscular strength and endurance of the arms.

Occasionally pull buoys can be used with more advanced swimming lesson groups. When considering pulling practices the teacher/coach should be aware of the effects of adding buoyancy to the legs. Firstly the pull buoy elevates the lower half of the body. This may have the effect of pushing the head of a weaker swimmer underwater. Secondly, in the alternating stroke the leg action provides the balance to the stroke. Pupils may find it difficult to maintain a streamlined position with their body following a straight path.

Kicking Boards – much larger versions of the polystyrene floats mentioned earlier in this chapter. They are used to isolate the leg action in order to develop its power and endurance. In isolating the leg action a kick board also provides the opportunity for a swimmer to rest the arms. The experienced swimmer will normally rest their arms on top of the board and possibly maintain a head up position when swimming on the front. The large kick boards offer little assistance to swimming legs only on the back, and may become a hindrance rather than a help.

The teacher/coach should be aware that swimming butterfly legs only with a kick board could damage the lower spine and this activity is not recommended.

Hand Paddles – these are pieces of flat plastic, they are available in a variety of sizes, the most common is a little larger than the area of the hand. They are worn on the palm of the hand and kept in place by finger loops. Competitive swimmers use them to create added resistance to the arm action in order to improve muscular strength and endurance. They are controversial in that they alter arm action resistance and, therefore, require adjustments in the technique of the unaided action. Some claim they contribute to muscle soreness in the elbow and shoulder regions. They also pose a small risk to fellow swimmers when training under crowded conditions, in that the tough plastic edge can inflict scrapes to others close by if the arms are recovered carelessly. It may be wise to restrict their use to occasions when space and numbers allow and to avoid prolonged practice.

Fins – fins can be used by competitive swimmers in training to improve ankle flexibility or simply to add variation to a training session. They have the effect of increasing swimming speed which can be interesting and exciting in training. It is preferable for swimmers to have their own pair of fins as it is difficult for a swimming pool or club to hold the range of sizes required without purchasing large numbers of fins.

Aside from the competitive swimmer fins are occasionally used by beginners to increase propulsion from the legs in crawl type stokes, they can also be used very effectively in the development of butterfly at the improver/advanced level.

Swimmers need to be alerted to the possible dangers of wearing fins, they can deliver a nasty slap in the face to anyone close behind and there is a greater danger of the swimmer colliding with the wall due to the increase in speed of travel. Particular care should be taken in this area when the swimmer is on their back as they may have little or no protection for the head.

Anti-Chlorine Goggles – if water in swimming pools is kept in good condition goggles should not be necessary for people swimming for short periods. In fact they can be more of a hindrance than a help in the early stages of swimming lessons due to the inordinate amount of time spent adjusting them. Many teachers/coaches regard it as an essential early experience to deal with splashes to the face and to be able to open the eyes underwater with confidence.
Swimmers training for long periods of time for general fitness purposes or in preparation for competitions probably do need them. Goggles do protect sensitive eyes from the irritation of

pool chemicals and give clear underwater vision which helps to avoid collisions in crowded lanes. Competitors find them useful in practising and executing racing turns where a clear view of the wall is important.

To be effective goggles need to fit the boney structure of the face, there are a number of different types available to try and accommodate most individuals needs. The elastic of the goggles should also be worn around the widest part of the skull, this gives the greatest area of tension. Finally when removing goggles between swims they should be placed on the forehead making them easy to fit for the next swim.

Goggles are now proving to be a very welcome addition to the short sighted swimmer. Prescription goggles can be purchased and ordinary goggles make the wearing of contact lenses much easier when swimming.

Pace Clock – these come in a variety of sizes, probably the most popular model is the one which is fixed to the wall and powered by electricity. there are also portable battery ones which can be transported from pool to pool. The use of a pace clock will enhance any competitive training session by providing discipline for the lane, a measure of the pace the swimmer is working at, and an easy method of the swimmer taking the appropriate rest interval.

Backstroke Flags – wherever possible the backstroke flags should be set up in a competitive training session. They should be stretched across the pool 1.8 metres above the water and 5 metres from each end of the pool. They serve to warn backstroke swimmers that they are approaching the wall. This means novices are less likely to hit the wall with their head and competitive swimmers quickly learn the number of strokes to the turn or finish from the moment they pass under the flags.

Starting Blocks – starting blocks should conform to ASA specifications. They should be easily fixed to the starting point so they are absolutely secure and do not rock. Whenever possible the starting blocks should be fitted during training sessions. This give swimmers an opportunity to practice starting techniques appropriate to the race situation.

Teachers Equipment

Whistle – whether metal or plastic a whistle should have a sharp, penetrating note which will readily attract the attention of pupils during noisy conditions or in an emergency. It should be reserved for such situations and not used to indicate other procedures such as starting an activity. The whistle's power to attract attention or stop all activity should not be diminished or confused by a variety of uses.

Clip-boards – a clipboard is a useful memory aid, especially if sessions have a complex content, or a series of different activities follow on in succession. Session plans can be referred to quickly and it is also handy for noting down ideas, individual corrections or achievements as they occur. This, in turn, will lead to better planned future sessions. Although the teacher/coach must recognise this as a useful tool it should not become a prop to support the session and should be picked up and discarded as necessary rather than retained in the hand of the teacher/coach for constant reference.

Pole – in addition to the long rescue poles which are part of every pool's safety equipment, the teacher/coach may find a shorter light weight pole, such as a broom handle, a useful item when working with non-swimmers. It can be used to assist someone straying out of their depth, but, more often, it will be used as a "confidence booster" when held within easy reach of an inexperienced swimmer who is attempting something new, such as swimming without buoyancy aids.

Awards Booklet and Recording Sheets – the teacher/coach can use an awards scheme as a measure of progress and to motivate pupils. A good awards scheme, such as the ASA's, will provide a booklet which contains all of the information required for conducting the awards.

Visual Aids – the teacher/coach can use a variety of visual aids to assist his pupils to understand the verbal communication. Visual aids come in a variety of forms. Posters, models and flash cards are just a few examples. Some additional preparation and planning prior to the session may be necessary in order to make the use of visual aids as effective as possible.

Bag of Tricks – the teacher/coach can also carry around with him his own *"little bag of tricks"*. This will usually contain many of the items which assist the teacher/coach in obtaining the best from their pupils. Items such as hair ties, swimming hats, safety pins, plasters, simple learning toys, unusual artificial aids, goggles, a small box for collecting any jewellery, shoe laces to tie up loose straps on costumes. This type of teacher/coach is always prepared for any eventuality and his lessons will benefit greatly from their additional advance planning.

Learning Toys

There is a very familiar saying within education - *"Play should have a Purpose"* This should always be born in mind when setting up activities within a swimming lesson which involve play activities. There are many toys which can be adapted for use in a swimming lesson to assist in giving play a purpose. here are some examples:

Rubber Ducks – can be used to blow across the pool as an aid to getting the mouth in the water and teaching aquatic breathing.

Balls – can be used in a throwing game to encourage movement in different directions (throw the ball into a space) or to get the non-swimmer used to having their face splashed (throw the ball just short of the pupil's reach). They can also be used to introduce water polo skills in improver level swimmers.

Floating letters, numbers or different coloured toys – can be scattered around the teaching station and collected by pupils as instructed. This will encourage movement in different directions whilst searching for toys.

Plastic Watering Cans – can be used to pour water gently over pupils heads encouraging them to get their face wet. There are many other possibilities. A trip around some of the large toy stores keeping in mind the purpose of the play activity will help any teacher/coach to select learning toys appropriately.

CHAPTER 6

TEACHING THE NON-SWIMMER

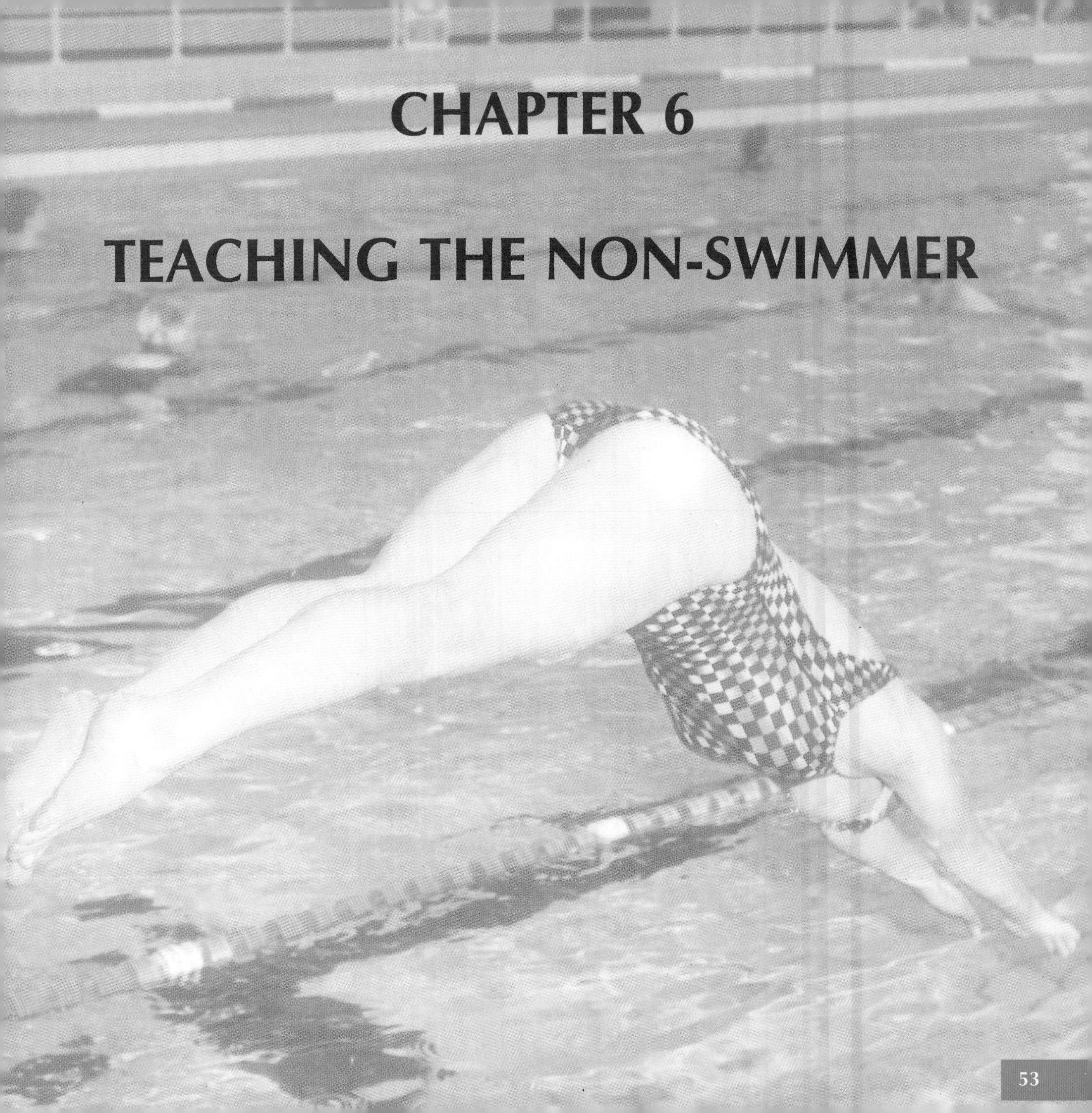

Introduction

If the needs of the non-swimmer can be properly identified then the possibilities of providing a comfortable, safe and stimulating learning environment can be greatly increased.

This chapter will look at factors which create an environment conducive to learning for the non-swimmer. The elements involved in introducing the beginner to the water and running a successful and enjoyable lesson, different methods used to teach the non-swimmer and finally the teaching of adult non-swimmers and the persistent non-swimmer. Although the last section of this chapter will provide a specific focus on the adult and persistent non-swimmer many of the details given in the remainder of the chapter will also be appropriate.

Factors which create an environment conducive to learning

- knowledge of the environment
- comfort
- swimming aids
- teacher/coach and pupil relationships

Knowledge of the Environment

Changing – learners are more confident if they are familiar with the procedure of attending the swimming pool and know the changing room, toilet and shower facilities. They need to know where and how their clothes are stored.

Pool – in the pool they should know where to go for their lesson. The teacher/coach should try to make this process as straightforward as possible by being available to welcome them and begin to develop a relationship with them.

Re-assurance – pupils need to feel safe, it will be helpful if a shallow learner pool is available exclusively for their use, or, in the case of adults, an environment which will not make them feel in any way threatened, and the appropriate area of water to suit their needs.

Quiet and friendly – a quiet and friendly environment is more welcoming to young or uncertain non-swimmers.

Roped Area – a roped off area should mark the extents of their class as non-swimmers are prone to wandering. This is not intentional but results from their lack of balance in the pool environment.

Comfort

Temperature – pupils are more relaxed if the air temperature in the changing room and pool surround is warm and slightly higher than the water temperature which should also be comfortably warm, say 29 degrees celsius.

Length of Lesson – early lessons, especially with younger children, should be short, active and enjoyable. Where the water temperature is less than ideal, the lesson should be shortened and activities chosen should be lively with the pupils' shoulders in the water.

Young Children – quickly adjust to this new and exciting environment if they are surrounded by brightly coloured and inviting toys and, sometimes, familiar music.

Adults – feel more comfortable in a class and pool on their own alongside other adults learning to swim. Onlookers should be kept to the minimum wherever possible.

Buoyancy Aids – availability, suitability and desirability

Support – a buoyancy aid can provide the necessary physical and psychological support needed at this stage to enable the learner to explore the water with greater confidence.

Type of buoyancy aid – the type of buoyancy aid chosen depends on the preference, age and size of pupil, the amount of support required or desired and the preference of the teacher/coach. Chapter five looks at buoyancy aids in more detail. The teacher/coach is are advised to read this chapter to help with the choice of equipment.

Position in the Water – it is important that the buoyancy aid chosen allows the pupil to float in the water, to have freedom of arm movement and buoyancy that can be progressively reduced. It is also important for the teacher/coach to observe the effect the buoyancy aid has on the swimmer obtaining a horizontal body position, and be aware of the effect that the unnatural assisted position that it creates may have on practices carried out.

Time without buoyancy aids – some time during each lesson should be spent without the buoyancy aid.

Teacher/Coach and Pupil Relationship

Confidence – A pupil needs to feel confident in the care of the teacher/coach. Welcoming pupils to a class and exchanging pleasantries and names helps to establish a relationship with the pupil.

Interest – the teacher/coach should take an interest in the pupil and encourage two way communication. This will help to put the pupil at ease and give the feeling that they are valued.

Enthusiasm – this is never more important than at the non-swimmer stage. Enthusiasm is infectious and can easily be transmitted to your class.

Teacher/Coach – **Pupil Ratio** – it is helpful if the numbers in a beginners class are low (eight – ten pupils) but preferably as low as six. Success and progress are closely linked to small class sizes at this level.

Teaching the non-swimmer

There are a number of essential skills which need to be incorporated into non-swimmer lessons. The lesson begins from the moment the pupil arrives on the poolside.

Methods of Entry into the water

- backwards down the steps
- from a sitting position twist one hand across the body, palms flat on poolside, rotate body and lower
- from a standing position drop or jump in, depending on the depth of the water
- in learner pools down the large steps which may run along the side or the end of the pool

Water Confidence

Pupils will attempt many more activities if they become water confident. This should play an important part in initial non-swimmers lessons. *"An introduction to Teaching & Coaching"* covers this area in detail. Reference to this text is advisable prior to planning non-swimmer lessons.

Movement

The initial movements done in the water should be in a standing position with shoulders under the water. These activities will assist the pupil with balance, the pressure of the water around them and resistance.

- walking, sliding feet with a wide base for balance, arms spread just under the surface in front of the body. Moving forwards, backwards or sideways or with a turn.
- arms begin to pull, push and scull, alternating or simultaneously.
- following a variety of patterns (circles, triangles, figures of eight etc).
- varying the speed of movement through the water (slowly, quickly).

Getting Feet off the Bottom

These practices can be performed with or without buoyancy aids as appropriate to the non-swimmer and the environment.

- marching on the spot, lifting the knees high, chin on water, arms spread and pressing down.
- head up, knees tucked in, turning on the spot. Pressing against the water with the arms helps turning.
- grasping the rail, trough or poolside and lifting legs.
- prone or supine floating positions.

Regaining the feet from prone and supine position

It is important at this stage, that pupils practice the skill of regaining their feet to enable them to regain balance, and stop. This should be done before they are required to push and glide or move into a horizontal position. Most young pupils will naturally perform the correct movements, but others, in particular adults, find it useful to know exactly what they are doing and why.

From the prone position at the rail the pupil will be able to press down against the rail to initiate the head lift. A full explanation of regaining the feet from the prone position is described in *"An introduction to Teaching & Coaching"*. The photographs which follow are provided as a reminder.

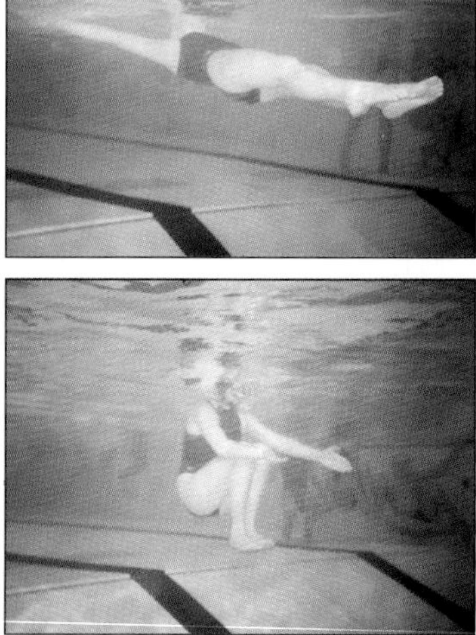

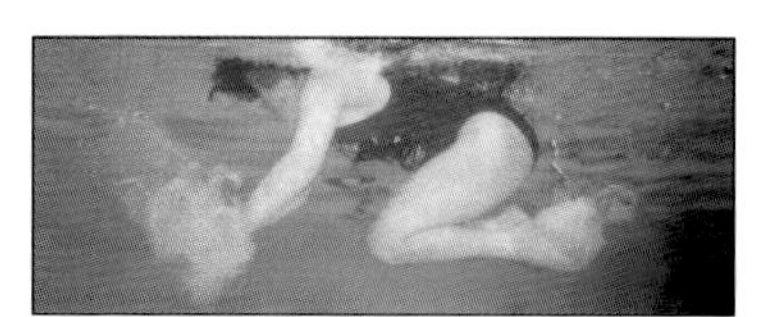

Push and Glide in prone and supine position

These are examples of other essential early skills; they provide initial momentum enabling the pupil to achieve a horizontal position and are a good method of starting off. These activities will continue to be utilised through more advanced lessons and even as part of competitive practices (transitions on starts and turns). It is very important that time is spent on these skills at the non-swimmer stage.

Push and Glide – Prone

- push and glide from pool floor to the poolside.
- push and glide away from wall to a partner.

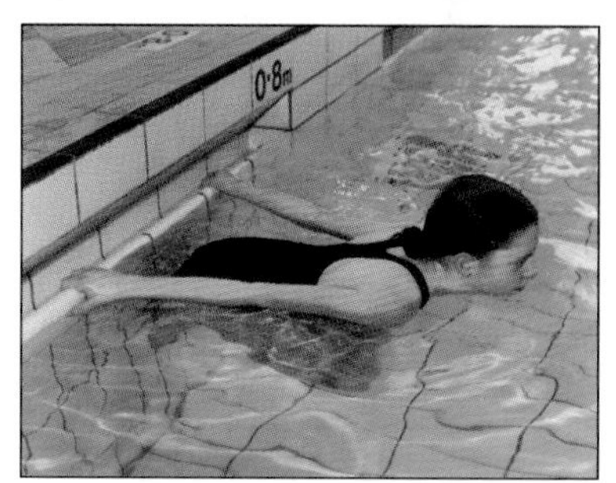

- push and glide away from wall and regain feet on own.
- back to wall both hands on the rail, legs bent, feet high on wall, head down and push away from wall.

Push and Glide – Supine
- push and glide from pool floor gently backwards towards the rail.
- push and glide away from wall towards a partner.
- push and glide away from wall and regain feet on own.
- facing the wall, both hands on rail, legs bent, feet high on wall, head back and push away from wall.

Push and glide practices can be performed with or without buoyancy aids, as appropriate.

Propulsion

The initial aim is to enable pupils to propel themselves on fronts, backs or sides, on and under the surface. Progressing on from this, the ability to change direction and bodyshape. Movements used at this stage may resemble recognised stroke patterns but need not be accurate and precise.

Exploration of Leg Actions

Using a number of different support positions (two floats, woggles etc.) pupils can attempt leg actions from a prone or supine push and glide. The types of actions suggested are alternating kicking resembling crawl type action and simultaneous kicking resembling breaststroke and butterfly.

As pupils gain in confidence and watermanship they can then progress to practices with buoyancy aids offering less support.

Exploration of Arm Actions

At this stage all recovery movements of the arms should be completed under the water surface. The effect of lifting arms out of the water during recovery is that of sinking the body which is not recommended at this level and will delay success.

Simple paddling or circling movements with the hands and arms will produce head first travel.

Submersion

The ability to submerge and surface in a variety of different ways will assist the pupil to develop new skills. Pupils should already have been taught a range of water confidence activities and be happy to place the face in the water.

Face in water and breath control – before pupils are asked to explore under the water surface they need to be able to hold their breath with their faces out of the water initially, they can then try with their faces in the water.

Eyes open under water – counting objects on the pool floor: collecting different coloured objects or ones with particular markings on them, partner games with fists open/closed.

Regaining the surface – through pressing feet down and standing up. Pupils can also be taught to press down with the hands and arms then raising head or hand to the surface.

Early submerging practice – holding the side of pool/partner's hands, kneel, sit on the pool floor and then touch pool floor with other body parts, e.g. tummy, elbow etc.

Push and glide to submerge – feet high on wall, head down, push down to the pool floor, straight arms, hands leading, keeping chin on chest.

Re-surface from underwater, push and glide – tuck knees, lift head, place feet on the pool floor and stand up, swim up or raise head, point hands to surface and glide to surface.

Under and through games – using hoops, partner's arms, partner's legs astride to go under and through.

Breathing

Following the breath holding skills tried earlier whilst pupils faces were in the water, pupils can be encouraged to breathe regularly whilst moving through the water, both in walking and swimming positions.

Young children – singing games and nursery rhymes in the water.

Adults – encouraging them to chat to each other whilst swimming.

All ages – ask your pupils to smile, it is impossible to smile without breathing.

Flotation

The most commonly taught floating positions for non-swimmers are:

Mushroom Float
Star Float – Prone
Star Float – Supine

Reference to the section on flotation in the Chapter thirteen *"Fundamentals of Swimming"* will help the teacher/coach to understand why these methods are used.

Floating helps pupils become aware of where their body is, the shape it is making and how this affects their balance in the water.

Front and Back Paddles

Depending on the progress of the individual within any group the time will arrive for introducing the basic actions of prone and supine swimming positions. Usually the movements take the form of Front Paddle and Back Paddle.

Details of these actions can be found in *"An Introduction to Teaching & Coaching"* where a full explanation is provided.

Structuring non-swimmer lessons

When beginning to plan lessons for non-swimmers and improvers it is important to be clear of the aim of the lessons at this stage.

Initial lessons should be focused on the development of water confidence and initial skills of movement. Continuation lessons should gradually introduce skills of flotation and propulsion progressing on to front and back paddle or circular actions. Increasing opportunities should be given for pupils to practice skills without buoyancy aids. Lessons can then begin to develop a whole, part whole structure with progressive practices which will begin to teach the strokes.

An example of the breakdown of an eight week scheme of work for a class of non-swimmers, who are attending lessons for the first time, is included at the end of this chapter.

The first lesson and the sixth lesson have been highlighted. An outline of these lessons is also included in this chapter to give an indication of the structure and breakdown of the lesson.

Important points when teaching a non-swimmer lesson

The lesson should be exciting, challenging and reassuring to the pupils new to the class.

There should be:

- safe confident entry.
- good organisation and supervision to ensure that each pupil has enough space and time to enter independently.
- a lively exciting warm up activity or game encouraging independent movement, vertical or horizontal.
- teaching at a level relevant to the individual pupil.
- an occasional testing of skills e.g. using the appropriate ASA Awards Scheme.
- a concluding game encouraging the basic practice of some of the previous skills.

Teaching Methods for non-swimmers

Shallow Water Method –Using this method pupils achieve a horizontal position in the water with their hands on the pool floor. An appropriate depth is such that the chin is on the water while the hands are on the pool floor with arms extended. This method can be used in learner pools, on the broad horizontal steps leading to pools or on the beach area in many of the leisure pools. The shallow water method is normally used without buoyancy aids and has the advantage of the pupils' face being out of the water.

Prone – the pupils move forwards by sliding their hands along the floor of the pool, progressing to making stepping movements with the hands. The legs float behind in an extended position. Eventually the arms pull the body forward without making contact with the floor. The pupils can then be encouraged to add a gentle kick.

Supine – from a sitting position, pupils can be encouraged to lie back putting their hands on the pillow of the water. The pupils' hands are flat on the pool floor with fingers pointing towards their feet. The progressions are as for the prone position.

Deep Water

With this method pupils wear inflated, close fitting buoyancy aids and could possibly swim out of their depth. The teacher/coach must be aware that pupils may require adult support in the water in order to ensure that the lesson progresses safely.

The advantages of the deep water method are:

- pupils are experiencing the upthrust of the water throughout the lesson.
- pupils breathe regularly while they are moving and tire less easily.
- pupils quickly learn the skills of using arms and legs for propulsion.

Partner Support

This method should be used only occasionally and with classes which are able to respond in a confident and responsible manner in a supporting role.

Children – can respond very positively when given this responsibility. This method can be useful if equipment is limited. Care must be taken to ensure that children are sufficiently confident to take the role of the partner.

Adults – respond very well to working with a partner and learn from helping each other. Partner work often gives them much needed rest as well as a chance to chat and share experiences with a fellow learner.

Limitations – when pupils are supporting or assisting a partner they are not actually practising. Water time is so valuable that it is essential to aim for maximum activity for all pupils.

Multi Stroke Approach

This method involves the strokes being introduced alongside each other with an equal emphasis on the basic technique for each stroke. The leg actions of the crawl strokes are combined with an alternating arm action with underwater recovery (front and back paddle) and the circular breaststroke leg action is combined with an arm action with a circular pathway. Pupils usually find the type of action and position in the water of one of the strokes more natural to them. This method is particularly advocated for the teaching of children as it promotes the importance of learning a number of skills. This will ultimately assist with varied stroke development at a later stage as well as provide the earliest possible opportunity for them to become water borne without buoyancy aids.

Single Stroke Approach

This method involves the learner selecting the stroke movements which are most appropriate for the particular individual and following a series of lessons which focus solely around the movements involved in that stroke. This method is not advocated for children as it restricts their continuing development, but it may be more useful for adults whose only desire is to be able to make progress through the water using the stroke to which they are most suited.

Adult Non-Swimmers

Adults join a learn to swim class for any number of reasons, but probably the most common reasons are:

- a desire to exercise for health benefits.
- in order to join the younger member of their family in the swimming pool.
- following advice from their General Practitioner.
- to participate in swimming activities whilst holidaying in the sun.
- to overcome a long time fear of the water.
- to socialise with other adults.

Often adults will arrive very apprehensive about their new activity. They may have stories of bad experiences with water as a child or just a long standing fear of water and the dangers surrounding it.

Whatever their reason for not being able to swim it must be remembered that they have made a huge step in attending a class and this should be respected. They may also lack a great deal in confidence, and despite the self motivation which has got them to the pool will need the teacher/coach to be encouraging, understanding and enthusiastic.

Other factors which influence that adult learner might be:

- that physical difficulties, perhaps related to joint mobility and muscle use in general, make exercise something to be approached with caution.
- that they are perhaps easily fatigued.
- that they are capable of longer attention spans than children.
- that they need to know why they are doing something.

Adult Lesson Structure

It is normal for the structure of an adult lesson to differ considerably from that of a childrens' beginners lesson. The teacher/coach will find that the physical ability of the pupils dictates far more the activities followed and the practices used. Even the choice of propulsive actions to be taught. More time will need to be given to each activity as an adults ability to learn a new skill is not as good as that of a child, and more rest will need to be allocated between activities (partner support is useful for this). The teacher/coach will also find that adults often like time to practice the skills they are learning on their own with the teacher/coach just keeping a watchful eye.

The lesson is likely to involve far more two way communication and the teacher/coach will certainly be able to devote more time to explaining the reasoning behind each activity practised. It is unlikely that there will be any discipline problems which allows organisation and control to be much more relaxed.

An outline of a possible structure for an adult lesson follows.

SESSION PLAN – Swimming

Class: Begs	**Session No.** 2 of 10			**Date**	**Time**	**Duration**
Age Range Adult	**No. in class:** Eight	**Male:** Three	**Female:** Five	10th Jan, 97	8.00pm	45 mins
Venue: Chesterton	**Type of Pool** – deck level – **conventional**	– leisure – other	**Water depth** 1.2m	**Safety equipment available:** Poles, Throw bags, Ropes		**Working area required:** Shallow end

Additional information (if any) provided by: participants, parents, teachers etc. including medical conditions Some adults suffering from arthritis – record made on register	
Aims of session To teach water confidence and basics of breaststroke	**Specific Objectives** To introduce aquatic breathing To teach partner support To introduce breaststroke legs and flotation
Ability of pupils (include any reference to lack of water confidence) Beginners, 3 lacking in water confidence	**Additional information**
Equipment required 2 floats per swimmer Woggles	**Assistants available (if any)** Non

Activity/Practices	Teaching Points	Organisation	Time
Warm Up Each adult to enter using own method preferred method Move around the space	Shoulders under water Say hello to everybody in the class	All moving at same time	10 mins
Main Theme **Aquatic breathing** When to breathe in and out Practice with face out of water Gradually submerge mouth & nose Continue above whilst moving **Breaststroke Leg Action** Kicking at rail – Breaststroke legs Kicking with 2 floats on front – breast legs, chin on water Introduce partner support In pairs – breast legs with partner Adults given time to practice each of above activities on their own or in pairs. Teacher circulating and giving feedback Group together as a whole One last attempt at each practice	Blow into water Breathe in through nose and mouth Blow out for the count of three Turn feet out Kick in circles Point toes to sides of pool Kick back with heels Knees and feet together in glide Pause and turn feet out Individual feedback and teaching points as appropriate Kick seat with heels Point feet east and west	The number of widths and number of repeats will depend on the progress. All at the same time in most cases. Allow adults to find their own space to work in.	25 mins
Contrast Introduce woggles & explain use Various floating positions with woggles	Emphasise relaxation when floating Encourage to float on back	Random spacing	10 mins

The Persistent Non-Swimmer

It is not uncommon for the teacher/coach to have a pupil or a number of pupils in his class who could be termed *persistent non-swimmers.*

These pupils appear to find the skill of moving through the water very difficult to achieve, often, for a number of different reasons:

- **fear of water** – this can manifest itself in different ways. The pupil may not be willing to leave the side, or may be very tense when trying to swim, which results in a poor body position.
- **poor co-ordination** – moving through water needs reasonable co-ordination of the arms and legs. A pupil who has difficulties with co-ordination may find progress difficult.
- **poor flotation** – there is little doubt that a poor floater will take longer to achieve the streamlined position than a good floater. This means that good unassisted travel through the water will require much more effective use of the arms and legs.
- **lack of flexibility** – this is particularly noticeable in adult non-swimmers. Often a limited range of movement means actions which create propulsion cannot be achieved easily.

The teacher/coach must assess the pupil carefully in the early stages of his lessons and ascertain their individual requirements. The assessment of ability and the understanding of individual needs is a very important skill of the teacher/coach throughout all of his teaching/coaching. The correct assessment of individual needs will allow the teacher/coach to set an appropriate programme of work.

Once the teacher/coach is clear on the programme of work for the pupil he must then use all of his different teaching skills to assist the pupil to achieve the work set.

Persistent non-swimmers can become very disheartened with their lack of progress towards their goal. The teacher/coach must be ready to motivate the pupil, perhaps by ensuring that the goals set are appropriate to the rate of progress of the individual. The teacher/coach should ensure that he does not become despondent with the lack of progress but remains positive focusing on the progress being made, however slow this may be.

The teacher/coach may find it more fruitful to work with the pupil on a 1:1 or 1:2 ratio, this avoids the pupil making comparisons with other class members and permits the teacher/coach to dedicate more time to their specific needs. A teaching assistant can be very beneficial in this situation, particularly in the water.

The teacher/coach may establish lessons specifically for the persistent non-swimmer, this is often a successful approach as it brings together a number of pupils who are experiencing similar difficulties.

The persistent non-swimmer sets the teacher/coach a real challenge. In order to meet this challenge it is necessary to be willing to experiment and be open to different ideas and methods for approaching the problem. If the teacher/coach maintains an open mind the likelihood of success will be increased.

Summary

The teacher/coach will see from this chapter that there are many elements involved in teaching/coaching the non-swimmer. Well thought out enthusiastic teaching/coaching of the basic skills is essential at this stage as these lessons provide the basis for all swimming activities which follow and are also the pupils' first real experience of swimming. It will be this experience which will shape their thoughts and feelings about the sport of swimming. It is essential the experience is an enjoyable one.

Scheme of Work – Non-swimmers

Aim:	Safe entry & exit	Movement in water
	Develop confidence	Basic swimming movements

Session	Content		Date of Session
1.	**Warm Up**	**Safety rules and entry down steps** **Jumping up and down at rail**	**29th October**
	Main Theme	**Movement Games – exploring space and changing direction**	
	Contrast	**Water confidence games and activities**	
2.	Warm Up	Slide in entry Running, hopping & jumping around the pool	5th November
	Main Theme	Flutter kick leg action on front Star floats on back	
	Contrast	Blowing bubbles and breathing practices	
3.	Warm Up	Slide in entry Running, hopping, jumping, touching all of the corners	12th November
	Main Theme	Flutter kick leg actions on front and back Introduction to arm movements	
	Contrast	Picking objects up from pool floor	
4.	Warm Up	Slide in entry Running across the pool. Swimming across pool, with aids	19th November
	Main Theme	Front paddle and back paddle, with flotation aids Regaining standing	
	Contrast	Jumping in	
5.	Warm Up	Slide in or jump in entry Swimming across the pool, with aids, on back or front	26th November
	Main Theme	Front paddle and back paddle, with flotation aids Star floats on back	
	Contrast	Picking up sticks from bottom	
6.	**Warm Up**	**Jump in entry** **Swimming across the pool, with aids, on back and front**	**3rd December**
	Main Theme	**Intro to circling arm and leg actions** **Push and glides**	
	Contrast	**Simon says – movement and confidence**	
7.	Warm Up	Jump in entry Swimming across the pool, with aids, on back and front	10th December
	Main Theme	Swimming on front or back unaided Push and glides	
	Contrast	Star floats & mushroom floats	
8.	Warm Up	Jump in entry Trying to swim across the pool without aids on front or back	17th December
	Main Theme	Swimming on front and back unaided Badge testing	
	Contrast	Statues – movement games	

SESSION PLAN – Swimming

Class: Begs	**Session No.** 1 of 8			**Date**	**Time**	**Duration**
Age Range 4-5 yrs	**No. in class:** Six	**Male:** Two	**Female:** Four	29th Oct, 96	5.00pm	30 mins
Venue: Parkside Pool	**Type of Pool** – deck level – **conventional**	– leisure – other	**Water depth** 0.9m	**Safety equipment available:** Poles, Throw bags, Ropes		**Working area required:** Learner Pool

Additional information (if any) provided by: participants, parents, teachers etc. including medical conditions Non	
Aims of session To introduce to swimming pool environment and lessons	**Specific Objectives** To outline safety rules To enter water safely To initiate movement around pool
Ability of pupils (include any reference to lack of water confidence) No previous swimming lesson experience	**Additional information**
Equipment required 2 floats per swimmer Learning toys	**Assistants available (if any)** Non

Activity/Practices	Teaching Points	Organisation	Time
Warm Up Explain safety rules Enter down steps Jumping up & down at rail	 Explain how to do this safely See how high you can jump	All at same time	5 mins
Main Theme		Activities will use free form organisation with random spacing	20 mins
Movement Games Follow the leader *Confident child to be leader.* *Follow the leader wherever he/she goes*	 Copy what the leader does Keep in a line Try and fill the empty spaces		
The quick change game *Children change direction and activity every time I beat the drum*	Large strides forward Large strides sideways Bunny hops with shoulders under		
"How big is our space" game *Children have got to touch special marked places around the class space. All children to touch every place*	Find the quickest way around Touch the places in any order Touch the places in number order		
Float tag *One child has a float and must tag others. Float must stay on surface. When tagged he/she also becomes a tagger.*	Keep float in front of you in water Stretch arms out to tag someone Keep shoulders underwater Move around in any direction		
Giants & Pixies *Children have to be giants and pixies. They must take large steps and stand tall when giants and takes small steps and be small when pixies.*	Pixies keep shoulders under Giants stretch arms above head		
Contrast Washing the face Simon says – water confidence activities			5 mins

SESSION PLAN – Swimming

Class: Begs **Age Range** 4-5 yrs	**Session No.** 6 of 8 **No. in class:** Six **Male:** Two **Female:** Four		**Date** 3rd Dec, 96	**Time** 5.00pm	**Duration** 30 mins
Venue: Parkside Pool	**Type of Pool** – deck level – leisure – **conventional** – other	**Water depth** 0.9m	**Safety equipment available:** Poles, Throw bags, Ropes		**Working area required:** Learner Pool

Additional information (if any) provided by: participants, parents, teachers etc. including medical conditions Non	
Aims of session Water Confidence Movement	**Specific Objectives** To develop movement on front and back To improve water confidence
Ability of pupils (include any reference to lack of water confidence) Experience from previous lessons in this course	**Additional information**
Equipment required 2 floats per swimmer Learning toys	**Assistants available (if any)** Non

Activity/Practices	Teaching Points	Organisation	Time
Warm Up Entry by steps or slide in Run around the pool and touch all four sides	Move in different directions	Free form organisation	5 mins
Main Theme 2 widths try to swim on your front	Keep hands underwater Stretch arms forward		
Kicking with 2 floats on front – flutter kick	Stretch knees straight Floppy angles (kick your socks off)	The number of widths and number of repeats will depend on the pupil's progress. All at the same time in most cases. Occasionally cannon formation	20 mins
Kicking with 1 float on front	Legs like a wooden soldier Use float like a steering wheel		
Walking across using arms underwater	Arms under water Chin on water		
2 widths – try to swim – front paddle	Keep chin on water Blow bubbles		
Star floats – using two floats	Push tummy to ceiling Ears in water		
Kicking with 2 floats on back – flutter kick	Splash the ceiling Look up, eyes open		
Kicking with 1 float on chest	Push tummy up to float Imagine your float is a teddy bear		
2 widths – try to swim – back paddle	Lean back and stretch Kick hard and fast		
Contrast Disappearing sticks. Throw the sticks in, swimmers collect sticks. Close eyes. Throw sticks in, pretend they have disappeared	Go cand collect you own magic stick	Free form	5 mins

CHAPTER 7

INTEGRATION OF PUPILS WITH A DISABILITY

Introduction

The ASA has a general policy of equal opportunities for all. Integration of swimmers with a disability is very much encouraged in the belief that everybody should have the opportunity to achieve their full potential.

Swimmers with a disability cover the same range of ability as their able counterparts, from non-swimmers to the elite performer. At developmental levels many have now had the opportunity to experience and enjoy swimming in specialist groups, integrated classes and normal pool recreational sessions. At the elite level, their success has been proven with excellent results at international competitions across the world.

There is, therefore, a need for the teacher/coach to become better informed in this area, in order that all can access the best possible teaching/coaching practices, regardless of any disability which they may possess.

There are many areas which should be considered when planning sessions to integrate pupils with a disability. This chapter is broken down into the following sections:

- pre planning
- disability access
- facilities
- awareness of safety, assisting and handling techniques
- teaching and learning
- common disabilities
- the parent

More detailed information regarding stroke adaptations, coaching swimming with varying disabilities and the competitive structure can be found in the publication *"Integration of Swimmers with a Disability – ASA 1996"*.

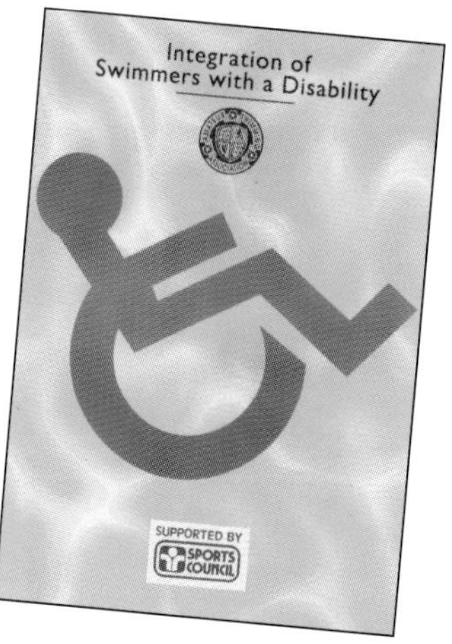

Pre planning

Pre planning is an important aspect of successful integration. In exactly the same way that the teacher/coach plans sessions for able bodied swimmers, prior to their arrival at the pool, plans need to be made for the integration of a pupil with a disability. The teacher/coach needs to be aware that he must spend additional time in planning to integrate a pupil with a disability, as there are additional considerations over and above the actual swimming session itself.

When the teacher/coach is gathering the initial information for the class the following key points need to be considered with regard to the pupil:

- medical condition
- age
- medical approval
- previous experience in the water
- movement ability
- swimming ability and effect of disability on swimming
- communication – hearing, speech, sight
- need for help in the water
- congenital or recent disability
- ambulant or wheelchair
- method of entering the water
- performance in competition (if appropriate)

Once the teacher/coach has developed a clear picture of the requirements of the pupil he can then begin to ensure that the experience will be enjoyable, by making any necessary arrangements prior to the session.

The pre planning does not stop at this point, the information gathered will tell the teacher/coach whether any special arrangements need to be made with regard to the access, facilities, etc. More detailed information in a number of areas follows. This should help the teacher/coach to understand better the requirements with regard to a range of people with disabilities.

Disability Access

There should be convenient arrangements for those arriving by transport, wheelchair or on foot. There are two important points to be considered for arrival by transport. Firstly, a clearly marked drop-off point adjacent to a non stepped building entrance should be provided, and secondly, properly sized parking bays should be available. These should also be near a non-stepped entrance.

For wheelchair access, ramps should be introduced wherever more than one shallow step is required, a landing should be provided at the top of the ramp. The ramp should have a non-slip surface and a preferred gradient of 1:12 is acceptable. Some ambulant disabled people prefer steps to a long ramp and so a combined ramp and step facility may be considered. The convenience of handrails and door handles for wheelchair users should also be considered.

Signs should denote accessible entrances, lifts and toilets as well as manageable routes through the building. Sign posting is particularly important for people with sensory disabilities and the availability of an induction loop will assist those with hearing impairment. For those with a visual impairment "signs" should be included to indicate changes in floor surfaces at stair heads and entrances to lifts. Signs should be in contrast to the general background.

Routes into the facility which eliminate doors and corridors, wherever possible should be planned.

Facilities

Facilities should be available for the use of every potential customer. Pupils with disabilities may have special needs which will require specialist equipment/facilities or slight adaptations to the equipment/facilities in order to enjoy a successful swim.

Points for the teacher/coach to consider:

Car Park
Is it close to the entrance?
Are the parking bays wide?
Are there designated disabled spaces close to the entrance?

Access - facility
Is there a ramp into the building?
Is there a handrail?
Are the doors suitable for access by wheelchair?
Are the doors wide enough for access by pupil and helper?

Access – changing room
Is the access acceptable for all types of disability?

Access – to poolside
Is the access suitable for different abilities?
Is the access suitable for wheelchair users?
Is there a handrail for less able ambulant swimmers?
Can a wheelchair be parked without becoming a safety hazard?

Access – to pool
What is the normal mode of entry?
Is there a hoist available and is it available at all times?
Are instructions on its use clear and easy to follow?
Is specialist training required, and, if so, provided?
Is there a ramp, ladder, graduated steps?

Changing Area
Is the area big enough?
Are there any big cubicles?
Is there a special changing area for swimmers with disabilities?
Does the area have tables, bins and mats to assist changing?
Is the temperature appropriate?
Are there handrails?
Is the changing area clean and fairly dry?
Are the showers easily accessible?
Are shower chairs available?
Are the toilets suitable with adequate space?

Poolside
Is there sufficient space to manoeuvre for assisted entries?
Are the floors non slip?
Is the pool deck level or is there a drop?
If there is a drop is the distance appropriate?

Pool
Is the water/air temperature suitable?
Is there deep water available?

Is there any specialist equipment available, e.g. flotation aids?
What other equipment is available, e.g. swimming aids?
Is a helper available if needed?

Awareness of safety, assisting and handling techniques

The adult human form is an awkward burden to lift or carry. It has no handles, it is non rigid, and is liable to severe damage if mishandled or dropped. In a swimming pool the pupil may have to be placed inconveniently for lifting.

The law states, employers have a duty to ensure the health and safety and welfare of their employees. This means that a "suitable and sufficient" assessment of the risks to staff and others affected by work activities must be completed. This includes swimming clubs which may have disabled swimmers as members. Risk assessment should be carried out in any teaching/coaching situation where there may be a need for a pupil to be assisted into the water manually. This assessment should be carried out by a suitably experienced person at regular intervals and all possible steps taken to minimise the risks of manual handling.

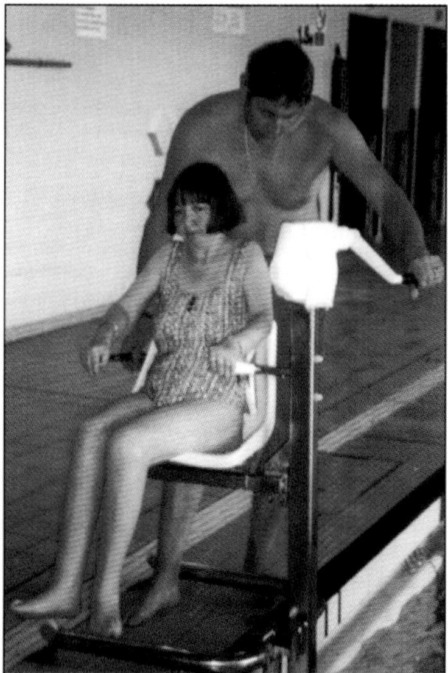

Initial considerations for the teacher/coach

- Ideally all lifting operations should be avoided by using mechanical lifting aids.
- A suitable and sufficient assessment must be made, and recorded, of any lifting operation that cannot be avoided.
- Following the assessment, the risk of injury should be reduced as far as is reasonably practical by introducing mechanical assistance or, if necessary, changing the way the task is carried out.
- The teacher/coach should be trained, by suitably qualified staff in the correct use of any equipment.
- The teacher/coach should have regular training by suitably qualified staff in moving and assisting.

Some common sense principles for the teacher/coach

- Disabled swimmers may often need help to participate but avoid lifting wherever possible.
- Always encourage disabled people to help themselves and teach them how to do so.
- Make use of swimmers own arm and leg strength.
- Make use of graduated steps, sliding boards, shower chairs, etc.
- Use mechanical aids as much as possible.
- Some swimmers will need lifting but the teacher/coach should always think, plan and prepare before he lifts.
- Lift the shortest possible distance.
- If a lift has to be done, the teacher/coach should never lift on his own.
- Two is always easier and safer providing they are of equal ability and size.
- The teacher/coach should not carry pupils across a wet poolside.
- Use appropriate equipment to assist, e.g. transit seats, shower chairs.
- The teacher/coach should make sure that any participants with balance problems are always assisted when walking on a wet poolside.
- Amputees should not be allowed to hop along the poolside.
- Pupils with paraplegia, spina bifida or those with minimum control of their lower limbs should not enter feet first in shallow water. Head first or forward entries in water of sufficient depth should be taught, with regard to normal safety precautions.
- Lock wheelchair brakes or lock the wheelchair before assisting pupil to stand.

- The teacher/coach should observe continuously those participants who are subjected to seizures.
- In early learning stages it is sometimes necessary to teach/coach essential features of safety on a one to one basis.
- Teachers/coaches should remember to give the required information to visually impaired participants.

The teacher/coach should be aware of the *"Manual Handling Operations and Guidance on the Regulations (1992)"* and of the *"Disability Discrimination Act (1995).*

Before assisting or handling the teacher/coach should think about:
- the task
- the person
- the environment.

Teaching and Learning

Although there is an ever growing involvement of pupils with disabilities in conventional teaching/coaching sessions, there is still a place for alternative arrangements, either long term or on a temporary basis, for participants who require specialist help, or prefer segregated sessions. A range of provision may be both possible and preferable.

Participation may be:

- fully integrated
- integrated and supported
- specialist disability club

The swimming programme, time and the content will have a bearing on participant choice. Choice may be associated with personal preference and interests e.g. Aquafit, adult improvers, beginners, recreation, swim fit, etc

Assessment of Need
Determining the specific needs of any pupils is an essential pre-requisite to their successful involvement in any swimming session. Specific needs may be determined by:

- direct consultation with the individual
- swimming background
- completion of enrolment/registration forms
- observation of how disability affects swimming style

As with any other pupils, constant monitoring of progress and achievement of goals should be reviewed by the teacher/coach on a regular basis.

Swimming Fundamentals and Safety Skills
All swimming sessions regardless of ability should include practices to ensure the pupil is proficient and happy performing the basic safety skills. For some disabled pupils the mastery of basic safety skills may take some time. These skills include:

- adjustment to the water
- progression in breath control
- submerging
- buoyancy and balance
- supine float and recovery to safe breathing practice
- prone float and recovery to safe breathing practice
- turning over
- vertical and horizontal rotation
- combined rotations e.g. rolling forward, then sideways and finishing on the back

- movement in supine and prone positions
- simple propulsion
- changing direction when moving through water

The teacher/coach should be aware of hidden disabilities which might present unexpected problems e.g. asthma, epilepsy, diabetes, cystic fibrosis, etc. The safety requirements of the pool and specific knowledge about the individual will determine whether there is a need for a watchful parent, spotter, etc.

Teacher/Coaching Principles
The basics of successful teaching is dependent upon:

- good technical knowledge
- willingness to be adaptable
- willingness to expand knowledge of disabilities where appropriate
- sound knowledge of fundamentals as they apply to promoting adapted stroke performance in people with disabilities
- acknowledgment of importance of basic safety skills
- ability to produce sessions with differentiated content for specific individual needs
- alertness to hidden disabilities.

Common Disabilities and Swimming Consideration

Teaching/coaching swimming is teaching/coaching swimming regardelss of whether the pupil is able bodied or disabled.

All pupils should go through the same initial process of becoming happy and contented in the pool environment. The practices used are the same. The important factor is that every pupil is an individual and the teacher/coach must consider how the swimmer's physique, mobility and application affects the swimming technique. This knowledge should then be used to maximise propulsion and reduce resistance for all swimmers.

Common Disabilities – Key Points

Asthma	● participate fully – awareness of tiredness and possible breathing difficulty
Diabetes	● may tire easily ● diet – exercise – insulin balance is important
Epilepsy	● constant observation ● appropriate action if fit occurs
Amputee	● full participation ● select appropriate strokes ● strength development
Spina Bifida	● degrees of lower limb paralysis ● care of limbs on rough surfaces ● reliance on upper limbs for propulsion
Blind	● auditory emergency signal guidance for end of pool ● buddy system ● care in lane swimming ● may be disorientated underwater
Deaf	● visual emergency signal ● visual communication
Learning Difficulties	● slow to learn skill ● constant repetition ● can become physically able

The table gives some examples of common disabilities and their possible effect on the pupil. The teacher/coach should be aware that this list is only a small sample of the range of disabilities which may be seen. The teacher/coach is advised to consider each pupil individually and obtain as much information as possible with regard to the disability, then, from his experience of teaching/coaching able bodied participants, make the necessary adjustments to activities.

Additional information with regard to different disabilities can be found in the *"ASA Teacher Certificate Log Book"* and *"Integration of a Swimmer with a Disability – ASA 1996"*.

All of this information could be obtained via an enrolment form/registration form, which is completed by all pupils attending the swimming session. It is important for the teacher/coach to ensure that those responsible for collecting this information understand the importance of this being transmitted to the teacher/coach. The teacher/coach is the person who is working closely with the swimmer and it is vital he has all of the relevant information to hand.

The aims and objectives of the parent should be discussed prior to the session commencing. This will help the teacher/coach to identify if the session is working towards similar aims and objectives. If the aims of the session are different to those of the parent and pupil it may be necessary for the teacher/coach:

- to recommend more suitable groups
- to obtain specialist help at a special needs club until the required standard is achieved
- to obtain suitable volunteer helpers to make the session suitable

Both parents and the teacher/coach have to be aware that, for some swimmers with a disability, the time taken to learn to swim, improve and compete can be considerably longer than for their able peers. This can lead to worries for parents and sometimes frustration from the pupil. The teacher/coach needs to be sympathetic to these worries whilst at the same time acknowledging the present ability of the pupil.

Summary

Many teachers/coaches will be integrating pupils with a disability into their everday teaching/coaching on a regular basis. Disabilities such as asthma and hearing problems are very common and it is rare for the teacher/coach not to experience one of these conditions during his teaching. The principles which are used in these cases need to be extended in order to cater for the largest range of disabilities possible. Additional planning and preparation may be necessary but the outcomes can be very rewarding.

The Parent

Parents obviously have a key role to play, they are a vital link between the pupil and the teacher/coach. The parent must believe in and support the integration of swimmers with a disability.

There is an amount of information that the parent can share with the teacher/coach which is relevant to the swimming situation, some examples might be:

- is the swimmer able to cope in a group?
- does the swimmer require one to one assistance to move in the water?
- does the swimmer require one to one assistance to understand instructions?
- in other situations outside swimming, which method of teaching has worked best? (visual, verbal, manual or a combination of everything)
- does the swimmer have any special need which is not apparent?
- has the special need been recently acquired and so is new to the swimmer?
- are there any restrictions or limitations on/in under water?
- does the swimmer require medication?

CHAPTER 8

ORGANISING AND MARKETING SWIMMING COURSES

Introduction

Once qualified any teacher/coach could establish his own swimming courses. A teacher/coach could often find himself in a position were he may have to do this. This could be for a number of reasons:

- he decide to set up their own swim school
- he is put in charge of the lessons at the pool where they are employed
- he is asked to organise the swimming lessons for their club
- he is asked to coordinate lessons for a school

Whatever the reason, this can be a daunting task if the teacher/coach has only previously experienced managing his own class. This chapter aims to look at all of the areas involved in setting up a course of swimming lessons and sets guidelines which any teacher/coach could follow.

Pool Time

The first consideration of the teacher/coach must be to obtain pool time or to examine the pool time which is available and consider how it can be best utilised. Some of the points listed below must be taken into account when organising pool time:

- what is the age group to be targeted?
- what is the cost of the pool hire?
- does the cost include a lifeguard?
- what lifeguarding cover and qualifications are necessary?
- has the pool got an NOP & EAP?
- what equipment is available at the pool?
- what are the dimensions and the depth of the pool?

Once the pool time has been booked the next consideration must be how to make the best use of the water time available. The diagrams give some examples of good utilisation of water for swimming lessons.

The teacher/coach must remember that water is an expensive and valuable commodity and should be utilised fully when

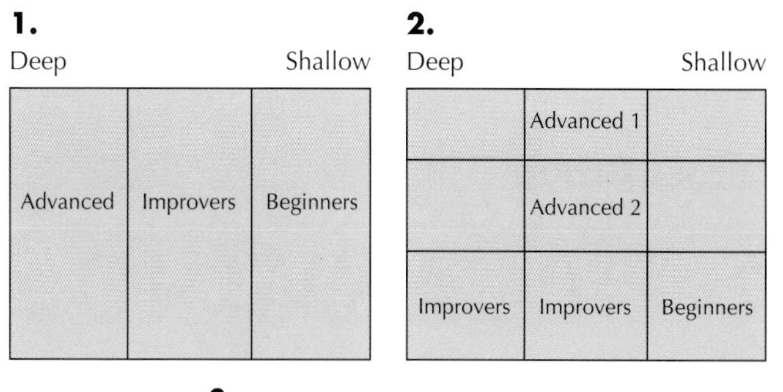

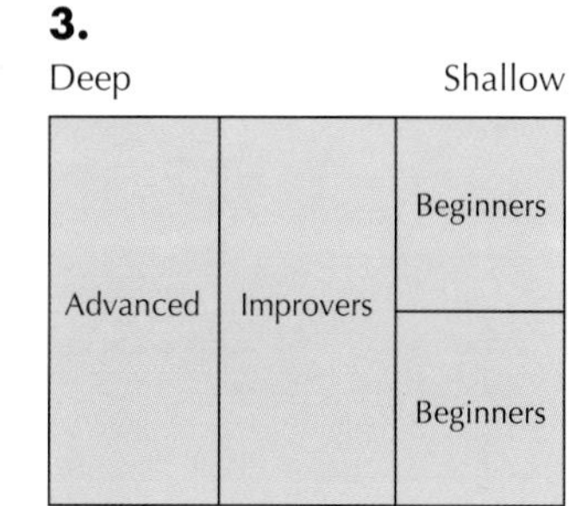

4.

Shallow Deep Shallow

Advanced 1			
Advanced 2			
Beginners	Improvers	Advanced	Beginners

5.

Main Pool

Deep Shallow

P.Survival Class	Advanced	Improvers

Learner Pool

Shallow

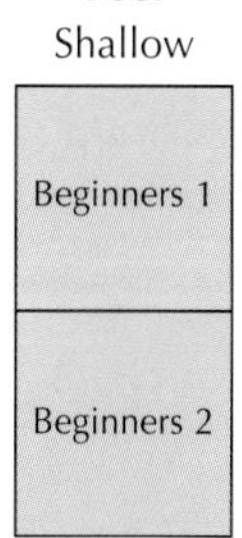

available. Full usage of the space available will also make any swimming course more cost effective.

Target Group

Swimming lessons are normally focused at a specific target group/groups within one session. This allows participants within this target group to progress through a variety of stages and still remain at the same or a similar session.

The choice of target group for a swimming lesson will depend on some of the following:

- the time the pool is available
- the location of the pool
- the accessibility of the pool
- the population breakdown
- the demand for a particular type of session/s
- the structure of the planned session/s

If the pool time available is in the latter part of the evening it is unlikely to be attractive to children and older adults, equally if parking is not easily available, families may find it very difficult to bring young children.

It is wise for the teacher/coach to carry out some simple form of market research, prior to marketing the lessons, in order to ascertain the needs of the people living in the vicinity of the pool, and to help identify the particular type of session to be run and the target group.

Planning the Classes

Once the target group has been established the teacher/coach can then consider the actual classes to be held in more detail. If there are a number of swimming lessons available at the same time these would normally be progressive in nature (beginners, improvers, advanced etc.). This allows pupils to continue to attend at a similar time and day whilst progressing through the classes. However, this is not always possible, due to lack of time available or the limitations of the facilities.

The teacher/coach organising the lessons will also need to consider how many pupils should be in each class. The number in each class needs careful consideration taking into account the space available and the overall finances of the sessions. Most swimming lessons work on a ratio of approximately one teacher to between eight and twelve pupils. A set of guidelines relating to pupil ratios and supervision is now available *('Safe Supervision for teaching and coaching swimming' - ASA,ISRM,ISTC,RLSS - 1996)*

Teaching/Coaching Staff

The ASA strongly recommends that qualified staff should be used to teach/coach swimming. An ASA Teacher (Swimming) is the minimum qualification which should be accepted for any teacher/coach who has full responsibility for a group. ASA Assistant Teacher (Swimming) is an acceptable qualification for any person who is to work in an assistant role, perhaps in the water with the non-swimmers group.

If, as part of the swimming lesson programme, the teachers/coaches are to be employed, an appropriate rate of pay should be negotiated. Guidelines may be available from the ASA or the ISTC with regard to recommended rates of pay for teachers/coaches

Marketing the Lessons

Without effective marketing of the lessons it is unlikely they will be successful, but marketing can come in many different forms:

- advertising in the local newspaper
- advertising on local radio
- placing posters in relevant places
- delivering fliers to homes in the area
- placing fliers in public access places
- distributing fliers to schools, clubs etc.
- distributing fliers to existing customers
- feature in newspaper or on the radio
- word of mouth

The last item on the list *"word of mouth"* can be a very powerful marketing tool as the opinion of the customer/participant will be valued by other potential customers. Equally if the product which is being delivered is of a poor standard existing customers/participants will not be backward in pointing this out to others. In the fullness of time a quality product (good swimming lessons) will market itself through *"word of mouth"*. However, this method of marketing is difficult to use when initially setting up and establishing swimming lessons as there is no past history to base this on.

Normally, the organiser of swimming lessons will use a variety of methods of marketing to ensure information is spread to the widest possible audience. When the teacher/coach is deciding which marketing methods to use, the target group needs to be considered. For example, if the target group is children aged 4 - 6 years leaflets could be distributed to primary schools, after schools clubs and pre school child minding services.

If the teacher/coach is inexperienced at marketing swimming courses it is useful to observe the effectiveness of the marketing of other organisations, possibly by visiting the local pool or leisure centre and observing their advertising displays.

The other consideration when marketing courses is the finance available. This can often be quite limited at this stage as, to date, no income would have been received. Reference should be made to the section in this chapter entitled "Costing the Course".

Finally, the teacher/coach planning the course needs to design and produce an eye catching leaflet, poster or advertisement. Some swimming pools now have leaflets etc. professionally designed and printed, such as the ones below, but this is not always necessary. The main consideration should be to include all of the main features of the courses, whilst still making the leaflet etc. easy to read and understand. Too much information at this stage can be confusing. Additional information can always be given at a later stage. The list below covers some of the key points to be included:

- Dates & Times
- Venue
- Target Group
- Price
- Contact Number.

Costing the Course

Whether the teacher/coach is organising a course for the local pool which involves large numbers of pupils, or for the swimming club, which just wants to fill a small space in the pool, it is essential that it is cost effective. A cost projection should be produced at the planning stage of the course to ensure that appropriate charges are made etc. There are a number of items which must be included into the cost projection. Costs, such as administration are often forgotten as they are not always clearly visible. It is normal for an organiser of courses to plan a break even point at about 75% of maximum capacity, This permits courses to go ahead even if they are not completely full. An example of a cost projection is given below to indicate the areas which need to be considered.

Cost Projection for a 10 week course of Lessons

● pool hire	£26.00 per hour x 6 hours	=	£1560.00
● equipment	£20.00 per week	=	£200.00
● staff	£10.00 per hour x 6 x 4 teachers	=	£2400.00
● publicity	£20.00 per week	=	£200.00
● administration costs	£25.00 per week	=	£250.00
			£4610.00

No. of pupils per hour: Maximum 80
(4 classes of 10 pupils per 1/2 hour)

Cost per pupil per session: £2.00 per session = £20.00 per course

Maximum Enrolment on Course = £9600.00
Break Even Point = 50% take up

Running the Course

Once the course is planned, costed, staffed marketed and has enough participants to make it viable, the teacher/coach must now consider some of the responsibilities of managing a course on an ongoing basis.

- Preparing registers
  It is useful for every teacher/coach to have a register to check off pupils as they arrive.

- Ensuring teaching/coaching staff are available
  Although the staff may have been planned, occasionally a teacher/coach may not be able to attend due to illness. The course organiser needs to provide cover for the lesson affected.

- Keeping staff up to date with any changes
  From time to time it will be necessary to make changes. All staff should be advised, ideally by holding a staff meeting to explain any changes and answer any queries. It is useful if the staff meeting is supported by a written notice of changes.

- Dealing with complaints
  Even the best swimming lesson programme will receive complaints occasionally. If a complaint is received, the teacher/coach or organiser of the lessons should listen to the complaint, ideally in a quiet place away from other customers. The complaint should then be investigated and any necessary action taken. The teacher/coach or organiser should then write to the complainant and advise them of the course of action taken.

- Organising Awards Sessions
  Most swimming courses are supported by an awards scheme. The ASA promote the largest and most successful sports awards scheme in this country. It provides progress across a range of skill learning. The teacher/coach should give some consideration to incorporating awards in to the normal lesson structure and providing the opportunity for awards to be taken whenever possible.

Summary

Hopefully this chapter will have provided some guidelines to assist the teacher/coach to plan organise swimming lessons should the occasion arise. There are many elements involved in organising a course of lessons, regardless of the reasons for doing this. The underlying principle behind successful organisation is planning. The teacher/coach who plans carefully, taking into consideration the points raised in this chapter, is more likely to succeed in his endeavours.

CHAPTER 9

ANATOMY AND PHYSIOLOGY

Introduction

Teachers/coaches spend a great deal of time developing skills which require the human body to function in particular ways. It is vital that every teacher/coach has an understanding of how the body functions in order to, firstly, provide safe and suitable activities and secondly, to take appropriate action related to an individual's physical make up.

The subjects of anatomy and physiology are huge, and the information in this chapter will only be scraping the surface of these areas. This chapter will, however, provide the teacher/coach with a good working knowledge of the human body, in understandable terms, closely related to the activity of swimming.

The physical effects of exercise

In Chapter One *'Health, Safety and Hygiene'* reference was made to the three 'S's. A fourth 'S' for speed might also be added. For all round fitness an individual should possess an adequate amount of each. This can be achieved by ensuring that all of these components are included in an exercise programme on a regular basis. Simply by swimming regularly, suppleness, strength and stamina will be improved. However the demands of a serious competitive programme will need a much more detailed and structured approach than just simply swimming regularly. Chapter 20 will deal with the training process in more detail.

Within a swimming session the teacher/coach is trying to develop the swimmers physical well being in addition to developing skills and techniques appropriate to swimming activities.

The Framework of the Body

The human skeleton is made up of more than 200 bones which vary considerably in size and shape. The human skeleton performs a number of functions:

Support – Most of the tissues and organs of the body are fairly soft. The skeleton provides support to ensure that the human body is not just a shapeless lump.

Movement – The bones, with the moveable joints and muscles, form a series of powerful and complex levers. These allow the body to operate with a high degree of accuracy and control.

Protection – The body depends upon the functioning of a number of different systems. Some of these are structurally very delicate. The bones of the skeleton provide protection to many of these systems. An example of this would be the skull (cranium) protecting the brain. Many other examples can also be found if the structure of the skeleton is examined carefully.

Mineral Storage – The bones are largely composed of calcium phosphate. The body will normally obtain sufficient calcium from a balanced diet. If the body runs short, calcium can be absorbed from the bones. Calcium storage is an important function and reduced storage in later life can lead to brittle bone disease. A sports person with low calcium levels may be at greater risk of breaks or fractures.

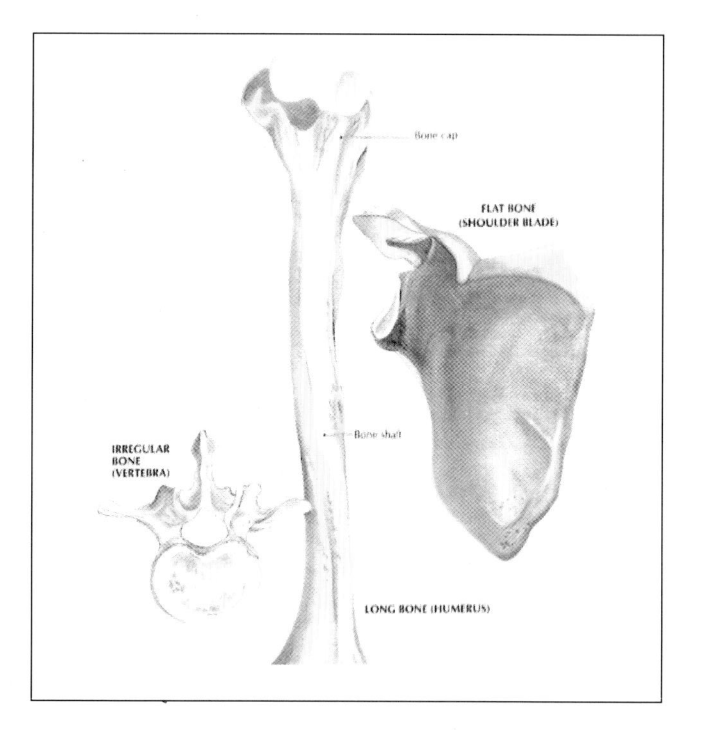

Blood Cell Production – This essential function of the bones is concentrated in the red marrow within them. Red blood cells and certain types of white cells are produced.

Bone Types

There a three main types of bones in the body:

Long – such as the bones in the arms (Humerus, Radius, Ulna) and legs (Femur, Tibia, Fibula). The length of these bones makes them very effective levers.

Flat – such as the bones of the skull (cranium). These frequently have a protective function.

Short – such as the carpals of the wrist. These are small bones which are very strong and well adapted to resist compression forces.

Joints

A joint is where two bones meet. Joints are classified under three main headings:

Fixed – where no movement occurs for, example in the skull

Cartilaginous – for example between vertebrae and discs

Synovial – movable joints, for example the knee

The main concern with regard to swimming are the movable joints (synovial). The movements of the body are diverse and complex, therefore, there are a number of different synovial joints:

Ball & Socket – this joint permits the widest range of movement

Hinge – this joint permits movement in one plane only

Pivot – as its name would indicate it allows a certain amount of turning (pivoting)

Condyloid – this joint permits movements in two planes at right angles to each other, (up and down and side to side)

Gliding – this is a small joint. Movement is limited to small gliding movements

Saddle – this joint permits movements in two planes at right angles to each other. (the base of the thumb)

Whilst it is important for the teacher/coach to appreciate that there are a number of different synovial joints functioning within the body, it is of greater importance to understand the range of possible movements at each joint. This helps the teacher/coach to recognise the need for movements within swimming strokes to be performed in particular ways. For example, the amount of movement possible at the shoulder when the arm is beginning recovery is limited. The stroke of frontcrawl assists with the recovery by adding body roll. This permits the arm to be recovered over the water more easily even though joint movement is restricted.

Joint Movements

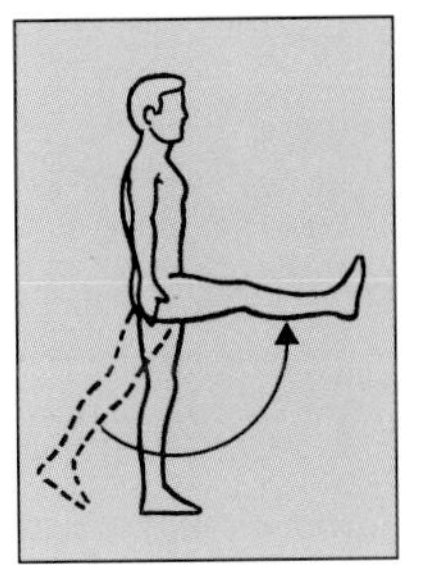

Flexion
Reducing the angle at the joint

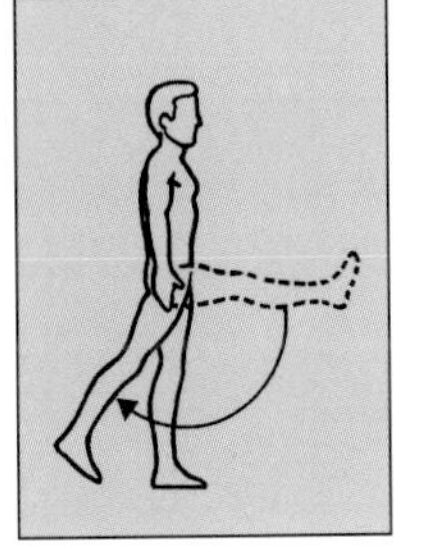

Extension
Increasing the angle at a joint

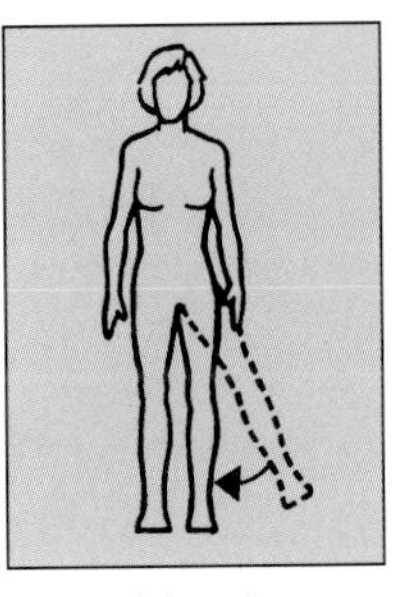

Adduction
Movement towards the body mid line

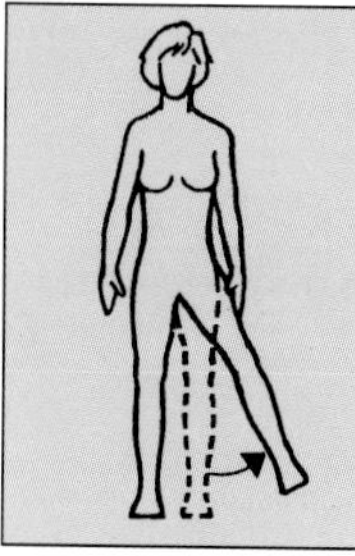

Adduction
Movements away from the body mid line

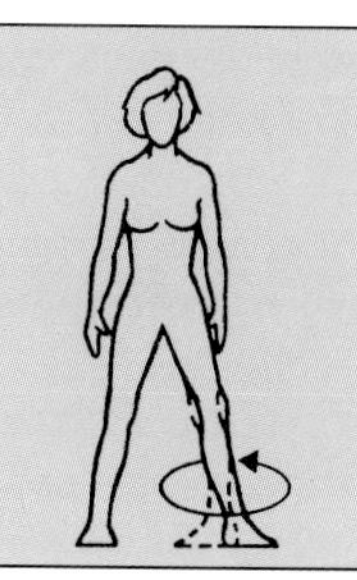

Rotation
A joint which rotates about a pivot

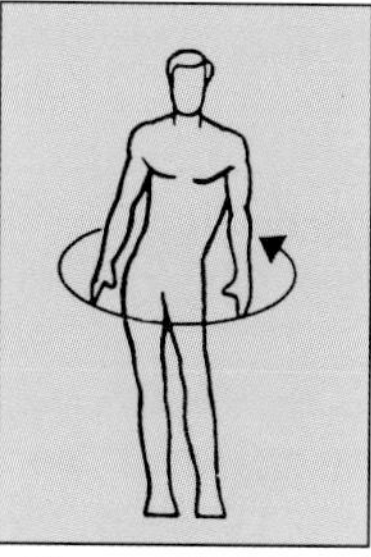

Circumduction
A combination of adduction, abduction, flexion and extension

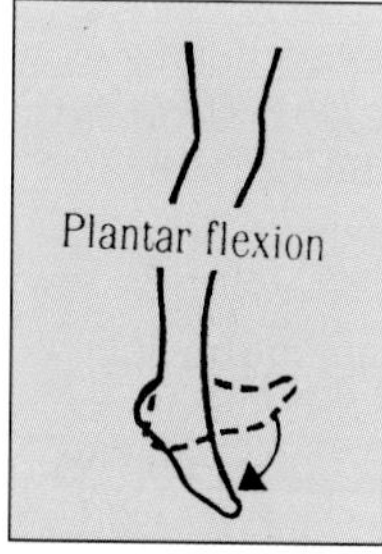

Plantar Flexion
Extending the foot away from the body

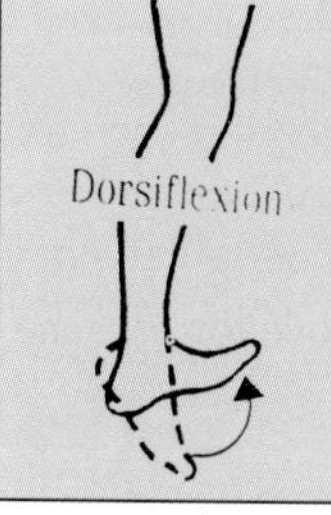

Dorsi Flexion
Pulling the foot upwards towards the skin

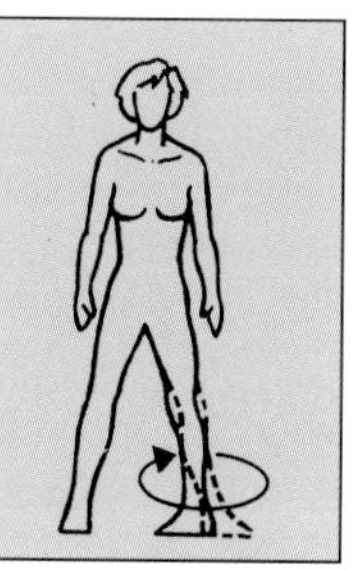

Inversion/ Eversion
Turning the soles of the feet inwards/ outwards

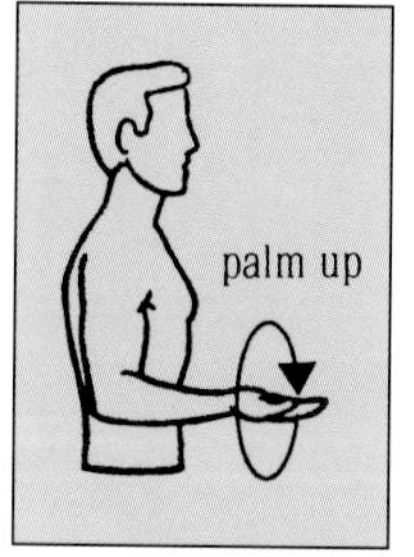

Supination
Turning the palm of the hand up

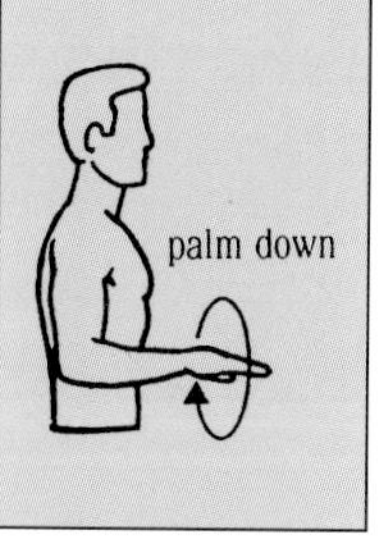

Pronation
Turning the palm of the hand down

Muscles

The muscles exert power both to move parts of the body by means of levers and to transport material within the body itself.

There are three types of muscle:

Cardiac – this type of muscle is found only in the heart. It can be classified as an involuntary muscle

Smooth – this type of muscle can be found in areas such as the digestive system. It is also an involuntary muscle

Skeletal – This type of muscle supports or moves the skeleton. It is a voluntary muscle and is the type which the teacher/coach should be concerned with.

Muscle Structure

A muscle is a collection of long fibres which are made up of cells grouped in bundles. Each bundle is separately wrapped in a sheath which holds it together and protects it. The muscle comprises:

- muscle tissue to enable contraction
- connective tissue, to bind it together
- nerves to receive messages from the brain
- blood vessels to carry oxygen and remove waste

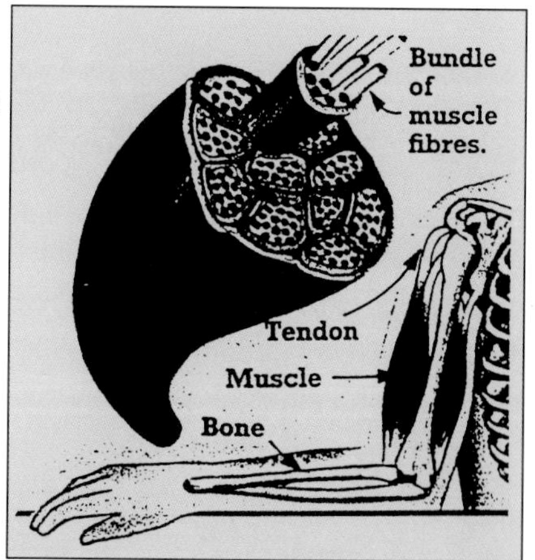

It has been recognised for a long time that there are different types of voluntary muscle fibres. This is because human beings need to function in different ways. For example a swimmer who is going to swim for a long distance needs to use voluntary muscle fibres repeatedly, whilst a swimmer who is purely going to perform a fast push and glide needs to use voluntary fibres for only a short time, but quickly.

The fibres in the muscles are commonly referred to as **fast twitch** and **slow twitch:**

Fast Twitch – can produce high speed movement for short periods of time e.g. a sprinter cannot continue at maximum speed indefinitely.These fibres are utilised during anaerobic activity.

Slow Twitch – produces lower speed movement but for longer periods of time e.g. distance swimming. These fibres are utilised in aerobic activity.

The teacher/coach should be aware that there are two types of fast twitch fibres, often referred to as A & B. This will become more obvious later in the chapter when the words anaerobic and aerobic are described in more detail along with the different energy systems.

How Muscles Work

Muscles are attached to bones by tendons, usually running between two bones and crossing a joint. Muscles contract because the muscle fibres shorten. This develops tension within the muscle. The human body ascertains the appropriate amount of effort to make and transmits this information from the brain to the muscle. The muscle then contracts the appropriate type and amount of fibres for the action to be effective. Examples of this can be seen when an inexperienced swimmer attempts a new action. At this stage the brain is unable to calculate the amount of fibres to contract as it is unfamiliar with the action. This usually results in the swimmer using far too many fibres and muscles and becoming tired very quickly. As the swimmer begins to understand the necessary movements the messages sent by the brain become much more accurate and just the appropriate fibres and muscles are contracted.

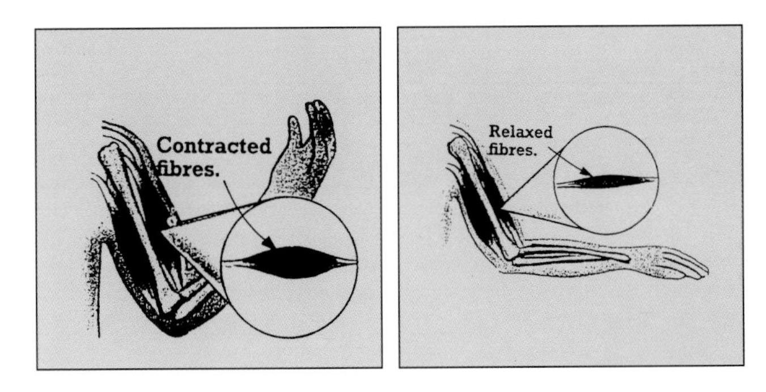

As the fibres contract one end of the muscle normally remains fixed, this is known as the origin, whilst the other end, the insertion, moves towards the origin. It is quite easy for the teacher/coach to feel the contraction of a muscle such as the bicep by placing the thumb at one end of the muscle, close to the armpit, and the first finger of the same hand at the other end, close to the inner elbow. As the muscle is contracted the finger can be seen to move towards the thumb and the gap between finger and thumb is reduced.

Group Action of Muscles

Muscles tend to work in groups of opposing action. The group which produces the movement is referred to as the agonist, whilst the group opposing the action is known as the antagonist. The word antagonist has been adapted for every day use to indicate a person who is against something or opposed to something. This is often an easy way for the teacher/coach to remember the words used to describe the action of muscle groups.

Types of Muscle Action

All muscles act by contraction of the muscle fibres to exert a force. However, this does not always mean that the muscle itself contracts or shortens overall. Muscles are able to contract in different ways:

Concentric

The muscle shortens and thickens, end attachments move closer, the angle of the joint decreases

Example:
The elbow bending in breaststroke to make the down sweep

Eccentric

This is the opposite of concentric, the muscle is lengthened and the end attachments move apart, the angle of the joint increases

Example:
The straightening of the elbow in frontcrawl after entry

Isometric

The muscles contract with no resulting movement, because the tension in the muscle exactly balances the opposing force

Example:
The muscles in the arms which support the swimmer when they perform the action of kicking at the rail

Isokinetic

The muscle contracts and works at maximum tension throughout its range

Example:
When using specialised apparatus which provides resistance throughout the range of movement

Circulatory System

There is a need for certain elements e.g. oxygen, to be transported to the muscles in order for continual energy to be produced. The circulatory system consists of:

- heart
- transporting vessels
- blood

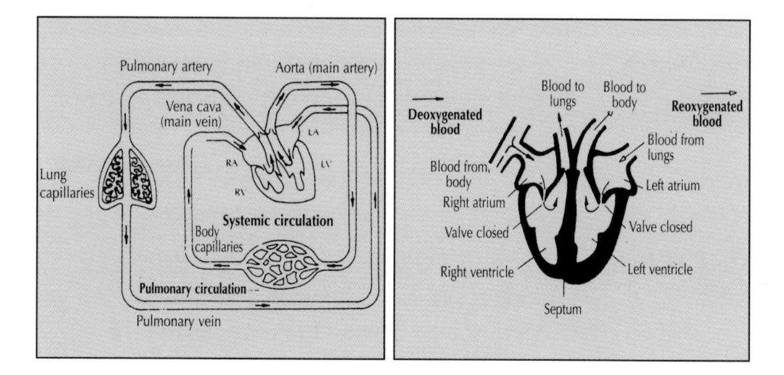

The circulatory system works in conjunction with the respiratory system, its main functions are:

- to provide the muscles with oxygen
- to remove the waste products of lactic acid, carbon dioxide and water
- to dispense the heat from the core to the periphery
- to provide the muscles with a source of energy

Heart – the heart is a muscular pump which is divided into two halves. The right side pumps blood into the pulmonary circulation system. A gaseous exchange takes place at the lungs which oxygenates the blood. The blood returns to the left side of the heart and is pumped around the body through the systemic circulation system.

Blood Vessels – Collectively the blood vessels are known as the "vascular system". This consists of arteries, taking blood to the muscles or organs, veins, returning blood to the heart, and, in between, the smallest vessels which are known as the capillaries. It is in the capillaries that the gaseous exchanges take place.

The blood vessels have an amazing ability to adapt to the needs of the body through a process known as "vascular shunting". The vascular shunt is the body adjusting its priorities and re-routing the blood to the areas it is most needed. An example of this would be when a swimmer begins to warm up on frontcrawl, the body would shunt additional blood to the chest and shoulder muscles to permit the swimmer to carry out an effective arm action.

Blood – The blood has a number of functions:

- transports oxygen from the lungs to the body tissues
- transports carbon dioxide from body tissues to the lungs
- transports digested food to meet the body's requirements
- transports naturally made poisons to the kidneys
- regulates the body temperature

The swimmer will probably be most concerned with the blood's ability to carry and transfer oxygen to the muscles as it is this function which will assist the swimmer in continuing his exercise for a longer period before the onset of fatigue.

The Respiratory System

The respiratory system enables the body to take in oxygen and expire carbon dioxide. The diagram shows the chest cavity and details the parts of the body which make up the respiratory system.

The respiratory system is made up of:

- lungs
- bronchi
- bronchioles
- alveoli

Mechanics of breathing

Inspiration – To permit air to be inhaled the ribs move upwards and outwards, the diaphragm moves downwards and flattens. The volume of the thoracic cavity is increased and the pressure decreased. The lungs inflate and air rushes in.

Expiration – To permit air to be exhaled the ribs move downwards and inwards, the diaphragm moves upwards and becomes dome shaped. The volume of the thoracic cavity is decreased and the pressure is increased. The lungs deflate and air is forced out.

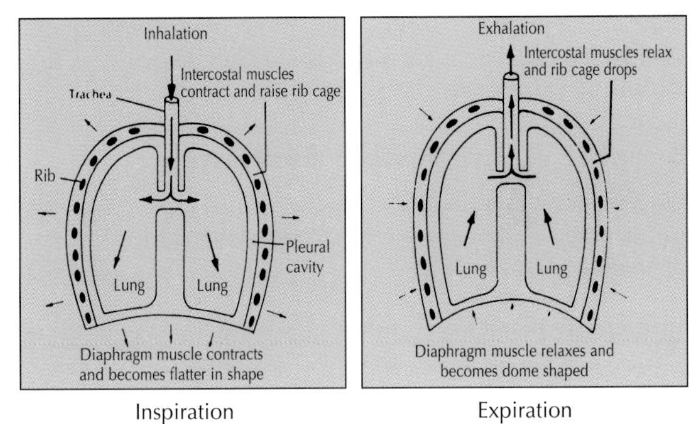

Inspiration　　Expiration

The flow chart which follows indicates the steps taken during the process of respiration.

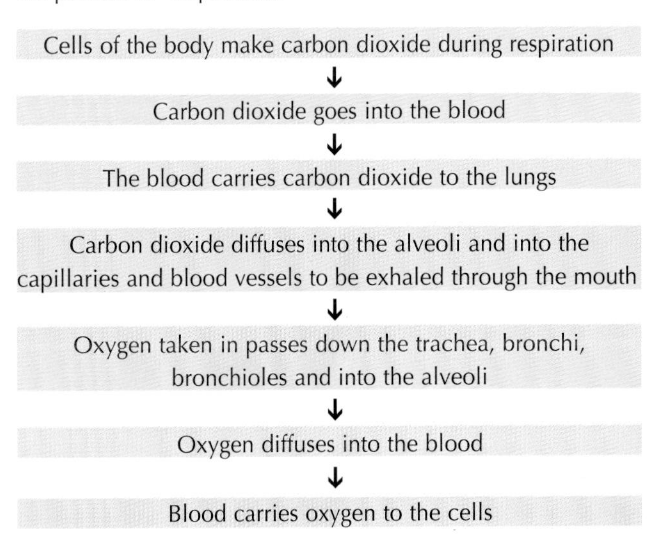
Cells of the body make carbon dioxide during respiration
↓
Carbon dioxide goes into the blood
↓
The blood carries carbon dioxide to the lungs
↓
Carbon dioxide diffuses into the alveoli and into the capillaries and blood vessels to be exhaled through the mouth
↓
Oxygen taken in passes down the trachea, bronchi, bronchioles and into the alveoli
↓
Oxygen diffuses into the blood
↓
Blood carries oxygen to the cells

The respiratory system at work

At rest, about 10 litres of air is breathed in per minute. During really hard exercise this can be increased to around 120 litres per minute, perhaps more. It is more effective for a swimmer to take fewer larger breaths, than a large number of small ones.

It should also be noted that aerobic training makes little difference to the lung capacity. Most of the improvements relate to the transporting of the oxygen rather than in efficiency in air intake.

Aerobic & Anaerobic Systems

The body has three systems of producing energy. Two systems are anaerobic and one is aerobic. These systems are commonly referred to as:

Anaerobic (without air)	System 1	–	ATP - CP
	System 2	–	Lactic Acid
Aerobic (with air)	System 3	–	Aerobic

System 1 – This system produces energy very rapidly and for a very short space of time, possibly up to 20 seconds. It uses stores readily available in the muscle. The energy is produced by a very simple chemical reaction which utilises Creatine Phosphate (CP) stored in the muscle. An example of the ATP-CP system in action in swimming is at the beginning of a swim (push off or dive). These actions are short in duration and very explosive so require a quick release of energy. The initials ATP stand for (Aderosine Tri-Phosphate).

System 2 – This system also produces energy from existing muscle stores. The chemical reaction is slightly more complex, and there are enough stores for approximately 2 minutes of exercise, although the effects of lactic acid, a by product of the chemical reaction, usually begin to inhibit performance after approximately 50 seconds. Energy is created by converting glucose into lactic acid via pyruvate. Some of the lactic acid goes into the blood stream during anaerobic exercise. An example of the lactic acid system in action in swimming is in a maximum effort swim lasting around 30 seconds (50m frontcrawl). This activity is of a duration of more than 20 seconds and less than 50 seconds performed at high intensity requiring energy to be produced as quickly as possible.

System 3 –This system produces energy by the complete breakdown of glucose. The chemical reaction requires oxygen to be present. The chemical reaction is the most complex of all three systems, therefore, it is a much slower process, but has not got any upper limits providing an ample supply of oxygen continues to reach the muscles in order to produce energy at the rate required. An example of the aerobic system in swimming is a swim or number of swims lasting for longer than 2 minutes, performed at sub maximal effort. This type of activity requires energy to be produced more slowly but on a continual basis.

The Effects of Exercise

There are a number of changes to the body's functioning which occur as a result of exercising. Some of these changes are only temporary and occur as the body is actually exercising. Other changes are more permanent and result from a structured programme of exercise over a period of time. They are often referred to as short term responses and long term effects of exercise:

Short Term Responses – These can be classified as the changes seen in the body whilst it exercises or shortly afterwards.

★ **Heart Rate Increases** ★

Providing more oxygen to the muscles and removing waste products more effectively,is achieved by an increase in the heart rate. (Amount of beats per minute).

★ **Stroke Volume Increases** ★

The stroke volume is the amount of blood pumped per beat. Not only is the heart beating faster but each beat of the heart pumps a greater volume of blood.

★ **Cardiac Output Increases** ★

The output of the heart per minute is increased.

★ **Breathing Deepens** ★

In order for the increase in heart rate to be useful it is necessary for the breathing to become deeper and permit more air to be inhaled with each breath.

★ **Amount of Air Breathed in per minute Increases** ★

The total amount of air breathed in per minute is greater than when the athlete is at rest.

★ **Vascular Shunting Occurs** ★

The body shunts more blood to the working parts of the body, hence allowing more oxygen to be available for use.

Long Term Effects – These can be classified as the changes seen in the body after a period of regular exercise, but whilst the body is at rest.

★ **Heart Rate Falls** ★

At rest the heart is able to beat more slowly but still achieve the output necessary to sustain the normal activities of life.

★ **Stroke Volume Increases** ★

A greater volume of blood is pumped per beat of the heart.

★ **Cardiac Output Increases** ★

A greater volume of blood is pumped per minute.

★ **Heart Size Increases** ★

The heart is a muscle and becomes larger and stronger when subjected to exercise.

★ **Muscles Increase in Size** ★

All muscles will increase in size when subjected to regular exercise.

★ **Ventilation per minute Improves** ★

The amount of air breathed in and out per minute, at rest, is greater.

★ **Gas Transfer at Lungs and Muscles Improves** ★

The transfers of oxygen and waste gases which occur at the lungs and the muscles become more effective.

★ **Number of Capillaries Increases** ★

Capillaries surround the muscle fibres. The number of capillaries increases as a result of exercise. This enables oxygen to be supplied more readily to each fibre.

★ **Transport Systems become more Efficient** ★

Many of the above effects make the overall transport system of the body more effective and efficient.

★ **Blood Pressure Reduces** ★

As the cardiac muscle of the heart is less stressed this reduces the blood pressure.

Summary

The body is a complex but clever machine, it is able to adapt to many different situations and conditions. When teaching/coaching swimming a number of different demands are placed on the body. It is important that the teacher/coach has an understanding of how the body functions at rest and during exercise in order to permit him to set the appropriate programme of activity.

CHAPTER 10

BASIC HUMAN GROWTH AND DEVELOPMENT

Introduction

A child is not a mini adult. This is a very important statement to understand when working with children in any situation. Understanding this will enable the teacher/coach to set a programme of work, which considers the needs of children, with regard to their stages of growth and development. In 1976 D.L. Gallahue stated:

"Without a clear understanding of children we become teachers of content rather than teachers of children"

Development

The development of an individual needs to be considered under a number of different headings:

Skill Development	– an increase in skill and complexity of function occurs as part of the progress towards maturity
Physical Development	– the growth and development of the muscles, bones and energy systems of the body
Social Development	– the development of relationships with peer groups and the adult world
Emotional Development	– the development of an individual's self concept

Everybody has a chronological age, which represents the age of the person in calendar years. The teacher/coach should already be aware that an individual's chronological age does not always represent his stage of development. This is because individuals develop at different rates. For example, some children will find learning the frontcrawl very difficult where as others will make it look relatively simple. Some children will be more physically developed than others of the same age.

This is true for all of the different areas of development, although it can often be found that if a child is slow to develop in one area others may also progress slowly.

Skill Development

It is very important for the teacher/coach to understand the level of skill which can be expected from an individual, in relation to his stage of development. A good understanding in this area enables the teacher/coach to set realistic goals, and ensures that tasks which would be impossible for the child to achieve are not included at inappropriate stages.

Here are some key points:

First two years	– rapid motor development
Pre school	– all basic locomotor skills normally established: development of range of eye and limb co-ordination
8 years - adolescence	– wide range of physical skills developed
adolescence - adult	– reinforcement of previously learned skills – introduction of new activities

When the teacher/coach considers the development of skill he should also look carefully at the adolescent growth spurt. This often results in a decrease in skill levels for a short period of time whilst the child adjusts to his new body shape and develops the necessary motor control.

Physical Development

Growth can be defined as:

> An increase in physical size of the whole or any parts, dimensions or tissues, that occurs as part of the child's progress towards maturity.

There are a number of factors which affect the rate of growth of an individual:

- maternal nutrition
- abuse during pregnancy e.g. smoking
- nutrition during early months/years
- physical activity during childhood
- genes – inherited characteristics

The rate of growh of a child up to post adolescence is continuous but not consistent. The teacher/coach will be familiar with growth spurts. A child in the class completes the last course of lessons before the summer break and on returning after the break appears to have grown in height quite considerably. Growth can be divided into a number of recognised stages:

- early foetal stage – rapid growth
- birth – growth slows down
- early years – growth speeds up
- early years to pre adolescence – growth slows down
- adolescence (puberty) – growth speeds up
- post adolescence – growth slows down

The peak rate of growth for a girl during adolescence will be, on average, at age 12 years, with the peak rate for boys being 14 years of age. If the teacher/coach is involved with children at the age of adolescence there is a noticeable change in the girls who, for a period of time are ahead of the boys in physical growth. In general terms females will reach full height at around 16 years whilst boys will continue to gain height up to about 18 years.

Exercise, if carried out in an appropriate manner, will have an effect on growth:

- size and structure of bones positively affected
- flexibility and strength of joints maintained and extended
- development of muscles
- increase in strength
- development of cardio-respiratory system

Physiological and Performance Capacities

The physiological and performance capacities are influenced by the growth and development of:

- bones
- muscles
- nerves
- organs

As all of these increase in size so does the individual's:

- motor ability
- strength
- aerobic capacity
- anaerobic capacity

One of the ways in which children differ from adults is with regard to the energy delivery systems. Children have little anaerobic capacity. Energy System No.2 *"The Lactic Acid System"* develops during puberty. The teacher/coach needs to be aware that, prior to puberty, children do not work effectively at high rates of intensity for long periods of time. An aerobic and skills based programme is recommended for development prior to adolescence, with the gradual introduction of anaerobic work of between 10 seconds and two minutes duration at the onset of puberty.

The teacher/coach should also be aware of the effects of the adolescent growth spurt on a child's swimming ability. Although the growth spurt is rapid many of the physiological developments are much slower. For example, a swimmer's arms and legs may increase in length, but it will take time for the muscles to develop the strength to use these limbs effectively.

Social and Emotional Development

Children's social development is influenced by a number of factors, their home life, their school life, their friends and also their own stage of emotional development. Although a child may be an early physical developer, the teacher/coach must remember that their social and emotional development may not have reached the same stage. A good example of this would be the five year old child who is tall for his age and, as a result of this, has also developed motor skills above the level of most children of the same age. It is easy for the teacher/coach to expect this child to behave in the manner of an older child just because of his appearance. If his social and emotional development is also taken into consideration the teacher/coach may be able to establish a better relationship based on lower expectations of his social abilities.

Summary

An awareness of all aspects of a child's development is important if the teacher/coach is going to assist the child in his development stages towards becoming an adult.

CHAPTER 11

THE ACQUISITION OF SKILL

Introduction

This chapter is concerned with the factors which influence the learning of physical skills. If the teacher/coach is to teach/coach skills effectively he must first understand how these skills are acquired. It is this understanding which will permit the teacher/coach to apply the principles of skill acquisition more effectively when structuring teaching/coaching sessions. The outcome of this will ultimately be, *"better swimmers sooner"*.

What is Skill?

Skill is a learned ability to reproduce specific patterns of movement which achieve desired outcomes.

This statement may need some additional explanation to make it more understandable to the average teacher/coach:

- a learned ability
  something which has been learnt
- reproduce specific movement patterns
  to repeat a given movement a number of times
- desired outcomes
  the ideal action

When teaching/coaching a skill the teacher/coach is constantly comparing a learner's performance with the ideal model.

Skilful swimming has the characteristics of efficiency, using just as much effort as is needed, and permanence, can be repeated consistently.

The old adage *"Practice makes Perfect"* is only true to a certain extent. This is only the case when the practice carried out is perfect or near perfect. There is also another saying which goes hand in hand with the last one *"Practice makes Permanent"*. This can definitely be seen to be correct because poor practice makes poor skills, which become almost permanent. Perhaps a better saying would be *"Perfect Practice makes Perfect"*.

Correct patterns of movement are usually referred to as techniques. Techniques become skills when the performer is able to adapt to changes to meet the circumstances around them, i.e. adjusting the length of the arm action when approaching the wall to perform a turn. In the early stages of learning the priority is to establish the solid foundation of good techniques upon which is built the progression towards a skilful swimmer.

How is Skill Learned?

The learning of skills for most individuals is a progression through definite stages and when teaching/coaching a skill it is important for the teacher/coach to remember the following points:

- individuals will start at different points
- individuals will learn at different rates
- individuals will have different desires to learn
- individuals will have unique levels of potential
- the teaching/coaching methods used will influence success

When teaching/coaching swimming it is quite easy to see evidence of all of the points above. The class of beginners who arrive for the first lesson with differing background experience. The swimmer who moves through the classes very quickly, whilst others take a number of courses to progress. The swimmer who, regardless of how hard he tries, does not have the potential to make the swim team. The factor common to all of these individuals is the process that they go through in order to acquire a skill.

Performance of a skill results from the successful processing of relevant information and the selection of the correct muscular responses. The statement may be a mouthful and the teacher/coach may wonder where this fits into a swimming lesson. In more basic terms:

A skill has to be taught – when an individual decides to learn a new skill he has a number of teaching/coaching methods at his disposal:

- self teaching/coaching
- teaching/coaching with the assistance of resource materials such as books and videos
- going to a person qualified to teach/coach the skills he wishes to acquire.

Being told how to perform a skill is not enough on its own, the individual must also practice the skill. If this skill is practised under the guidance of a qualified teacher/coach he will provide the initial information of how to perform the skill, followed by an opportunity to practice. After the practice the teacher/coach will then provide feedback, and possibly, further information. This circle of learning is the process the teacher/coach should follow when teaching/coaching a swimming session.

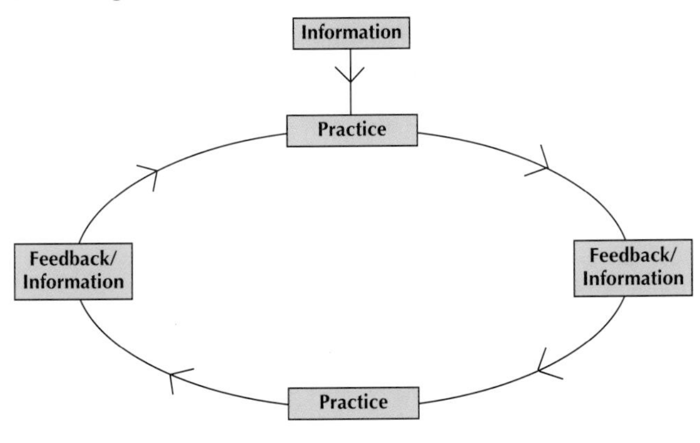

Feedback

Feedback provides motivation, e.g. praise combined with action for improvement, and a focus for the teacher/coach to draw attention on areas of performance to be considered during subsequent attempts. As the circle of learning progresses the pupil will be receiving feedback from two different sources:

Internal (Intrinsic) Feedback – this is experienced by the swimmer whilst actually trying to perform the skill. It could be explained as the information provided by the swimmer's muscles to the brain about how an action feels.

External (Extrinsic) Feedback – this is provided by the teacher/coach. To assist in improving the swimmer's skill it must contain information on which the swimmer can act.

For skill learning to occur:

- activities must be appropriate to the individual
- learners must see a good model
- there must be ample opportunities to practise
- learners need to know how they have performed
- learners must experience the enjoyment of success

In order for feedback to be effective it should be provided:

– during the performance	most effective
– immediately after the performance	
– some time after the performance	least effective

Earlier in this chapter it was mentioned that there are clear stages in the process of skill learning. The flow diagram helps to define these:

Learning a new skill – muscle tension initially high.
As the pupil begins to learn a new skill they are not aware of which muscles to use or the amount of effort to be exerted. The consequence of this is that he uses more muscles than necessary and creates a lot of tension in all of the muscles.

Continued learning – unnecessary muscle action reduced.
The internal and external feedback which the learner receives enables him to establish which muscles need to be used and the amount of effort required to make the movements.

Continued learning – apparently effortless movement
The pupil now knows exactly which muscles to utilise and the precise amount of effort required. The pupil has now grooved the movements and is able to perform them repeatedly without apparent effort.

Early Swimming – in the early stages of swimming the participant can be easily distracted by external factors which inhibit learning, e.g. the pool environment. As learning progresses there is a move from external factors to internal factors, such as how the body floats and maintains a horizontal position. As confidence grows basic techniques can be developed which lead to skill learning. At this stage the teacher/coach can encourage "feel" for the water. The ongoing success of the participant leads to an increase in confidence.

Competitive Swimming – at this stage skills will have been acquired which require continued development. It is now important for the participant to grasp the concept of a standard or goal to work towards. The participant should also be able to begin to develop skills of self assessment of his own performance against recognised standards. The teacher/coach should be aware that movement patterns are likely to deteriorate under pressure, e.g. fatigue or racing. Competition should be used to help continued development of skills but the teacher/coach and swimmer should be selective in the choice of competitions and cover a full range of events. There are additional skills involved in competitive swimming aside from those of technique. Skills such as concentration, strategy and coping with the environment. These also have to be developed in the same manner as technical skills using the "Circle of Learning"..

When is a Skill Learned?

A skill is learned when the performer can repeatedly perform the action, and, make adjustments as necessary to allow for differing circumstances. How is this achieved?

The brain works a little bit like a video recorder. Each time the pupil performs a skill a recording is made of the movement. This recording continues as the skill is developed. Once the skill can be performed well the brain then stores this recording and replays it each time the skill is to be performed.

As the performer becomes more competent at the skill he begins to feel as if he can do it without thinking about it. This to a certain extent is true, because the skill has now been stored in the memory bank. The brain is now able to focus on other activities in addition to the basic skill. An example of this may be a competitive swimmer who is able to concentrate on swimming a tactical race, and have an awareness of the other swimmers also competing, whilst performing the skill (i.e. Frontcrawl) automatically.

When a beginner first attends swimming lessons much of his attention is taken up with focusing on the surroundings and basic activities relating to water confidence. He finds it difficult to process any additional information related to acquiring the movement skills. As the pupil becomes accustomed to his new new environment, and feels comfortable in his surroundings, he is then able to focus on the techniques required to swim.

Role of the Teacher/Coach

For most pupils learning a skill, the teacher/coach plays a big part in their development. This means that the teacher/coach needs to understand his role in developing skill very well. A good teacher/coach will be aware of this and constantly put it into practice, giving the learner the best possible opportunity of acquiring the skill.

The teacher/coach needs:

- to be aware of individual needs and abilities
  Watching and assessing participants carefully and setting appropriate levels of work for each individual. The individual rather than the blanket approach

- to control the amount of information being processed by the learner
  Focusing on one particular aspect of a skill and limiting the quantity of information and feedback to an amount with which the learner can cope

- to present learning experiences which will provide essential pre-requisites for skill learning
  Essential pre-requisites are part of the circle of learning and all should be included whenever possible

- to select activities that are appropriate to the developmental stage of the learner
  It is easy for the teacher/coach to look at the technique of a world class swimmer and then try to teach/coach the same style to a swimmer in the early stages of skill development, regardless of the fact that this skill may be wholly inappropriate at this stage

- to present good "models" of skill performance
  A good model of skill performance could be the teacher/coach performing a good demonstration, pupils watching a more competent swimmer, or through the use of visual aids such as video

- to provide ample opportunities for repetition of good practice
  When learning a skill, repetition of the appropriate practices is important to allow the brain to record and groove the correct pattern of movement

- to provide learner with knowledge of how he performed (feedback)
  A section on feedback has already been written in this chapter. The teacher/coach is the swimmer's eyes and it is his feedback which will motivate and inform

- to provide the learner with an opportunity to develop a variety of skills concurrently
  There has already been a mention of the multi stroke method of teaching in Chapter 3 and Chapter 6. This method is recognised as the best way to develop a range of skills, providing the learner with a broader skill base

- to provide an enjoyable experience
  Skill learning will be accelerated if the lesson is enjoyable and fun.

Transfer of Skills

It is recognised that the learning of one skill can have a positive or negative effect on the development of other skills. This is commonly known as **Positive** and **Negative** transfer.

Positive Transfer – transfer occurs when the movements of one skill can be easily transferred into another, or can assist with the development of future skills. Some examples of this are teaching/coaching:

- the breaststroke leg action, which transfers to the method of treading water with breaststroke leg action

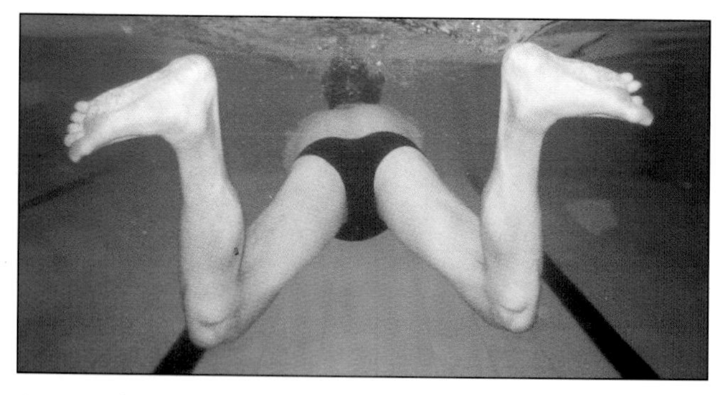

- a surface dive, which transfers to the arm action of butterfly
- frontcrawl leg action, which transfers to the butterfly dolphin kick
- a somersault, which transfers to a frontcrawl tumble turn

Negative Transfer – occurs when the movements of one skill may have a detrimental effect on another. Some examples of this are teaching/coaching:

- a surface dive and breaststroke arm action. The differing arm paths used can have a negative effect on each other if the teacher/coach uses the two skills in close proximity to one another

- frontcrawl leg action and treading water with a cycling action. The differing actions used can have a negative effect on each other.

When planning sessions the teacher/coach should pay attention to the activities in the main theme and contrasting activity, and, wherever possible, make these complimentary to one another.

The teacher/coach should also ensure that a scheme of work displays positive transfer throughout the sessions, possibly with the contrast activities being a series of progression to a final aim, for example:

6 week scheme of work:

Final Aim of Contrasting Activities – A tumble turn

Contrasting Activities for each lesson:

1. Mushroom floats
2. Somersaults in deep water
3. Somersaults from swimming
4. Push and glides in prone position
5. Push and glides into frontcrawl swimming
6. Tumble turns at the wall.

Summary

The development of skill is the most important role of the teacher/coach. Swimming is a complex skill with many simple skills being bonded together to produce a complete activity i.e. frontcrawl swimming. The teacher/coach must be constantly aware of the need to progress at the pace suited to each pupil within his class. The competitive swimmers of the future need to be very skilled in order to compete effectively. The recreational swimmer will find swimming a much more enjoyable activity if he is able to perform the actions in a skilled manner. Finally, the teacher/coach must not lose sight of the fact that many skills can have a positive effect on others, he should be willing to experiment with a range of activities to develop skill learning.

CHAPTER 12

SKILL ANALYSIS

Introduction

The ability to analyse skills is fundamental to teaching/coaching. It is a major part of the teaching/coaching process. Without this skill it would not be possible to identify a fault and its cause. It would be difficult to ascertain the appropriate practice for each individual within a session.

Observation may be defined as accurate watching and the collection and recording of facts. These are the first key points in skill analysis

- to observe carefully
- to collect and record facts

Analysis is the process of dividing an object or action into component parts or elements and the minute examination of each part. This is precisely the process followed when analysing a skill. Skill analysis, therefore, can be defined as the dividing of a skill into component parts, and the examining of each part carefully in order to collect the facts and record them. There is no great mystique involved in skill analysis once the methods of breaking down the skill and looking at what happens above and below the water level are mastered.

Analysis Methods

Poolside analysis – This is the simplest and most common method of analysis. It has been in use for many years and the teacher/coach can use it. Viewing from the poolside, i.e. above the water provides a variety of angles which build up a complete picture:

- from the front
- from the back
- from both sides
- from above e.g. a balcony

However the disadvantages of this method are:

- water refraction can make underwater movements deceptive
- over water action is clear, underwater action is blurred
- lighting within swimming pools is often not ideal

Underwater analysis – Facilities for underwater analysis are scarce. The willing teacher/coach can don snorkel mask or goggles and view technique from all sides. Underwater analysis allows true observation of the mechanical principles of lift and drag.

Video analysis – Over or underwater video analysis can be of great assistance to the teacher/coach. It provides opportunity to watch technique repeatedly and also, to use slow motion, freeze frame and single frame advance.

Approach

The teacher/coach must find a simple method of approach. Once the skill analysis is complete the teacher/coach should be able to "picture" swimmers without being able to physically observe them. The analysis should also enable any other person, with a basic knowledge of swimming skills, to read it, and picture that particular swimmer's technique. The comments and the words used should relate accurately to the stroke patterns observed.

The teacher/coach spends a considerable amount of time within a normal swimming session correcting faults, for this reason he often finds it difficult to observe without making an initial judgement of what he sees. It is important for the teacher/coach to understand that analysis is a none judgemental process and that all information should be recorded regardless of the teacher's/coach's opinion of whether this particular part of the technique is desirable or not.

Drawing a picture in words

This chapter has already mentioned the concept of being able to picture the skill and the swimmer from the descriptive words which have been used. In order to draw this picture in words, the words used must be descriptive. Here is an example: First of all the teacher/coach should read the description then try to picture the stroke and the actions which have been described. When this exercise has been completed the teacher/coach should turn to the end of this chapter and see if the picture in his mind is the same as the one at the end of the chapter.

Table 1

Frontcrawl

The water is crossing the head between the forehead and the crown

The swimmer's head is steady and in a central position

The shoulders are rolling to approx. 30 degrees

The right leg has just kicked down

The right hand has just entered the water thumb first, palm out

The elbow of the right arm is slightly bent

The left arm is towards the end of the insweep

The elbows of the left arm is bent to approx. 110°

The fingers are together and the thumb is out

The swimmer is breathing out through the nose

In describing something it is easy to use words such as good, poor, correct, incorrect, low, high, weak, strong. All of these words are judgemental and may mean something different to each person reading the analysis. For example, if the teacher/coach looks at the three pictures of the underwater arm action on butterfly, he will observe that they are all keyhole shaped. They are all limb tracks of world class swimmers, so all could be considered to be good, but if a true description was made of each it would be considerably different.

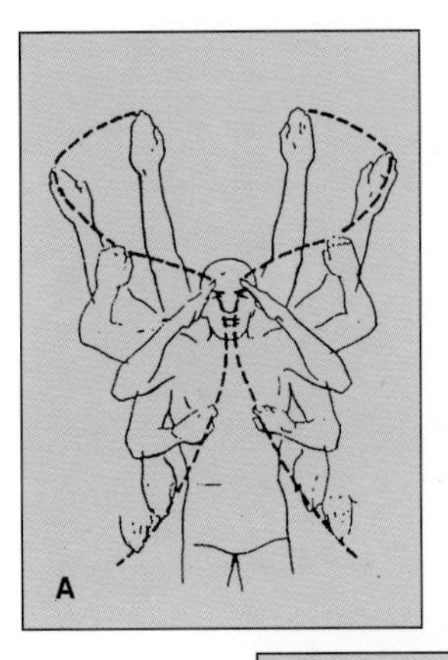

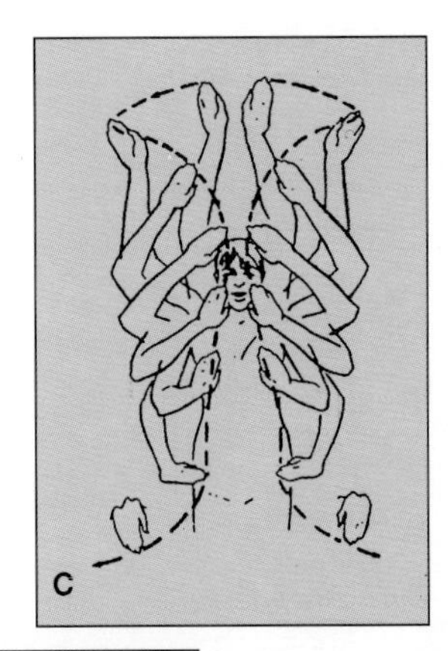

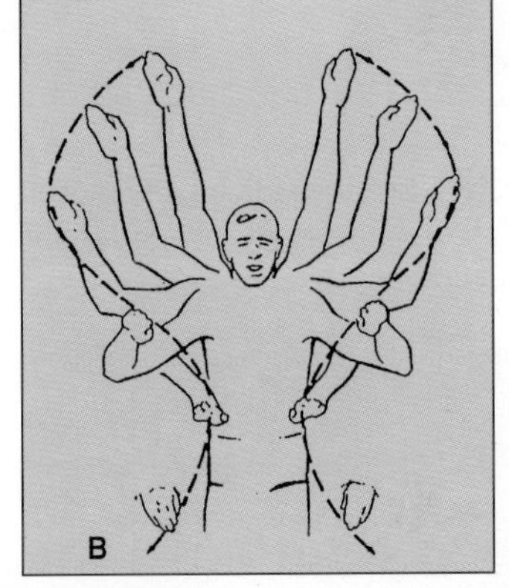

Analysis Format

There are a number of standard formats which have been developed to assist the teacher/coach to analyse a wide range of skills. Probably the most well known is BLABT, this represents the key headings used when analysing a stroke (Body Position, Leg Action, Arm Action, Breathing, Timing). All of the regular formats follow:

Stroke Analysis
- Body Position
- Leg Action
- Arm Action
- Breathing
- Timing

Dive Analysis
Stance
Take Off
Flight
Entry

Competitive Start Analysis
Stance
Take Off
Flight
Entry
Transition

Turn Analysis
Approach
Touch/Turn
Push Off
Transition

General Analysis – heading which can be used for skills which do not fall into any of the categories above, e.g. surface dives, treading water.

Preparation
Action
Recovery

All of these formats give a logical sequence to follow when analysing a skill. The addition of a first impression and a final assessment completes the picture. Analysis becomes therefore:

OBSERVE	–	First Impression
ANALYSE	–	Examine Component Parts
ASSESS	–	Final Picture

Beginning Skill Analysis

The skill of analysing has to be developed, in exactly the same manner that any skill needs to be practiced. The best way for the teacher/coach to become proficient in analysing skills is to practice, initially watching a swimmer perform a task and trying to analyse what is happening may be difficult without some form of guidance. This section of the chapter takes each of the standard formats and gives additional information with regard to observations in each section.

Stroke Analysis

In the same manner that the stroke is divided into component parts in order to observe it, the parts are sub divided and viewed in a logical sequence.

Body Position

Head	– position in relation to water level – position in relation to the rest of the body – type and amount of movement when swimming
Shoulders	– position in relation to water level – position in relation to the rest of the body – type and amount of movement when swimming
Hips	– position in relation to water surface – position in relation to the rest of the body – type and amount of movement when swimming
Legs	– position in relation to water level – position in relation to rest of the body, in particular the hips

Leg Action

Upbeat	– description of leg during the upwards movement
Downbeat	– description of leg during the downwards movement
Propulsion	– does the leg action aid propulsion?

– is the leg action the main or secondary source of propulsion?

Balance – does the leg action balance the stroke?

Depth – in relation to the range of the swimmer's body
NB – a deep kick on a tall swimmer is different from a deep kick on a short swimmer

Rhythm – is the kick continuous or interrupted?

Source – from where does the kick originate?

Arm Action

Entry of Hand – in strokes with over water recovery
- position in relation to shoulder width
- position of hand on entry, e.g. palm out
- distance in relation to head position

Propulsive Phase
- limb track – the path followed by the hand/arm throughout propulsion
- limb state – is the arm straight or bent in the main propulsive section?

Recovery
- hand/arm position as recovery begins
- hand/arm position during recovery, e.g. high elbow
- type of recovery – in or over water
- muscle state – tense or relaxed

Breathing
- inhalation in relation to stroke cycle
- exhalation in relation to stroke cycle
- position of inhalation, e.g. to the front
- type of breathing, e.g. explosive

Timing
- number of leg beats per arm cycle (Backcrawl), Frontcrawl, Butterfly)
- relationship of arm action, leg action and breathing (Breast)
- type of leg beats (Butterfly – major, minor)
- continuity of arm and leg action
- is there a catch up in the arm action? (Frontcrawl and Backcrawl)

Dive and Competitive Start Analysis

Stance
- position of feet
- position of hips
- position of head
- position of arms
- knee bend
- shape of back

Take off
- position of head
- position of arms
- angle of take off
- knee bend during take off
- amount of thrust

Flight
- changes in head position
- rotation
- streamlining
- body changes during flight

Entry
- position of body on entry
- angle of body at entry

Transition – on competitive starts only
- streamlining
- transfer of momentum
- speed of body during transition to stroke
- transitional movements

Turn Analysis

Approach
- head position
- speed of approach
- timing of last inhalation
- timing of approach

Touch/Turn
- hand position
- rotation
- movement of arms
- movement of legs
- feet plant

Push Off
- knee bend at point of push off
- leg thrust
- position of body during leg thrust
- position of arms

Transition to Stroke
- streamlining
- speed of body during transition to stroke
- transitional movements

General Analysis

Preparation
- positioning used to take up the skill
- the initial actions which lead to the main skill

Action
- body position
- leg action
- arm action
- breathing (if relevant)

Recovery
- movements to complete the skill
- movements to resume standing or swimming position

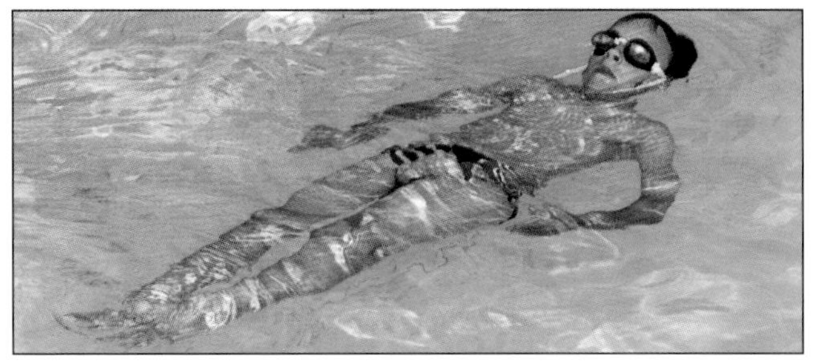

Final Picture (assessment)

Having completed the observation and analysis by looking at both strengths and weaknesses in the swimmer's technique a final assessment can be made. The assessment will determine the technique to be recommended for that particular swimmer and any changes necessary.

Text Book versus Individual Style
When the teacher/coach makes the assessment it is important that he remembers that every individual performs skills with their own style. The aim of a good teacher/coach is to convey to the swimmer a technique which is as near to the *"text book style"* as is possible, i.e. mechanically efficient, within the constraints of the individuals capabilities, strength etc. The teacher/coach should be clear in his knowledge of the text book techniques before observing the swimmers' techniques.

Contributory Factors

There are a number of other factors to be taken into account when making the final assessment and deciding on the technique to suit the individual swimmer:

Flexibility – the range of the swimmer's movements will have a bearing on the way a stroke is performed.

Age/Strength – the age and strength of a swimmer may affect his ability to perform certain stroke movements.

Buoyancy – the natural buoyancy of a swimmer varies and can affect the body position, e.g. low floating position.

Tiredness – a swimmer's stroke will deteriorate when tired. This could result in an incorrect analysis of an individual's technique.

Speed – a swimmer's stroke may look very different when swum at speed rather than at a steady pace. When working with early competitive swimmers it is very important for strokes to be analysed at speed as well as in a training situation.

Summary

- In skill analysis it is important to observe, analyse and assess in a logical sequence throughout the skill in order to obtain a true picture of the swimmer
- Observation should be made from all possible angles to obtain a complete picture for analysis.
- All contributory factors need to be taken into account before deciding on the style to suit the swimmer being analysed
- Ultimately, practice at analysing skills will develop a teacher/coach who is more able to adapt to the needs of the individual and correct faults more effectively

The following pages give examples of completed analysis sheets for all of the standard formats previously described.

Stroke Analysis

SWIMMER	DATE	STROKE
Lisa Nunn	30 May 1996	Frontcrawl

GENERAL IMPRESSION	Very streamlined and straight Looks easy and relaxed Good technique but slow
BODY POSITION	Water crossing above forehead and hairline but not to crown Shoulders out of water with body roll. Hips at surface occasionally break with roll. Roll to approx. 60 – 70 degrees. Very slight snaking, almost straight. Body streamlined.
LEG ACTION	Alternating, continuous, legs close together. Shallow and balancing body. Possibly propulsive but doubtful. From hip, bent on downbeat, straight (almost) on upbeat. Toes pointed and intoeing.
ARM ACTION	Palm out on centre line, elbow bent. Arm stretches forward. Palm faces backwards slight scull, downsweep, insweep occasionally over centre. Exit elbow first at hip. High elbow recovery. Arms sweeps slightly sideways. Little finger exists first.
BREATHING	To the left. On the upsweep of one arm and scull and downsweep of other arm. Head turned to breathe.
TIMING	6 beats per arm cycle. Breathing every two strokes.

Skill Analysis – Starts – Liam Smith – Frontcrawl Grab Start

Stance

Feet approx. one foot apart, toes over edge
Knees bend to almost 90 degrees
Leaning back – hips pointing backwards
Back almost flat and in line with ceiling
Head looking at water below hands
Hands grabbing over edge of pool, arms straight

Take Off

Springs forward by swinging arms out to point at water
Legs stretch out and swimmer pushes with feet
Pushes hips up and pushes off slightly up and out (only very slightly up – mainly heading for water)
Looks up slightly in push off

Flight

In flight the body is slightly to one side, leaning to left
Hips slightly up
Head down in flight
Body straight
Flight mainly downwards to water

Entry

Entry approx. 1m front end of pool
Hands enter followed by head and hips
Feet drop in water slightly behind the hips

Transition

Pauses in streamlined position after entry
Elbows slightly bent in streamlined position
Hands side by side in streamline
Body still leaning slightly to one side
Legs begin to kick first – Frontcrawl action
Pulls with right arm first
Ready to swim when surfacing

Skill Analysis – Turns – Emma Leftly – Breaststroke

Approach

At normal swimming speed
Arms fully outstretched for touch
Arms shoulder width apart
Eyes looking at wall, head up

Touch/Turn

Touch with two hands. Grabs trough to turn
Elbows bend body moves towards wall
Turns to left side
Pauses before beginning turning movement
Left hand leaves wall underwater, right arm thrown over water
Head remains above water for turning movement
Legs tuck under body. Feet planted on wall sideways

Push Off

Push off slightly over, slightly on surface
Throws body away from wall
Pushes off on side with legs, legs straighten

Transition

Legs streamlined, arms slightly bent
Very short streamlined period before starting stroke
Transition is on surface of water
Arms begin to pull first with normal breaststroke action
Legs follow and continue with normal stroke
Face down when streamlined. First stroke with face down

Skill Analysis – General – Vikki Green – Treading Water

Preparation

Push & glide from side of pool Breaststroke action Takes up upright position Begins with sculling arms and adds kick

Action

Almost upright, slightly sitting in water Head always out of water Chin on water Breaststroke type leg action, heels kick down Knees always bent, legs always apart, slight screw action Knees come up to chest Arms scull with wide sculling action from centre to well outside shoulder width Almost a large breaststroke pull Very relaxed and easy action

Recovery

Swimmer stretches out onto breaststroke Breaststroke swum to side of pool

A picture in words – This is the picture which was described in Table 1

CHAPTER 13

FUNDAMENTALS OF SWIMMING

Introduction

It is essential for a teacher/coach to appreciate that everyone will move in water in a different way. As human beings we differ in flexibility, strength and natural skill. However, the underlying principle which should be appreciated is that all movement in water is governed by the basic laws of mechanics. A good understanding of these will enable the teacher/coach to analyse movements, in and out of the water, evaluate more carefully those movements and take appropriate corrective action based on a sound understanding of those same mechanical principles. A sound knowledge of mechanical principles will permit the teacher/coach to take advantage of a swimmer's natural ability, whilst taking into account individual swimmers' anatomical differences. When examining the mechanical principles involved in movement these can be looked at under the following headings:

- buoyancy
- resistance
- propulsion
- rotation

Buoyancy

A teacher/coach would probably accept the concept that most people can float to some degree. A swimmer, on the other hand, may need some considerable work on confidence to accept this statement in practical terms. In order to understand why it is possible for a human being to float it is, perhaps, first best to appreciate a simple scientific term of "density".

Density – The ratio of the mass of an object to its volume.

In simple terms it should be appreciated that steel is more dense than wood, which in turn is more dense than polystyrene, so every substance has density and, indeed, water itself has its own density, which can vary, sea water has a greater density than fresh water.

What decides whether something will float in water is whether or not it has a greater density than that of water. If its density is greater than that of water it will sink. If its density is less than that of water it will float to a greater or lesser degree, but the amount of flotation varies dependent on how close the density is to that of water.

Density can be measured in grams per cubic centimetre. When using such measurements the density of fresh water is 1.0gm/cc whilst the average density of a male and female is 0.97gm/cc and 0.98gm/cc respectively. The lower the density the higher the swimmer will float, the higher the density the lower the swimmer will float. To simplify this even further if the density of water is considered to be 100% then a male will float with approximately 98% of the body under water. From this example it is clear to see that the human body floats in the water rather than on it.

Some typical densities:

	g/cc
fresh water	1.00
sea water	1.03
male	0.98
female	0.97
human fat (adipose tissue)	0.90
iron	7.90
granite	2.70
alcohols	0.85
oil (ave)	0.95
wood	0.70
cork	0.24

With the exception of fatty (adipose) tissue and air the human body is composed of sinking materials, i.e. they have a greater density than that of water:

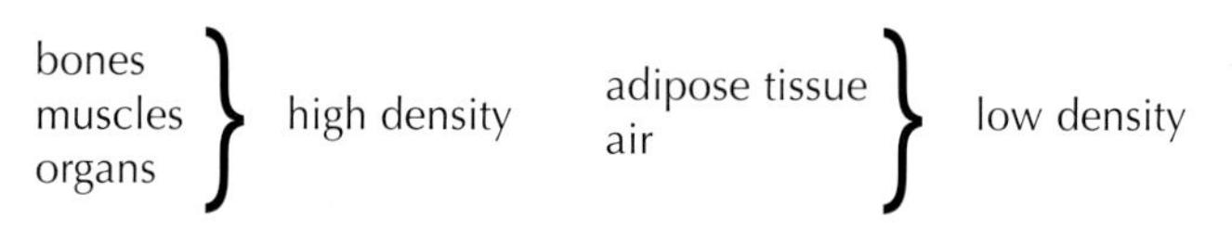

The teacher/coach will probably be familiar with the differing floating positions naturally adopted by different individuals. The "sinkers" who float with the legs suspended downwards, and the "floaters" who float with the body high and horizontal on the surface of the water. The differences in individual floaters is related not only to their body composition but the distribution of the materials from which the body is made. As a very general rule, women tend to float better than men as they have more adipose tissue on their hips and thighs. Men have a tendency to have more muscular legs which causes them to float in a vertical position. With children the differences are not so marked. It is fair to say that more rounded children tend to float more easily than children who are very thin.

Buoyancy can also change with age. Older people who are "sinkers" may have been "floaters" in their early years.

It is important for the teacher/coach to consider a participant's buoyancy when teaching/coaching swimming. This may have considerable bearing on the tasks planned for that particular individual and the type of technique to be taught.

The mechanical principles which underpin all of the information in this section relate to external forces which act on the body:

Body Weight – this force is due to the gravitational pull of the earth on the swimmer. The force acts directly downwards through the centre of gravity.

Bouyancy Force – this force acts vertically upwards through the centre of buoyancy.

The size of the buoyancy force is equal to the weight of water displaced by the swimmer's body (Archimedes Principle). Consequently, if the weight of the water displaced by the swimmer's body is greater than or equal to his body weight, he will float. However, if when fully submerged, the weight of water displaced by the swimmer is less than body weight he will sink. It is for this reason that when a human being sits in a bath of water only partially submerged his seat will remain on the bottom.

Resistance (Drag)

In everyday life little thought needs to be given to the mechanical principles of walking or running. However, it is a very different matter if a runner tries to run through water. In water there are considerable forces resisting movement. Resistive forces are sometimes called drag forces because they act in the opposite direction to the movement of the swimmer's body or body part.

A good understanding of these forces by the teacher/coach is essential because good teaching/coaching is aimed towards minimising resistance and maximising propulsion. There is more than one type of resistance (force) working against the body, each resistance has slightly different properties whilst all, ultimately, carry out the same role, that of slowing the swimmer down and making movement through the water quite difficult and energy consuming.

Profile (frontal) Resistance – This resistance is influenced by the shape of the body presented to the water, a large cross sectional area will create a higher resistance. For example the front of a canoe is pointed and smooth with a gradual widening, where as the front of a human body presents very square wide shoulders to the water.

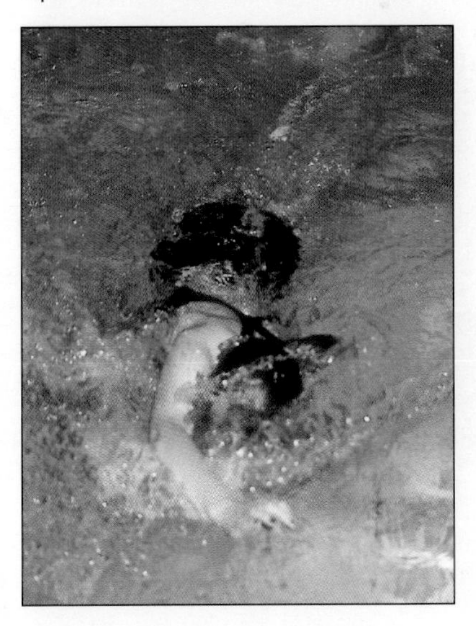

Example 1 – A swimmer who snakes (laterally deviates) when swimming frontcrawl is presenting a larger area to the water (head, shoulders and hips) causing greater resistance.

Example 2 – A swimmer who displays a poor body position in breaststroke is presenting a very large surface area to the water (head, shoulders, upper legs) causing greater resistance.

Example 3 – A swimmer who performs a push and glide with one hand on top of the other, elbows straight and body horizontal will be subject to only a small amount of resistance.

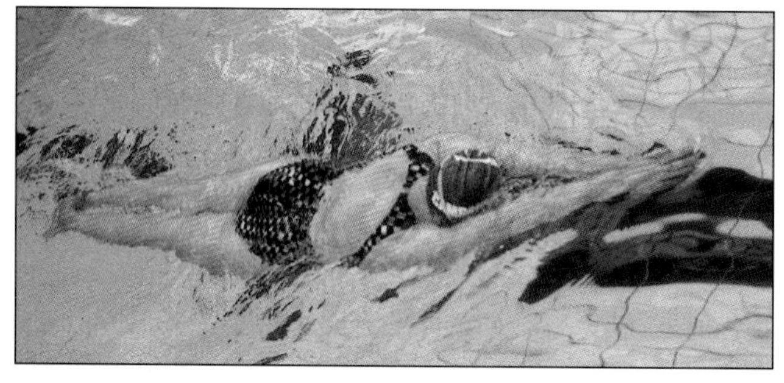

Eddy Currents

Movement of the water has a tendency to create eddy currents which are caused by the water filling in behind the swimmer as he moves forward. This tends to pull the swimmer back, as the hole behind the swimmer needs to be filled. Turbulence is the enemy of a swimmer who wishes to move quickly through the water and a streamlined body position offers the least turbulence.

Example 1 – A swimmer who swims frontcrawl with his face out of the water creates a large hole behind the body and legs, causing eddy currents to work in opposition to the swimmer.

Example 2 – A swimmer who swims backcrawl with his hips just below the surface and feet breaking the surface leaves little space for eddy currents to be created.

Viscous Drag (Skin Friction)

As the body moves the water exerts a frictional force on the layer of fluid next to the body which, in turn, slows it down. The amount of viscous drag is determined by, amongst other things, the roughness of the swimmer's body, consequently swimmers wearing tight fitting costumes composed of smooth fabric should be subject to less viscous drag. Viscous drag makes only a small contribution to the overall resistive force acting on the swimmer.

Example 1 – A child who attends swimming lessons wearing long, baggy cotton shorts would be subject to more viscous drag.

Example 2 – High level competitive swimmers have been known to shave their body hair prior to racing to reduce viscous drag. Having said this it is still uncertain whether this is of real benefit, except perhaps psychologically.

Wave Drag

This drag force acts where the air and water meet. It makes a large contribution to the overall resistance experienced by the swimmer. When a swimmer moves a body part at the water's surface a wave is created. The force exerted on the swimmer as a result of this wave is known as wave drag. The bigger the wave created the more force exerted consequently the more resistance to forward movement. In many of the swimming actions performed vertical movements of the limbs at the surface of the water are unavoidable but these should be minimised wherever possible.

Example 1 – A swimmer enters his hand on frontcrawl with palm down, and presses downwards (vertical movement). The teacher/coach suggests to the swimmer that he enters thumb first and extends the arm forwards (horizontal movement).

Example 2 – A swimmer buries his head in the water when swimming frontcrawl creating a large bow wave. The bow wave exerts a larger resistive force on the swimmer than if he had held his head with the water crossing the forehead. When teaching swimming the teacher/coach should always consider how to reduce resistance as a first priority, some possible ways are listed below:

- horizontal body position
- good streamlining
- limb movements
- well fitting swimwear
- wave reduction

It should also be noted that an increase in speed produces a larger increase in the resistive forces. This accounts for the fact that a recreational swimmer may be subject to a lot of resistance due to a poor body position, but, as he has no desire to swim at speed, it is relatively unimportant, whereas a competitive swimmer must work to minimise resistance as much as possible.

Propulsion

The teachers/coaches understanding of how swimmers propel themselves through the water was, for many years, largely based on copying the particular swimming style of a successful performer. However, in recent years a great deal of scientific study has been undertaken on the major factors which allow a swimmer to propel himself through the water. Through much improved underwater photography techniques the teacher/coach has come to appreciate more clearly how propulsion is achieved, and this has enabled him to modify stroke patterns by the application of sound mechanical principles. The job of a teacher/coach is to constantly analyse stroke movements and, by comparison with sound mechanical principles, encourage swimmers to adopt patterns of movement which provide for maximum propulsion and efficiency with minimum resistance.

To understand this more clearly it is important to have an understanding of the three laws of motion formulated by Sir Isaac Newton.

First Law – Inertia

A swimmer will remain stationary or move with a constant speed (in a straight line), unless acted upon by external forces which are not in equilibrium.

An example of this law within swimming would be when a swimmer takes up a stationary position on a starting block prior to a race. At this point the forces acting upon the swimmer are balanced, hence the swimmer remains still.

Second Law – Acceleration

When the external forces acting on a swimmer are not in equilibrium, the swimmer will accelerate in the direction of the resultant (net) force.

This means if the propulsive force is greater than the resistive force the swimmer will accelerate, and if the propulsive force is less than the resistive force the swimmer will decelerate.

Propulsive force greater than resistive force
Leg thrust in breaststroke kick

Propulsive force less than resistive force
Leg recovery in breaststroke kick

Third Law – Interaction (Action and Reaction)
For every action (force) exerted by the swimmer on a second body, there will be a reaction (force) equal in magnitude but opposite in direction exerted by the second body on the swimmer.

For example when a swimmer changes the hand position after entry on frontcrawl and begins to make an action backwards the reaction is that the swimmers body travels forwards. Teachers/coaches should remember that this law relates to action in any direction, this can sometimes be detrimental to forward movement, i.e. if a swimmer presses directly outwards in frontcrawl their body will snake at the hips.

Propulsive Forces

The only way a swimmer is going to move through the water without the aid of a push off or a mechanical aid is to create propulsion with the body's levers, the arms and legs. The theories behind movement in the water relate to the biomechanics of the body. The exact methods of propulsion have been the topic of debate amongst sports scientists for many years with a number of theories being proposed. The two theories examined in this chapter are thought to be the methods used for propulsion when a body moves through water.

Propulsive Drag Theory

This theory is based on Newton's 3rd Law of Interaction. Swimmers use their hands as paddles and gain propulsion by pulling and pushing them directly backwards through the water. This type of action can be observed as a swimmer carries out particular phases of the arm stroke and also at particular points within the leg action, i.e. the lower leg whips downwards in frontcrawl. Theoretically swimmers could obtain all of propulsion from propulsive drag, but in reality it is unlikely as it is a very inefficient source of propulsion. Strokes such as doggie paddle rely heavily on this particular type of action. The teacher/coach will be aware that there is little forward motion for a large energy expenditure.

One of the main reasons for this particular type of propulsion being ineffective is because as the hand presses backward, the water begins to accelerate. Once the water is accelerating the swimmer is faced with the problem of having to continually exert a greater force on the water. This may be possible in the early part of the movement but is impossible to sustain throughout the arm or leg action of any competitive stroke.

Propulsive Lift Theory

Research into swimming in the 1970's reported that paths followed by the hands of elite swimmers did not follow a straight line but involved a significant number of sculling type actions. This research also observed that the hand did not particularly move backwards along the body but appeared to be stationary as the swimmer's body moved over it. As a result of the research another method of propulsion was introduced termed the propulsive lift theory. This theory indicates that the hands could also be used as hydrofoils and that some of the propulsion generated comes from lateral and vertical sculling movements.

Lift forces can be generated when the hands or feet are shaped to resemble that of a foil. As the hands or feet are moved when swimming, the water at the leading edge separates. The water then travels under and over the hand to meet at the rear edge.

The diagram indicates that the path the water needs to travel over the knuckle side of the hand is longer, hence the water has to move at a greater speed than the water travelling over the palm side. An Italian scientist, Bernoulli, discovered that the faster a fluid travels the less pressure it exerts. The flow of water around the hand is uneven and therefore there is an imbalance of pressure. The pressure on the palm side is much greater. This results in a lift force begin exerted on the hand perpendicular to its direction of movement.

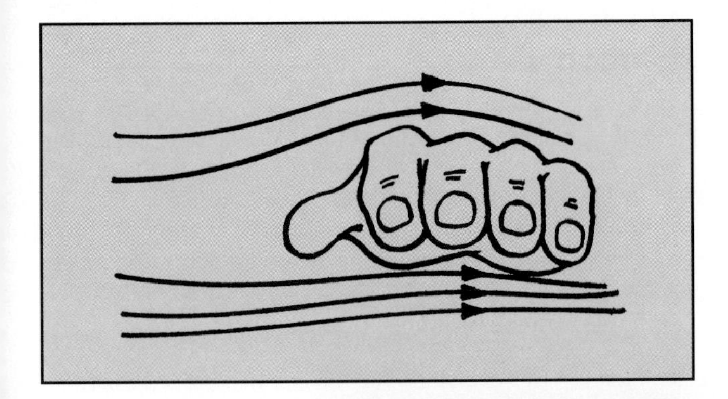

To look at this in swimming terms, if a swimmer treads water and moves the hands sideways, in a sculling action, a lift force is generated. This lift force would result in the swimmer's hand moving in an upwards direction. The swimmer treading water wants the body to move upwards not the hand, so he exerts a force downwards which permits the hands to remain in the same position and the body to move upwards.

Looking at this information, the teacher/coach can now relate this to forwards swimming movements by placing the swimmer treading water in a vertical position, into a horizontal position which resembles swimming. It can be seen that the swimmer will travel forwards by using a variety of sideways sculling movements.

The size of the lift force generated by the swimmer depends on:

- the speed of the hands or feet through the water
  In order to maintain the lift force the swimmer must move the hands or feet at the correct speed within the vertical and lateral movements.

- the size and shape of the hands
  Research suggests the hand should be slightly cupped with the fingers together to maximise lift forces.

- the angle of attack of the hands or feet
  This is the angle at which the hand or foot is inclined to the water flow, that is the angle between the palm of the hand/sole of the foot and its direction of movement. The diagrams show a range of different angles of attack. Picture (a) generates little or no lift force, whereas (b) shows the angle which is thought to generate the greatest lift force. Picture (c) does not permit a lift force to be generated as there is no flow under the palm and the water is merely deflected back from whence it came.

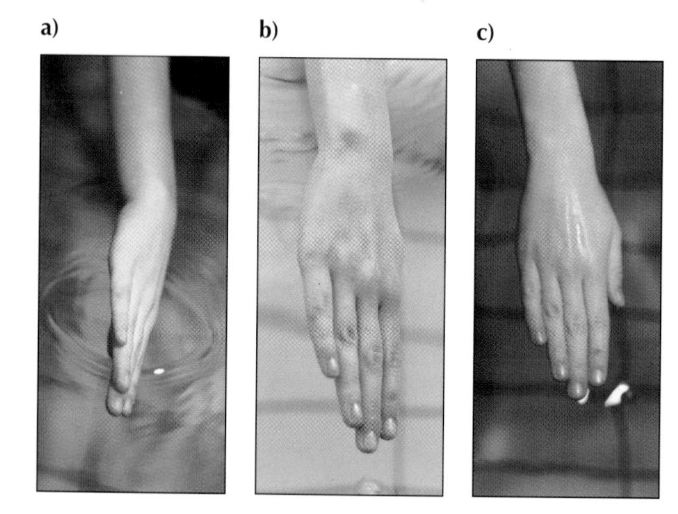

The teacher/coach may also use the word *"pitch"* when explaining the position of the hands and feet in the water. It is important that the difference between *"pitch"* and *"angle of attack"* is understood. Pitch refers to the direction in which the hands and feet are inclined, i.e. pitched outwards. Angle of attack refers to the number of degrees they are inclined in relation to the water flow, i.e. hand angled at 45 degrees.

Whilst the teacher/coach must understand the theory behind the propulsive actions he is clearly concerned with the practical teaching/coaching of these elements. From very early stages a swimmer should be taught to move his hands in sweeping movements directing pressure backwards and sideways. As the pressure is directed backward and sideways the hand is fixed in the water. The swimmer then uses the shoulder as a pivot point and allows the body to move forward over the hand. The shape of the hand and the pitch of the hand should also be emphasised. As a swimmer develops he will begin to gain a "feel" for the water and be able to adjust the pitch and the angle of attack accordingly in order to obtain the best results.

Rotation

A wide variety of rotational movements are used when performing aquatic activities:

- the body in frontcrawl rolls from side to side with the stroke
- the beginner attempting to stand up rolls from horizontal to vertical

These are just two examples, the list is endless. It is important for the teacher/coach to understand the variety of rotations which can be performed and the body shapes adopted when performing such rotations.

The body is able to rotate around a number of different axis:

Horizontal axis – as in a somersault

Longitudinal axis – as in a lateral roll

Vertical axis – as in treading water and turning to face another direction.

Of course, a combination of these rotations can be used to achieve a variety of movements. For example a swimmer can begin to rotate around the horizontal axis (leaning forwards with shoulders and pushing hips back) in order to regain standing from the supine position and complete this movement by rotating around the longitudinal axis (turning from back to front).

Body shape – Rotations can be performed:

with the body in a piked position, as in the rotation movement within the flight of a competitive start.

with the body in a tucked position, as in the rotation movement to regain standing position.

with the body in a straight position, as in the body roll in frontcrawl.

Summary

There are many different facets to consider when looking at the fundamentals of swimming. The principles are based around scientific theories which often make them complex and difficult to comprehend. The swimming teacher/coach should have a clear understanding of the principles and the effect on the participant within the swimming lesson. It is the application of the principles in the practical situation which is of the utmost importance.

CHAPTER 14

FRONTCRAWL

Introduction

Frontcrawl is the fastest and most efficient of all swimming strokes. This is due to a number of reasons:

- it has the most streamlined body position
- it employs continuous propulsion from the arm action
- the majority of the action takes place within the body range
- it puts the body in the most advantageous position to use the strong chest and shoulder muscles (pectoralis major, deltoids and trapezius)

Frontcrawl is the stroke used for a large percentage of competitive swimming training because it develops aerobic conditioning at a greater rate than any other technique. In addition to this, the movements at the joints are executed easily within each joints' movement range, giving minimal risk of injury.

Frontcrawl is the stroke most commonly utilised within competitive freestyle events, primarily because it is the fastest. The large range of race distances available in freestyle (50m – 1500m) means that, at competitive level, the stroke has a number of variations to accommodate the different requirements of each distance.

Developing Frontcrawl

With regard to the teaching/coaching of frontcrawl, it is normally developed from a front paddle which introduces the alternating leg action and a shortened underwater phase of the arm action. The over water recovery cannot be developed until the novice swimmer is able to wholly submerge the face in the water and has an understanding of aquatic breathing. In teaching frontcrawl, problems are often encountered when breathing is introduced. This is due to the positioning of the body in the water and will be explained later.

Body Position

The body position is streamlined, very close to the surface of the water. The water crosses the head at the natural hairline and the eyes are looking forward and downwards. The shoulders and upper back should be visible above the surface of the water. The hips should be at the surface, or just below, and the legs close enough to the surface to permit the heels and toes to break the surface towards the end of the upbeat. As the swimmer performs the alternating arm action the body should roll around the longitudinal axis. Body roll will normally be between 45° and 60°.

Body Position – Key Points

- head in line with body
- eyes looking forward and down
- shoulders at the surface and rolling with the stroke
- hips close to surface and rolling with the stroke
- legs in line with the body
- body roll between 45° and 60°

Leg Action

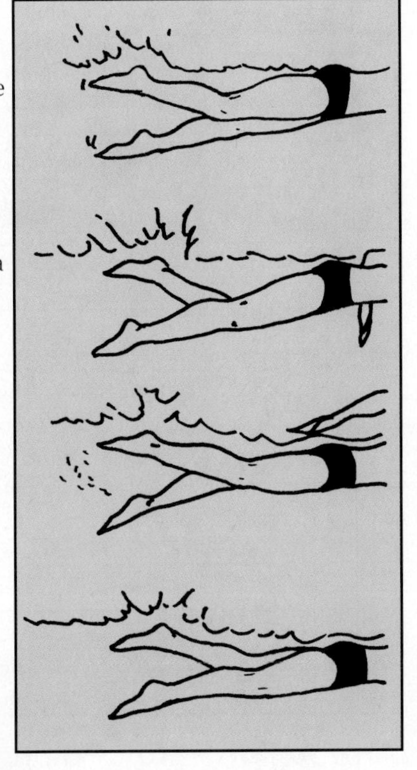

For many years there has been a long debate about the amount of propulsive force that the legs contribute to the overall propulsion. The legs in frontcrawl are mainly utilised as a streamlining and balancing agent, enabling drag to be minimised whilst executing the full stroke. It is, however, thought that the contribution from the legs to overall propulsion may be around 5%. Any propulsion which is derived from the legs is likely to be when one hand is at catch and the other sweeping upwards, this is the least propulsive part of the arm action and may permit some contribution from the legs.

The frontcrawl leg action is alternating and continuous. The legs remain close together whilst alternating.

The movement of each leg initiates at the hip and can be observed as an upbeat and downbeat.

Upbeat (Recovery) – each leg begins its upbeat with the leg extended and at its lowest point. This will normally mean that the foot and lower leg will be outside the body range. The depth of the leg at this point will vary dependent on the overall size of the swimmer, the length of limbs and the force of the previous downbeat. It is sufficient to say that the deepest point will be when the leg is completely straight with the toes pointed. As the swimmer begins the upbeat the hip lifts to allow the leg to move upwards towards the surface. The leg remains straight and relaxed with the toes pointed during this phase.

Downbeat (Propulsion) – the downbeat begins as the hip lowers, the upper leg follows the hip and the knee begins to bend. The knee bend is normally between 90° and 120°. The lower leg then presses down with the shin. The pressure at this point is a combination of downwards and backwards. Any propulsive force gained from the leg action will occur as the leg accelerates downward. The final phase of the downbeat is a straightening of the leg at the knee.

Leg Action – Key Points

- alternating continuous action
- kick is predominantly balancing
- upbeat and downbeat (recovery and propulsion)
- upbeat and downbeat initiated at hip
- legs straight and relaxed in upbeat
- knee bends in downbeat
- lower leg accelerates on downbeat
- toes are pointed and intoeing
- approximately 5% contribution to overall propulsion.

Arm Action

The arm action provides the main propulsion within frontcrawl, it utilises chest and shoulder muscles to the best possible advantage and each arm utilises the longest possible propulsive path which offers the least resistance.
The overall action is continuous and alternating. Each individual arm stroke can be classified under four main headings:

- entry
- catch
- propulsive phase
- recovery

Entry – The hand enters the water in line with the shoulder with the thumb and first finger first, this permits the hand to be pitched at 45° to the surface of the water. At the time of entry the elbow is bent. After hand entry the elbow begins to straighten and the hand extends, just below the surface.

Catch – The pitch and angle of attack is then changed via a small sculling movement to downwards and backwards. This permits the hand to purchase the water and gain catch. At catch the arm is fully extended. Catch is also assisted by the shoulder and hip rotation.

Propulsive Phase – The hand begins to apply pressure. This permits the body to begin travelling forward over the hand using the shoulders as the pivot point.

Downsweep – The hand now sweeps downwards and is pitched downwards and backwards. The elbow is bending to maintain the strongest force utilising the mid range of movement. As the hand reaches the end of the downsweep the elbow should be in a high position with approximately 90° elbow bend. The hand then presses momentarily backwards before changing pitch to inwards and downwards to commence the insweep.

Insweep – The hand sweeps inwards to the centre line of the body maintaining the elbow bend. Towards the end of the insweep the body begins to roll towards the opposite arm. This roll lifts the hip and allows the hand to change pitch to backwards, and then backwards and upwards to begin the upsweep.

Upsweep – At this point the hand can clearly be seen lifting up towards the surface. The initial elbow bend is maintained permitting the elbow to exit the water first, followed by the thumb. The palm turns inwards to release the water just prior to exiting. The propulsive phase is often referred to as an 'S' shaped pull pattern. Although this is essentially true a more realistic explanation would be a very thin letter 'S'.

Recovery – The exit of the hand is assisted by the hip and shoulder roll. As the hand exits the elbow remains bent and the shoulder joint rotates. The hand travels forward in a straight path, close to the body line and close to the water. The arm remains bent and the elbow high. Towards the end of recovery the hand position is changed to permit thumb and first finger entry.

Arm Action – Key Points

Entry

- thumb and first finger first
- elbow bent
- in line with shoulder

Catch

- just below the surface
- arm fully extended

Propulsive Phase

- three major hand sweeps (downsweep, insweep, upsweep)
- pitch of hand changes to accommodate sweeps
- high elbow at end of downsweep
- high elbow maintained throughout insweep
- body accelerates through each sweep
- water released near thigh

Recovery

- elbow exits water first
- little finger exits first on hand
- hand follows straight path close to body and water surface
- elbow is bent and high
- arm is relaxed

Breathing

Frontcrawl technique permits the inbreath to be taken to the side of the body. This ensures that there is minimum disturbance to the streamlined position. The head can be rotated in line with the body roll. As a swimmer progresses through the water the head position, partly submerged, partly exposed, creates a wave in front of the swimmer. Behind the wave is a trough in which the swimmer should try to breathe. The trough permits the swimmer to turn the head and inhale air. If the trough is large the swimmer will only need to turn the head slightly in order to obtain air. The larger the wave, the larger the trough, the faster the swim, the larger the wave. This goes some way to explaining why it is often difficult to teach/coach the technique of breathing. A novice will be progressing fairly slowly and so will only create a small wave, hence a small trough. Consequently, the novice will need to turn the head further in order to inhale air.

The head starts to turn as the swimmer begins the upsweep. At this point the body is rolling away from the propelling arm. The mouth should be clear of the water as the hand exits. The inbreath is taken quickly permitting the swimmer to return the head to a central position before the hand enters.

Breathing – Key Points

- head is turned to side to inhale
- inhalation taken in the trough
- head begins to turn at the start of the upsweep
- head returns to water before hand entry

Co-ordination

Frontcrawl is an extremely well co-ordinated stroke. Arms are co-ordinated with each other, leg kick co-ordinates with arm action and breathing co-ordinates with arm action and body roll.

Leg/Arm Co-ordination

There are a number of recognised kicking patterns to each full arm cycle:

- two beat
- two beat crossover
- four beat
- six beat

Two Beat – Each leg executes one downbeat per arm cycle. This kick contributes mostly to balance and almost nothing to propulsion. It is often used by distance swimmers, or by competitive swimmers in endurance training periods because it reduces energy expenditure in the leg muscles (Quadriceps and Hamstrings). It is not recommended that this kick is taught to novice swimmers.

Two Beat Crossover – This is a variation of the previous kick which permits the legs to assist with balance by crossing over with the roll of the body. This kick may be useful when teaching/coaching adults with limited ankle and hip joint flexibility. Other than this it is not recommended that this kick be taught to novice swimmers.

Four Beat – Each leg executes two downbeats per arm cycle. At times a four beat kick is often accompanied by a pause.

Six Beat – Each leg executes three downbeats per arm cycle. This kick, if any, will contribute the largest % to overall propulsion. In a competitive situation it is normally used in the more sprint orientated events (50m, 100m). Many swimmers will also use it to assist momentum into and out of turns. It is the pattern of kick most regularly taught to novice swimmers as it provides good balance and streamlining.

Arm Co-ordination – Frontcrawl arm action is often described as an alternating action in which the arms are always opposite. This is not technically accurate, the stroke adopts a style which permits continuous propulsion from the arm action. This means that one arm is at catch and beginning the downsweep as the other is completing the upsweep, hence there is a point when both hands are in the water.

Breathing Co-ordination – The most common breathing patterns are unilateral and bilateral.

Unilateral – The swimmer opts to breathe to one side only. The inbreath takes place as the arm on the breathing side completes the upsweep and the opposite arm is at catch and beginning the downsweep. An inbreath is taken once every arm cycle or two arm strokes.

Bilateral – The swimmer opts to breathe to both sides. The inbreath takes place with the arms in the same position as above. An inbreath is taken every one and half arm cycles or three arm strokes.

Although these are the most common patterns some swimmers will choose variations on these themes, e.g., breathing every four or five arm strokes, the principles still remain the same.

When teaching/coaching frontcrawl the technique of breath holding is often used prior to the introduction of breathing techniques.

Co-ordination – Key Points

- two, four or six beats per arm cycle
- continuous propulsion from the arms
- unilateral or bilateral breathing patterns

Variations in Technique

Clearly everybody is an individual and, consequently, is not able to adopt exactly the same stroke technique. This means there are accepted variations in technique which still fulfil all or most of the basic principles. Some of these have already been described, two beat or four beat kick, unilateral or bilateral breathing. Others have previously been mentioned, sprint and distance freestyle. This section of this chapter details some of the more common variations below:

Sprint freestyle – The stroke adopted for sprinting normally utilises a six beat kick. The turnover speed of the arm actions will be quicker and usually result in the swimmer using more strokes per length. The powerful kick and high rate of arm turnover give the swimmer an elevated body position, which permits easier breathing. The speed of travel will also create a larger bow wave also assisting breathing. The swimmer will often use the technique of breath holding, with only a minimal amount of breaths being taken during the swim.

Distance freestyle – The stroke adopted for distance swimming is normally much longer with a slower arm turnover. Swimmers often choose to utilise a two or four beat leg kick in order to conserve energy. The longer arm action and slower leg kick mean the body position will be lower in the water. Distance swimmers normally adopt a regular unilateral or bilateral breathing pattern to ensure they obtain sufficient oxygen to provide energy for the duration of the swim.

Straight arm/ballistic recovery – The swimmer recovers the arm with an almost straight elbow low to the surface, the hand follows an arc around the side of the body. Swimmers with a limited range of movement in the shoulder joint, due to a lack of flexibility or high muscle bulk, may be unable to recover the arm with a high elbow and may opt for a ballistic recovery. Although this can still be very effective the swimmer risks lateral deviation at the hips due to sideways movements of the arms.

Catch up technique – More recently competitive swimmers have begun to utilise a catch up action over the water. This is often seen when swimmers are carrying out large endurance training sets. As the hand enters the water it pauses, prior to the catch, permitting the other hand to complete the propulsive phase and begin recovery. This action conserves energy expenditure in the arms and permits a stronger upsweep and an early catch. It needs to be accompanied by a strong six beat kick to be effective.

Technique Development

There are a number of recognised practices/drills which develop the desired technique in all aspects of frontcrawl. The teacher/coach should use these practices/drills progressively at an appropriate level to suit the needs of the pupil. Examples of the most common practices/drills follow:

Common Frontcrawl Practices/Drills

Body Position

Push and glide in prone position

Leg Action

Frontcrawl leg action, holding rail

Frontcrawl leg action, two floats

Frontcrawl leg action, one float

Frontcrawl leg action, no float

Frontcrawl leg action, float held vertical to increase resistance

Arm Action

Frontcrawl arm action, standing

Frontcrawl arm action, walking

Frontcrawl single arm action, arm extended and supported by float or other buoyancy aid

Frontcrawl single arm action, arm extended, no buoyancy aid

Frontcrawl arm action, catch up over the water

Frontcrawl arm action, with pull buoy

Breathing

Holding rail or side with one hand, breathe to side

Holding float, frontcrawl leg action with breathing

Holding float in one hand, other hand by side, frontcrawl leg action with breathing

Holding float in one hand, single arm action with breathing

Full stroke, short distance, add one breath

Full stroke, increase distance and increase number of breaths

Full stroke with bilateral breathing

This list is intended to be a guide to the teacher/coach and should not be considered to be the only practices available. The teacher/coach should observe others teaching/coaching in order to broaden his knowledge of practices/drills available.

Many of the practices/drills listed in this chapter can be found in greater detail in *'An Introduction to Teaching and Coaching'* supported by photographs and teaching points.

Faults, Causes and Corrections

It is essential that the teacher/coach can identify faults, determine the cause and apply the appropriate correction. There is not always a simple answer as there may be a number of causes related to the same fault.

The information which follows identifies many of the more common faults in frontcrawl, provides possible causes and suggests the area and type of practices which may help in correcting the fault. Specific practices/drills are not listed for each fault. The teacher/coach needs to identify the type of practices/drills to be used and select the specific practice which is most appropriate for the pupil.

When the teacher/coach uses the practices/drills listed in a corrective manner he should always give teaching/coaching points, relating to the fault, which provide a focus for the swimmer.

Fault – Lifting head to breathe

Fault – Excessive body roll

Fault – Pulling across centre line

Fault – Head too high

Fault – Lower legs breaking surface

Fault – Dropped elbow during propulsion

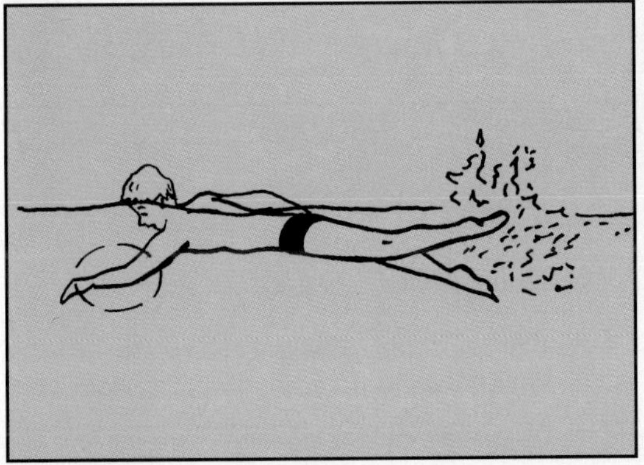

Fault	Cause	Corrective Practices
Head too high	Hips too low Fear of putting face in water Lifting head to breathe	Early leg action practices Water confidence practices Breathing practices
Hips too low	Head too high Weak leg action Lifting head to breathe	Body position practices Early leg action practices Breathing practices
Lateral deviation at hips	Hand entry over centre line Hand crossing centre line Ballistic recovery Weak leg action	Early arm action practices Early arm action practices Arm action practices Early leg action practices
Excessive body roll	Propulsive phase too deep Turning head too far to breathe	Early arm action practices Breathing practices
Weak leg kick	Kicking from knee No knee bend	Early leg action practices Early leg action practices
Lower legs breaking surface	Kicking from knee Excessive knee bend	Early leg action practices Early leg action practices
No movement when kicking	Cycling Action with legs Kicking with straight legs	Early leg action practices Early leg action practices
Excessive knee bend	Kicking from knee Cycling action with legs	Early leg action practices Early leg action practices
Legs apart on kick	Breaststroke type action Kicking sideways	Early leg action practices Early leg action practices
Entry over centre line	Excessive body roll Straight arm recovery	Body position practices Arm action practices
Entry wide of shoulder	No body roll Stiff shoulders	Body position practices Flexibility practices
Hand/elbow enter at same time	Low straight arm recovery Elbow dropped in recovery	Arm Action practices Arm action practices
Pulling across centre line	Excessive body roll Turning head too far to breathe	Body position practices Breathing practices
Dropped elbow during propulsion	Weak catch position Pulling arm backwards in water	Sculling practices Arm action practices
Lifting head to breathe	Difficulty in obtaining inbreath Unable to turn head far enough	Early breathing practices Early breathing practices
Turning head too far to breathe	Pulling over centre line Difficulty in obtaining inbreath	Arm action practices Early breathing practices

CHAPTER 15

BACKCRAWL

Introduction

Competitively backcrawl is the third fastest of the strokes. It originated from an old English style of backstroke. In the pursuit of speed the stroke evolved into a more effective alternating action, to give a stroke with reduced resistance and continuous propulsion.

The stroke of backcrawl is not governed by any specific ASA laws (the laws are applicable to backstroke), however there is a requirement to remain on the back whilst swimming. This can be anything up to 90° from the horizontal. As there are no specific laws governing the actions, the stroke is swum in such a way that takes maximum advantage of the mechanical principles of propulsion and resistance. Its speed is limited by the restricted range of movement at the shoulder joint and also the inability of the swimmer to utilise the chest muscles to their best effect.

Developing Backcrawl

With regard to the teaching/coaching of backcrawl it is normally developed from back paddle which introduces the alternating leg action. The overarm recovery is developed once the swimmer is able to maintain a streamlined body position and use an effective kick.

Backcrawl will often be the first choice stroke to be taught as it permits the face to be clear of the water and presents few difficulties with regard to breathing. Many swimmers are unwilling to attempt the stroke in the early stages due to a fear of swimming on the back.

Body Position

The body is supine, streamlined with the overall appearance from the side being similar to the cross section of a saucer. The head should be pillowed in the water with the water crossing the ears. The eyes should be focused on the horizon, looking upwards and backwards. The chin should be close to the chest. The shoulders are just below the water surface but will be visible as the body rolls and the arm recovers. The hips are below the surface being the lowest point of the body. The legs and feet will be close to the surface with toes breaking the surface. The body rolls around the longitudinal axis, anything up to 60° from the horizontal. This body roll assists in placing the hand in the best catch position enabling an effective underwater arm action and assisting the over water arm recovery. The body position can be seen to vary from the novice to the more competent swimmer. Often the novice will need to focus the eyes in a more upwards direction to ensure the body remains streamlined, whereas a competitive sprinter will often display a high position, almost resting the chin on the chest.

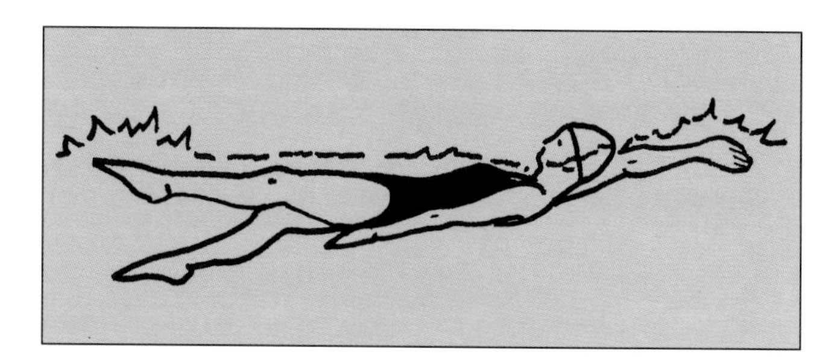

Body Position – Key Points

- streamlined, slightly saucer shaped
- eyes looking upwards and backwards
- body rolls around longitudinal axis

Leg Action

A good leg action is imperative when swimming backcrawl. The leg kick is mainly balancing and it is essential that the body is balanced. The arm action takes place outside the line of the body which causes lateral deviation. A good leg action is capable of disguising and minimising this deviation. It is also key to keeping the body flat and streamlined, enabling the swimmer to establish the correct head position.

The backcrawl leg action is alternating and continuous. The legs remain close together whilst alternating. The movement of each leg initiates at the hips and can be observed as an upbeat and downbeat.

Downbeat (Recovery) – the leg begins the downbeat close to the surface and almost straight. As the swimmer begins the downbeat the hip presses downwards and is followed by the upper leg, lower leg and foot. The downbeat of each leg is the recovery phase and so this movement is relaxed and carried out with minimal effort. At the end of the downbeat the foot will be at its lowest point, probably outside the body range. The depth of the leg at this point will vary dependent on the overall size of swimmer and the length of the limbs. It is sufficient to say that the deepest point will be that point at which the leg can be fully extended with the toes pointed.

Upbeat (Propulsion) – the upbeat begins as the hip begins to lift. The upper leg follows the hip and the knee begins to bend. the knee bend is normally between 90°and 120°. The lower leg then presses upwards with the shin and the top of the foot. The pressure at this point is a combination of upwards and backwards. It is at this point as the leg accelerates upwards that any propulsive force gained from the leg action will be achieved. The upbeat, of the kick ends as the toes break the surface.

Leg Action - Key Points

- alternating & continuous
- upbeat & downbeat (propulsion and recovery)
- legs straight & relaxed on downbeat
- knees bend on upbeat
- leg accelerates on upbeat
- upbeat & downbeat initiate at hip
- toes pointed & intoeing
- kick is predominantly balancing

Arm Action

The arm action provides the main propulsion within backcrawl. The overall action is continuous and alternating. Each individual arm stroke can be classified under four headings:

- entry
- catch
- propulsive phase
- recovery

Entry – The hand enters the water in line with the shoulder, this is often referred to as the 11 o'clock, 1 o'clock position. The hand is placed in the water little finger first with the palm facing outwards, the angle of attack is as near to 90° to the surface of the water. The hand moves downwards towards the catch position. As the hand moves downwards the pitch changes to outwards and downwards.

When teaching/coaching the novice swimmer the backcrawl arm action one of the most difficult areas to develop is the correct catch position and the downwards movement to the catch position.

Catch – the hand now begins to place a backwards pressure on the water, this permits the hand to purchase the water and begin to move the body forwards over the hand.

Downsweep – the elbow begins to bend and the hand continues to sweep downwards slightly. As the hand executes the downsweep the pitch of the hand will be downwards and backwards. When the downsweep is complete the elbow will be flexed to 90° and the hand will be in line with the shoulder. At this point the elbow is pointing to the pool bottom and the finger tips are facing outwards. The hand changes pitch into a backwards direction in the transition period, through to inwards and upwards, ready to begin the upsweep.

Upsweep – the hand then sweeps upwards towards the surface of the water maintaining the bent elbow. The upsweep progresses from shoulder line through to just above the waist. It is through this phase that the body roll is of prime importance, to ensure that a sweeping propulsive phase can be effective. At the end of the upsweep the pitch is altered in the transition phase to backwards and then to downwards and backwards.

Final Downsweep – as the hand sweeps downwards the elbow straightens. The propulsive phase is completed with the arm extended below the hip.

The overall arm stroke is often likened to a long letter "S" shape along the side of the body.

Recovery – the recovery begins with the hand below the hip the palm turns inwards and the hand recovers with thumb first and the arm straight. The hand then follows a straight arc over the water to the entry point. The arm is straight and relaxed during this phase. Towards the end of the recovery the shoulder rotates and the hand is placed in a position to enter little finger first.

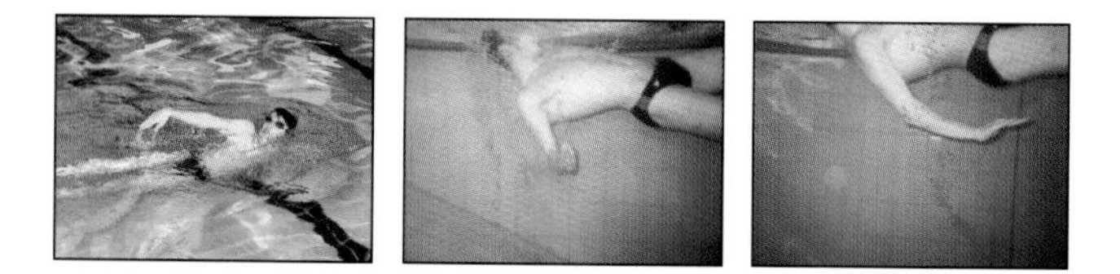

Arm Action - Key Points

- entry little finger first in line with the shoulder
- hand presses down to catch position
- propulsive phase follows "S" shape
- three major hand sweeps (downsweep, upsweep, downsweep)
- elbow bend to 90° in propulsive phase
- elbow points to pool bottom
- hand accelerates through each phase
- hand recovers thumb first
- relaxed straight arm recovery
- recovery in straight arc

Breathing

Breathing is probably one of the easiest areas to consider in backcrawl. The face is perpetually clear of the water enabling breathing to take place at any point in the stroke. It is important that a regular pattern of breathing occurs during swimming. Breathing needs to be taught and developed. The normal pattern of breathing in backcrawl is an inbreath as one arm recovers and an outbreath on the other arm recovery.

Breathing - Key Points

- regular pattern
- in on one arm out on the other

Co-ordination

There are two areas were the movements in backcrawl require co-ordination. The timing of the leg movements with the arm action, and the timing of each arm stroke with the other.

Leg Action Timing – The most common timing used on backcrawl is a six beat leg action to each complete cycle of the arms. As already mentioned a strong balancing leg kick is essential to balance the arm action which occurs outside the body range. Only a very small minority of swimmers will use any other timing pattern.

Arm Action Timing – Although throughout the arm cycle the arms can be seen to be almost opposite to each other there is a period in this cycle where both arms are in the water. This is the point at which one arm is moving towards catch and the other arm is releasing the water and beginning recovery. This slight overlap ensures that the stroke maintains almost continuous propulsion from the arm action. The photographs show the arms and hands at each stage of the arm action to highlight this point.

Co-ordination - Key Points

- six beat continuous leg action
- alternating arm action
- arms have slight catch up at beginning and end of propulsion

Variations in Technique

Although the technique described is that used by the majority of swimmers some individuals may use accepted variations of this technique, which still fulfill all or most of the basic principles. An example of this already mentioned is the technique adopted by a competitive backcrawl sprint swimmer. The more common variations seen are as follows:

Flat backcrawl – wide entry – This is sometimes executed by swimmers with limited flexibility in the shoulder joints. Their limited movement range means they are unable to enter in line with the shoulder but enter a little wide. The effect of this is to reduce body roll. Swimmers executing this type of entry will also often have a wider, shallower propulsive phase.

Flat backcrawl – straight arm pull – This is an action which is based on the traditional style of backcrawl. The swimmer uses a straight arm in an arc around the side of the body. It is not recommended that this action is deliberately taught as it does not use the fundamentals of resistance and propulsion to their best advantage, but the teacher/coach may find that some individuals automatically adopt this style. It is particularly useful for adults with limited shoulder flexibility or swimmers who are weak in the upper body.

Technique Development

There are a number of recognised practices/drills which develop the desired technique in all aspects of backcrawl. The teacher/coach should use these practices/drills progressively at an appropriate level to suit the needs of the pupil. Examples of the most common practices/drills follow:

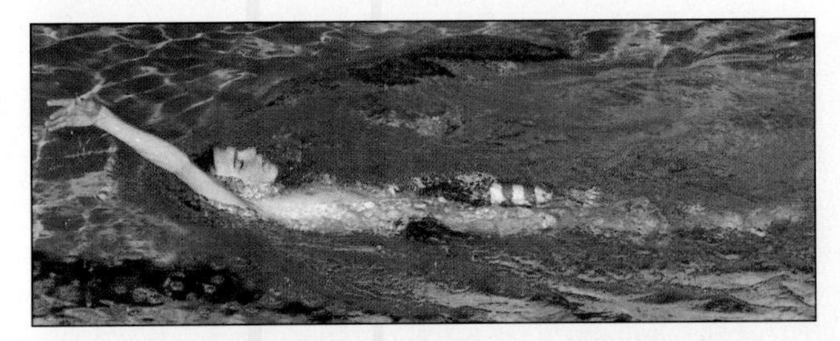

Common Backcrawl Practices/Drills

Body Position

Push and glide in supine position
Floating, in supine position

Leg Action

Backcrawl leg action, two floats
Backcrawl leg action, one float on chest or behind head
Backcrawl leg action one float held over knees
Backcrawl leg action, no float, hands sculling at swimmers side
Backcrawl leg action, float extended above head
Backcrawl leg action, arms extended above head

Arm Action

Backcrawl single arm action, float held on chest
Backcrawl single arm action, arm by side
Backcrawl arm action, pulling along a lane rope
Backcrawl arm action, with pull buoy

Co-ordination

Full stroke, concentrating on keeping arms opposite to one another

This list is intended to be a guide to the teacher/coach and should not be considered to be the only practices available. The teacher/coach should observe others teaching/coaching in order to broaden his knowledge of practices/drills available

Many of the practices/drills listed in this chapter can be found in greater detail in *'An Introduction to Teaching and Coaching'* supported by photographs and teaching points

Faults, Causes and Corrections

It is essential that the teacher/coach can identify faults, determine the cause and apply the appropriate correction. There is not always a simple answer as there may be a number of causes related to the same fault.

The information which follows identifies many of the more common faults in backcrawl, provides possible causes and suggests the area and type of practices which may help in correcting the fault. Specific practices/drills are not listed for each fault. The teacher/coach needs to identify the type of practices/drills to be used and select the specific practice which is most appropriate for the pupil.

When the teacher/coach uses the practices/drills listed in a corrective manner he should always give teaching/coaching points, relating to the fault, which provide a focus for the swimmer.

Fault – Entering hand thumb first

Fault – Entry over centre line

Fault – Knees breaking water surface

Fault – Hands stopping at thighs

Fault – Entry wide of shoulder

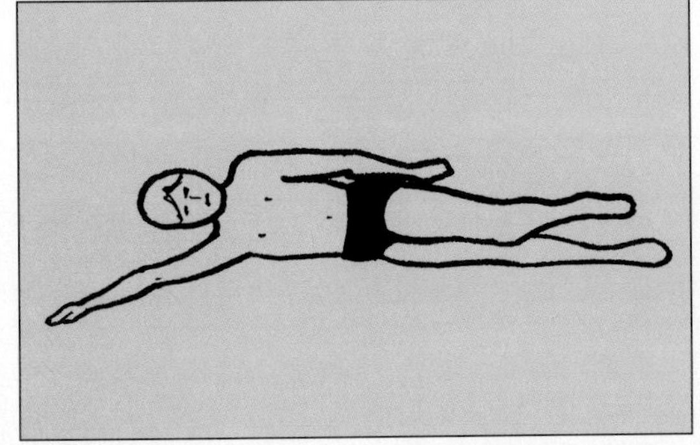

Fault – Pulling too deep

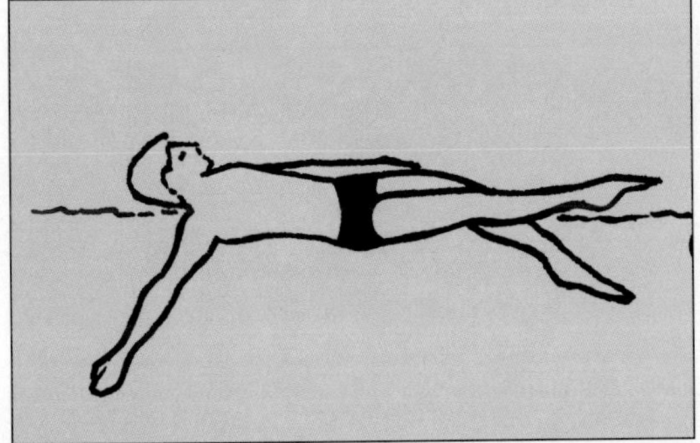

Fault	Cause	Corrective Practices
Head too high	Hips too low Fear of getting face wet	Early leg action practices Early water confidence practices
Hips too low	Head too high Weak leg action	Body position practices Early leg action practices
Lateral deviation at hips	Hand entry over centre line Weak leg action	Early arm action practices Early leg action practices
Excessive body roll	Propulsive phase too deep	Early arm action practices
Bobbing	Pulling too deep Holding breath	Early arm action practices Breathing practices
Weak leg kick	Kicking from knee No knee bend	Early leg action practices Early leg action practice
No movement when kicking	Cycling Action with legs Kicking with straight legs	Early leg action practices Early leg action practices
Knees breaking water surface	Kicking from knee Cycling action with legs	Early leg action practices Early leg action practices
Legs apart on kick	Breaststroke type action Kicking sideways	Early leg action practices Early leg action practices
Entry over centre line	Excessive body roll	Body position practices
Entry wide of shoulder	No body roll Stiff shoulders	Body position practices Flexibility practices
Entering with back of hand	Hand not turning in recovery	Arm action practices
Pulling too deep	Straight arm in propulsion Windmill type action	Arm action practices Arm action practices
Dropped elbow during propulsion	Weak catch position Pulling arm backwards in water	Sculling practices Arm action practices
Arm bent on recovery	Not finishing final downsweep	Arm action practices
Hands stopping at thighs	Incorrect timing of stroke Arm action not continuous	Full stroke practices Arm action practices

CHAPTER 16

BREASTSTROKE

Introduction

Breaststroke is the oldest of the competitive strokes, and also the slowest of the four major strokes used in competitive swimming. There are a number of reasons why it is the slowest, the first is related to the ASA laws which govern the way the stroke is swum. The laws relating to breaststroke are very specific and dictate that certain actions must be followed, for example the feet turning out in the propulsive phase. ASA Laws are based on FINA laws, FINA is the world governing body for swimming. Every four years stroke laws are reviewed and amended as necessary. Rather than risk this publication becoming inaccurate the laws have not been included. Up to date laws can be found in the publication *"Laws of Sport"* available from the ASA. If breaststroke is the slowest stroke it is important for the teacher/coach to understand why. Here are a number of reasons:

- the legs and arms are usually recovered under the surface of the water
- propulsion from the arms and legs happens consecutively rather than at the same time
- the underwater recovery of the heels to the seat creates a large frontal area
- the propulsive phase of the arms is shorter than any other stroke
- the front breathing technique inclines the body creating resistance

Breaststroke has always been the slowest stroke, because of this the teacher/coach has constantly looked at ways to increase its speed and efficiency. This has resulted in breaststroke being subjected to many changes in style over a number of years. Technical descriptions in old text books refer to changes in the leg action from wedge to whip. The arm action has changed from a wide sweeping action at the surface, to a straight arm deep pull, to the bent arm action which is currently being used. The general body position has also varied from a very flat position to a more undulating lifting style.

Developing Breaststroke

Breaststroke is often the stroke taught first, particularly to adult beginners, because it allows the face to remain clear of the water throughout the stroke, and permits the swimmer to look where they are going. Allowing for these possible advantages, the technical nature of the stroke makes the arm and leg action very difficult to master correctly, and swimmers must develop an ability to balance their bodies in a square position on the surface of the water.

The style of breaststroke taught/coached should be one which allows for further development into a more competitive style later, and provides a sound basis from which to progress. Although it may be desirable for the teacher/coach to develop the required competitive style from the outset he must remember that the swimmers at world level became proficient in the basic stroke patterns prior to developing a competitive style, and the actions used by a mature competitive swimmer may not be wholly appropriate for a young swimmer or adult stroke improver. The teacher/coach must also remember that not every swimmer will progress into the competitive field and may wish to use breaststroke for recreational or fitness swimming purposes only.

The descriptions of technique provided in this chapter will initially describe an ideal teaching/coaching stroke for the improver level pupil. Further development of competitive styles will be covered under the section entitled *"Variations in Technique"*.

Body Position

The body position should be as flat and streamlined as possible, with enough inclination from the head to the feet to allow the recovery of the legs to take place without bringing the lower legs out of the water. When the legs and arms are totally extended it is possible for the swimmer to be completely streamlined, just below the surface, with the head looking downwards. As the swimmer recovers the legs the upper body will be lifting, this will cause the legs to drop slightly and permit the underwater recovery.

The shoulders should remain square throughout the stroke and excessive head movement should be avoided.

In order to minimise the effects of drag the lower body should remain as streamlined as possible during the propulsive phase of the upper body and vice versa.

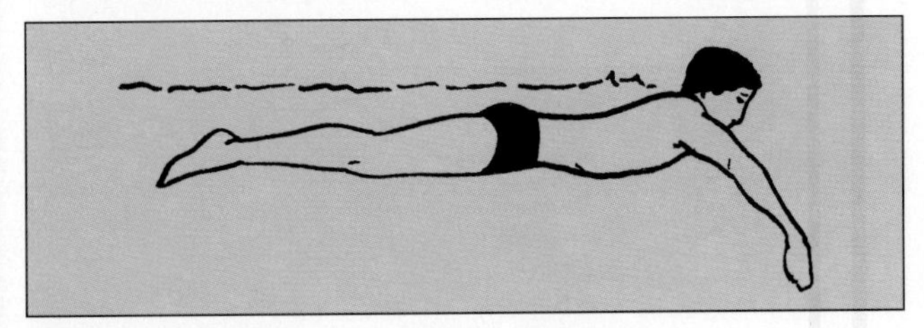

Body Position – Key Points

- as flat and streamlined as possible
- shoulders remain square throughout
- excessive head movement should be avoided
- as one end of the body provides propulsion the other should remain streamlined.

Leg Action

For many years teachers/coaches have argued over the whip and wedge action in breaststroke. Rather than prolong this debate it is sufficient to say that some swimmers employ mechanics which permit a narrow circular leg action, whilst others prefer to use a wider circular action. The important aspect here for the teacher/coach is the recognition that the kick is a series of sweeping movements which flow one into the next, rather than a number of individual actions.
There is still little doubt that the leg action provides the greatest contribution to propulsion, unfortunately the recovery action also offers the most drag.

Recovery

The recovery movement begins with the legs extended, straight and touching from thighs down to heels. After the completion of the leg kick the extended legs will be slightly inclined from hips to feet. The first recovery movement is a slight rise of the legs to bring the body into a streamlined position. The knees and hips relax and the heels are raised, under the surface of the water, to the seat by bending the knees. This results in a lowering of the upper leg. As the heels are lifting the hips are also dropping which permits the feet to remain under the surface. As the knees flex there will also be some outward rotation at the hips which will move the knees outside the body width. Throughout this phase it is important that the feet continue to point backwards, with slight intoeing, to maintain streamlining. As the feet approach the seat, they should part to approximately hip width and dorsi-flex in preparation for propulsion. This will allow the knees to remain just wide of the body. The effect of keeping the heels together is excessive rotation at the hip causing widening of the knees. The optimum hip flexion at the end of recovery is between 120 – 130 degrees, although this is often seen to be much more acute in the early stages of swimming.

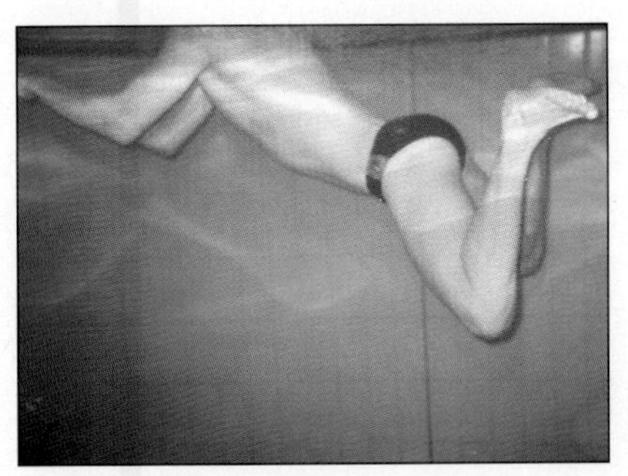

The Propulsive Phase

The propulsive phase comprises a series of sweeping movements which form a flowing circular pathway. The sweeps are outsweep, downsweep and insweep. At the end of the recovery the hips and knees are flexed and the feet are close to the seat and dorsiflexed.

Outsweep – the feet begin to move in an outsweep. In the early part of the outsweep they also move slightly backwards to catch the water, no propulsion is gained in this initial movement. The knees and hips begin to extend.

Downsweep – As the knees and hips extend the feet sweep downwards until the legs are at full extension. The downsweep helps to lift the hips ready to place the body in the streamlined glide position and also ensures the swimmer's heels do not break the surface of the water during propulsion.

Insweep – Throughout the downsweep the continually increasing pressure on the water is accelerating the body forwards at an ever increasing pace. The feet now move smoothly into an insweep whipping together quickly. Before beginning the insweep the swimmer must complete the extension of the knees in order to assume a streamlined position.

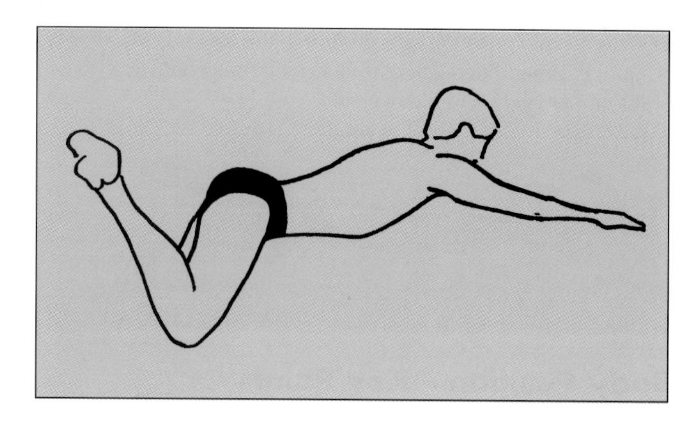

Leg Action – Key Points

- simultaneous flowing action
- kick is predominantly propulsive
- recovery and propulsive phases
- recovery begins with legs extended
- knees flex and heels lift to hips in recovery
- toes turn out at end of recovery
- legs sweep out, down and in following circular path
- feet place increasing pressure on water throughout propulsion.

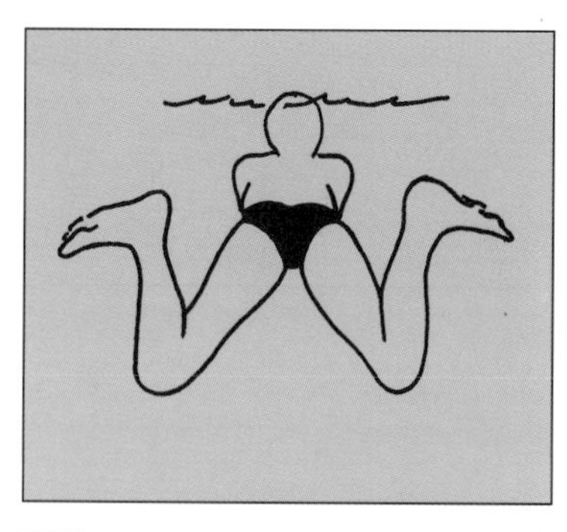

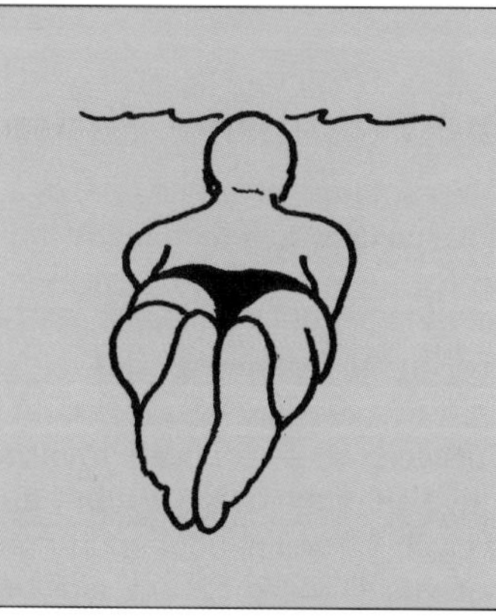

Arm Action

The arm action provides the secondary source of propulsion in breaststroke. The amount of propulsion gained from the arm action has gradually increased over a number of years. This is due to the more advantageous mechanics which are now applied to the stroke. The propulsive phase of the arms in breaststroke is the shortest of the four strokes as the laws indicate that the hands must not be pulled past the hip line.

The overall action is a simultaneous sculling action, it is normally described under the three main headings:

- catch
- propulsive phase
- recovery

Outsweep to catch – After the recovery the arms should be in a relaxed, fully extended position. The thumbs should be touching with the fingers pointing forward and the inside of the elbows close together. The first movement by the swimmer is to pitch the hands outwards and downwards with an angle of attack of approximately 45 degrees. The hands then sweep outwards until the catch point is reached and the hands fix on the water. The exact point of the catch will vary from swimmer to swimmer but, generally, it takes place when the hands are approximately shoulder width apart. The hands will be approximately 15-22 cms below the surface at this point. At catch several things happen which are fundamental to good technique. Firstly, the hands change pitch so they are pressing outwards, downwards and backwards. Secondly, the elbows start to bend and the shoulders rotate inwards.

Downsweep – From the catch position the hands sweep downwards with the elbow bend increasing to allow the swimmer to establish the high elbow position needed for efficient swimming. At the end of the downsweep the hands are pointing downwards and the hands are at their deepest point. The following illustration shows the swimmer at the end of the downsweep.

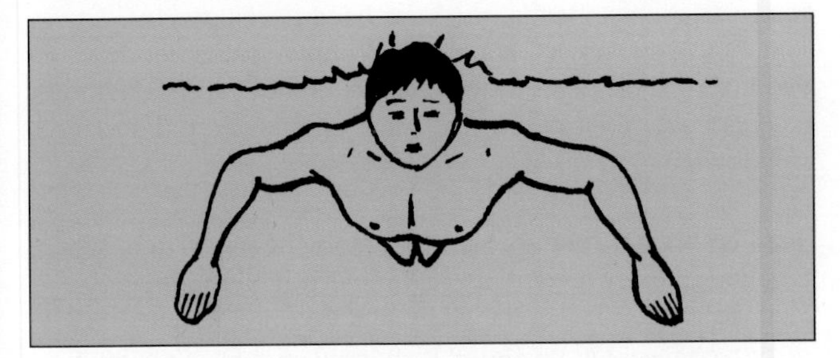

Insweep – The circular motion of the hands changes from sweeping downwards to sweeping inwards. The hands sweeping inwards and slightly upwards continue to accelerate. During the insweep the hands are pitched downwards and inwards. This hand pitch can be likened to a large sculling movement and provides a considerable amount of propulsion, so maintenance of the pressure on the hands and their acceleration is important. The path of the elbows will follow that made by the hands, but generally they should be brought inwards towards the chest and chin. The following illustration demonstrates the ideal position at the end of the insweep.

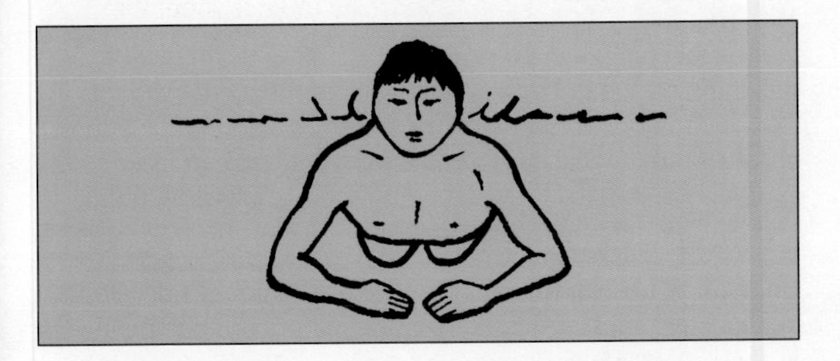

Recovery – the completion of the insweep brings the hands together under the chin. The hands have been accelerating continuously up to this point and the swimmer needs to control the first part of the recovery action so that a smooth transition from the end of the insweep to the start of recovery is achieved. The arms and hands are stretched forwards in the most streamlined manner possible. ASA Laws allow the hands to recovery on, under or over the surface of the water from the breast. During the recovery the pitch of the hands changes to downwards ready to commence the next propulsive phase. It is important that the swimmer completes the recovery with the arms fully extended.

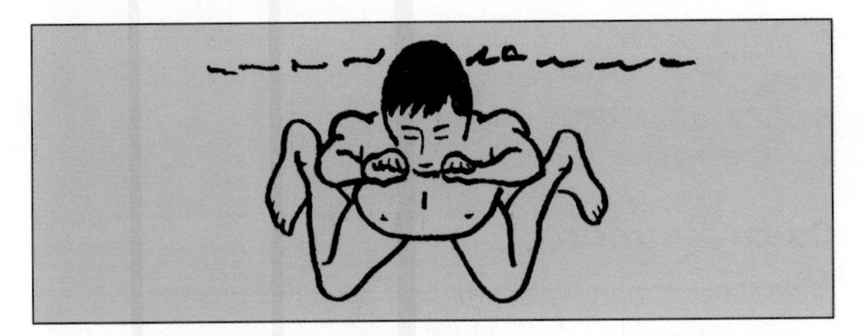

Arm Action – Key Points

- arms begin fully extended
- hands sweep out to approx. shoulder width for catch
- propulsive phase sweeps – downsweep and insweep
- elbows bend to 90 degrees in propulsive phase and remain high
- hands accelerate through each phase
- elbows follow hands inwards under chest/chin
- the overall movement is a circular pattern
- hands recover under, on or over surface from breast

Breathing

Breathing in breaststroke is usually not a problem. The insweep of the hands creates a natural lift in the body and this provides the ideal place to breathe. All breaststroke swimmers

should breathe in as the hands are completing the insweep, and lower their head into the water as the hands recover. In the initial stages of teaching breaststroke the face can remain clear of the water and the correct breathing action gradually introduced. Breathing in breaststroke can be either trickle or explosive and it would be normal to introduce breathing using the trickle style with a development to explosive breathing as the swimmer becomes more proficient.

Breathing – Key Points

- inbreath taken towards the end of the insweep
- head clear of the water as a result of natural body lift
- breathing can be either trickle or explosive
- head returned to the water during recovery

Co-ordination

Breaststroke requires the co-ordination of the arm and leg actions along with the breathing. It can be summed up in one short sentence:

Pull, Breathe, Kick, Glide.
The method of describing timing has been used for many years in the development of breaststroke and is a representation of the order in which each of the actions happens.

It is also important for the teacher/coach to understand that it is imperative that the arms and legs propel the body whilst it is as streamlined as possible. This allows the timing to be considered in a different light to that above, for example:

When the arms are propelling the legs are streamlined.
When the legs are propelling the arms are streamlined.

As breaststroke has developed the amount of glide used after the completion of the arm and leg action has changed. This will be covered in further detail in the section in this chapter which looks at variations in technique. For the moment it is sufficient to say that a swimmer in the early stages of development of breaststroke should strive to achieve the glide position with a short pause prior to the next stroke cycle.

Co-ordination – Key Points

- pull, breathe, kick, glide
- arms propel, legs streamline
- legs propel, arms streamline
- full extension is required prior to commencing each stroke cycle

Variations in Technique

In the pursuit of increasing the speed of the slowest stroke many variations in technique have been developed by competitive swimmers. Equally recreational swimmers have also made adjustments to the ideal technique to make it more acceptable for their needs. The more common variations are as follows:

Head up breaststroke – This is probably the most common variation used by recreational swimmers. It allows them to keep their face clear of the water and does not require the development of the breathing technique. It is this technique which is often used when first teaching/coaching breaststroke. The disadvantage of such a technique is the steeply inclined body position which causes a large amount of resistance.

Early breathing – Some swimmers may be observed lifting the head to breathe whilst the hands are in the glide position. Many years ago this was the technique of breathing which was taught in breaststroke. Although it can be quite effective for a swimmer with a prolonged glide it is not recommended that this style is taught in the future.

Mid breathing – In the era when many swimmers were taught breaststroke with a deep straight arm pull, a technique of breathing during the downsweep was introduced. With the introduction of bent arm actions this style has become almost obsolete but the teacher/coach should be aware of its existence as it may be displayed by some adults within the improver swimming lesson classes.

Undulating breaststroke – This style has now been developed to a greater or lesser degree with the majority of competitive swimmers. It is a style which permits increased speed due to an improved body position. The key points relating to undulating breaststroke are listed here:

- very streamlined body position in the extension
- eyes looking downwards in glide
- body possibly completely submerged
- fast acceleration of the feet
- wide angle of body to upper leg
- emphasis on downsweep in kick to assist dolphin action
- outsweep of arms often wide of shoulders
- hands and elbows accelerate inwards and forwards
- recovery is often on or over the water
- the swimmer drives the arms downhill during recovery
- head tilts forwards and downwards for breath
- there is a full extension but almost no glide

Although these are some pointers to help develop an undulating dolphin style the teacher/coach must recognise the need to make adjustments to suit each individuals specific needs.

Common Breaststroke Practices/Drills

Body Position

Push and glide in prone position

Leg Action

Breaststroke leg action, holding rail
Breaststroke leg action, two floats in prone position
Breaststroke leg action, two floats in supine position
Breaststroke leg action, one float extended
Breaststroke leg action, two floats in vertical position
Breaststroke leg action, arms by sides in prone position
Breaststroke leg action, arms by sides in supine position

Arm Action

Breaststroke arm action, standing
Breaststroke arm action, walking
Breaststroke arm action only suing a pull buoy
Push and glide and one complete stroke
Full stroke building the arm action from a small scull to a full action

Breathing

Standing in water, arm action, breathe to front
Full stroke, breathe every stroke

Co-ordination

Push and glide and one complete stroke cycle
Full stroke with pause in glide position
Two kicks, one arm cycle
Two arm cycles, one kick
Full stroke

Technique Development

There are a number of recognised practices drills which develop the desired technique in all aspects of breaststroke. The teacher/coach should use these practices/drills progressively at an appropriate level to suit the needs of the pupil. Examples of the most common practices/drills follow: This list is intended to be a guide to the teacher/coach and should not be considered to be the only practices available. The teacher/coach should observe others teaching/coaching in order to broaden his knowledge of practices/drills available.

Many of the practices/drills listed in this chapter can be found in greater detail in *"An introduction to Teaching and Coaching"* supported by photographs and teaching points.

Faults, Causes and Corrections

It is essential that the teacher/coach can identify faults, determine the cause and apply the appropriate correction. There is not always a simple answer as there may be a number of causes related to the same fault.

Fault – Straight arm shallow pull

The information which follows identifies many of the common faults in breaststroke, provides possible causes and suggests the area and type of practices which may help in correcting the fault. Specific practices/drills are not listed for each fault. The teacher/coach needs to identify the type of practices/drills to be used and select the specific practice which is most appropriate for the pupil.

When the teacher/coach uses the practices/drills listed in a corrective manner he should always give teaching/ coaching points, relating to the fault, which provide a focus for the swimmer.

Fault – Uneven leg action

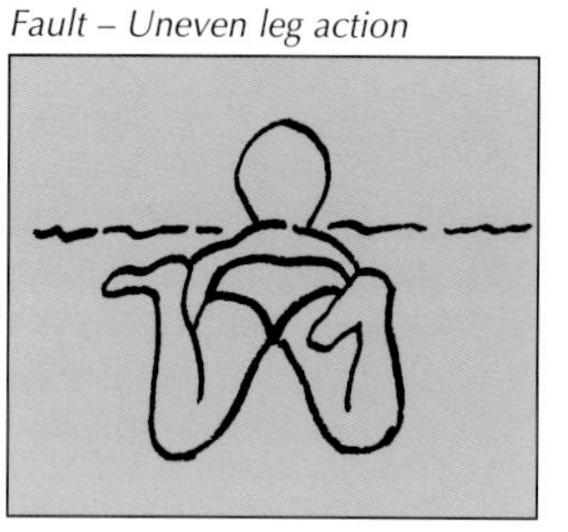

Fault – Pulling beyond shoulder line

Fault – Knees pulled forward of hipline

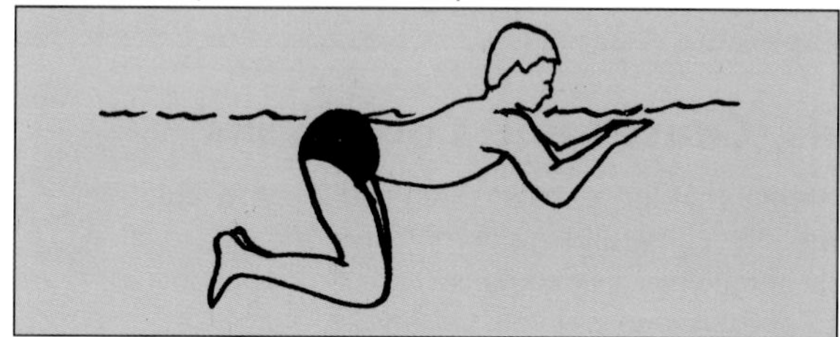

Fault – Incorrect timing of arms and legs

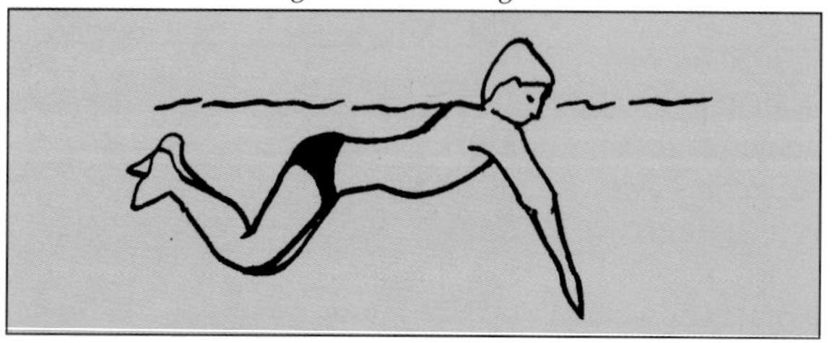

Fault	Cause	Corrective Practices
Head high, hips low	Fear of putting face in water	Early water confidence practices
	Lifting head too high to breathe	Breathing practices
Shoulders not level	Head turning to side to breathe	Breathing practices
	Uneven leg action	Early leg action practices
Uneven leg action (Screw kick)	Shoulders not level	Body position practices
	One hip lower than other	Body position and early leg practices
	Knee turned inwards	Early leg action practices
	Foot turned inwards	Early leg action practices
	Legs at different levels	Early leg action practices
Feet turned in during propulsion	Beginning kick with feet turned in	Early leg practices
Knees pulled forward of hipline	Bending at hip to recover legs	Early leg action practices
	Legs only bent slightly at knee	Early leg action practices
Legs kicking wide on outsweep	Feet not following circular path	Leg action practices
Legs not extended at end of kick	Poor insweep	Leg action practices
	Beginning next leg kick too early	Co-ordination practices
Pulling beyond shoulder line	No insweep in arm action	Arm action practices
	Outsweep wide of shoulders	Arm action practices
Elbows dropped in propulsion	No catch on water	Arm action practices
	Pulling elbows backwards	Arm action practices
Straight arm shallow pull	No downsweep in arm action	Arm action practices
No extension at end of arm cycle	Incomplete recovery action	Arm action practices
	Beginning next arm action early	Co-ordination practices
Not breathing every stroke	Incorrect timing	Co-ordination practices
Incorrect timing of arms and legs	Not completing arm action	Arm action practices
	Not completing leg action	Leg action practices
	Misunderstanding of timing	Co-ordination practices
Breathing too early in arm cycle	Lifting head during downsweep	Breathing practices

CHAPTER 17

BUTTERFLY

Introduction

Butterfly is the most recently developed of the four competitive strokes. It became a stroke in its own right in 1953. Prior to this the style was being increasingly used in breaststroke races, as laws at this time permitted the over water action and the dolphin leg kick. As one might expect from the most recently developed stroke it is very much a hybrid of the two other strokes swum on the front and displays features of both.

It is the second fastest competitive stroke, probably because it allows a long propulsive arm action and the undulating dolphin leg kick offers good propulsion whilst the arms are recovering.

Developing Butterfly

Butterfly tends to be considered a competitive stroke rather than a recreational stroke and is probably the least swum of all strokes as well as the least taught. Although the competitive butterfly can be physically demanding there are many aspects which can be taught without undue stress or difficulty. These aspects form an important part of an individuals skill acquisition and shouldn't be discarded so labelling the stroke difficult to teach/coach.

The butterfly is subject to a number of stroke laws, probably the best known of these is the law relating to the arms clearing the surface of the water in recovery. It is probably this aspect which creates the most difficulties when teaching/coaching as this action requires good watermanship and good co-ordination of the arm and leg movements.

Many aspects of the stroke can be taught prior to the necessity to lift the arms out of the water, so enabling the swimmer to develop the appropriate actions and timing progressively, in the same manner as the other strokes:

- the undulating body position can be taught once a swimmer is able to push and glide underwater
- the dolphin leg action can be taught once a swimmer has mastered the frontcrawl flutter kick.
- the underwater phase of the arm action can be taught once a swimmer has developed a breaststroke arm action.
- once the underwater arm action has been taught this can then be combined with the appropriate timing.
- the overwater phase of the arm action can be taught once a swimmer is able to perform the overwater recovery action on frontcrawl

Body Position

The body is in a prone, face down, horizontal, streamlined position with the crown of the head leading. The shoulders are level. The body is undulating from head to toe, this undulation is created by the movements of the head, the up and down leg action and the under and over water arm action. The undulating action means the body position varies throughout. The head moves from a position with the chin on the water to completely submerged. The hips rise and fall and the feet can be seen to break the surface during each cycle, but also to be down outside the body range.

Body Position – Key Points

- prone, face down with the crown leading
- undulating
- shoulders level

Leg Action

There is little doubt that the leg action on butterfly offers propulsion to the full stroke. The downward propulsive beats occur at a time when there is little propulsion being derived from the arm action so permitting the legs to add to the forward motion of the body. The positioning of the kicks is of vital importance as the leg action also assists in balancing the body at the surface of the water, permitting the swimmer to achieve an over water arm recovery. The positioning of the kicks will be detailed in the section in this chapter describing co-ordination.

The butterfly leg action is simultaneous with up and down movements being made in the vertical plane. The legs remain close together with the feet plantar flexed. The kick is very similar to the frontcrawl flutter kick, with the legs kept together and a greater degree of knee bend.

The movement of the legs initiates at the hip and can be observed as an upbeat and downbeat.

Upbeat (Recovery) – the legs begin the upbeat extended and at their lowest point. This normally means that the feet and lower legs will be outside the body range. The depth of the legs at this point will vary dependent on the overall size of the swimmer, the length of limbs and the force of the previous downbeat. It is sufficient to say that the deepest point will be the point at which the legs are completely straight with the toes pointed. As the swimmer begins the upbeat the hips will lift to allow the leg to move upwards towards the surface. The legs remain straight and relaxed with the toes pointed for the majority of this phase, towards the end of the upbeat the knees are bent slightly. At the end of the upbeat the hips will have lowered in the water.

Downbeat (Propulsion) – the downbeat begins as the hips lower, the upper leg follows the hip and the knee continues to bend. The knee bend is normally around 90°. The lower legs then press down with the shin, the pressure at this point is a combination of downwards and backwards. Any propulsive force gained from the leg action will occur as the legs accelerate downwards. The final phase of the downbeat is a straightening of the legs at the knee to place the legs in a position to begin the upbeat. The accelerating downbeat will have the effect of lifting the hips close to the surface.

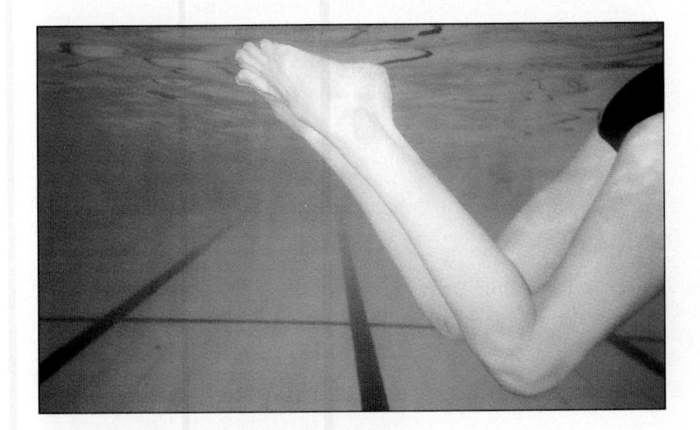

Leg Action – Key Points

- simultaneous action
- downbeat of kick provides propulsion
- upbeat and downbeat (recovery and propulsion)
- upbeat and downbeat initiated at hip
- legs straight at start of upbeat with slight bend at end of upbeat
- knees bend and straighten in downbeat
- lower legs accelerate on downbeat
- toes are pointed and intoeing
- approximately 30% contribution to overall propulsion

Arm Action

The simultaneous, continuous arm action provides the main propulsion within butterfly. The underwater phase is commonly known as a keyhole shaped action. The out, down and insweep resembling the breaststroke action and the up/outsweep which follows resembling the frontcrawl arm action. The entry could also be likened to frontcrawl and aspects of the recovery are similar to that of the frontcrawl recovery.

Entry – the hands enter the water in line with the shoulders with the thumb and first finger first, this permits the hands to be pitched at 45° to the surface of the water. At the time of entry the elbow is slightly bent. After hands enter, the elbows straighten as the hands travel slightly outwards.

Outsweep – from the entry position the arms extend forwards and sweep outwards and slightly downwards to the catch point. The hands are still pitched at 45° during this phase.

Catch – the catch occurs outside the shoulder width. At this point the pitch and angle of attack change to downwards and backwards. This permits the hands to purchase the water and gain catch.

Downsweep – after the catch the hands travel downwards with a downwards and backwards pitch. The elbow is bending to maintain the strongest force using the mid range of movement. As the hands reach the end of the downsweep the elbows should be in a high position with approximately 90° elbow bend. The hands now press momentarily backwards before changing pitch to inwards and backwards.

Insweep – the pitch of the hands is now inwards and backwards as they sweep inwards under the abdomen. The hands almost meet under the body somewhere between the chest and the stomach. The pitch of the hands changes to backwards before changing pitch to upwards and outwards.

Up/Outsweep – the hands now sweep outwards and upwards at the same time. At this point the hand acceleration speed is at its greatest having continuously increased throughout the propulsive phase. The hands continue until the arms are almost extended and past the hips. The wrists rotate the palms inwards leaving the little finger uppermost and the palms facing the thighs.

Recovery – this phase begins in the water with the elbows slightly bent. The shoulders are rotated to permit the elbows and little fingers to exit the water first. The arms recover low and almost straight with the hands relaxed. The elbow bend is increased slightly towards the end of the recovery to permit a thumb first entry.

Arm Action – Key Points

Entry
- thumb and first finger first
- elbow slightly bent
- In line with shoulder

Catch
- just below the surface
- outside the shoulder line

Propulsive Phase
- four major hand sweeps (out, down, in, up/out)
- pitch of hand changes to accommodate sweeps
- high elbow at end of downsweep
- key hole shaped action
- similar to breaststroke/frontcrawl
- water released past thigh

Recovery
- slight elbow bend on exit
- little finger exits first on hand
- low sweeping recovery
- elbow bend increases ready for entry

Breathing

The breathing on butterfly can disrupt the streamlining if executed poorly. It is vital that the swimmer employs a breathing technique which maintains streamlining and also permits the effective over water recovery of the arms.

The inbreath is taken as the arms complete the up/outsweep. Although this is the point at which the mouth clears the water it is important that the swimmer begins the head movement much earlier in the propulsive phase of the arms. The head movement should begin during the downsweep and insweep. The swimmer is permitted to take a breath either to the front or the side, providing the shoulders remain level. If the swimmer chooses to breathe to the front the chin should be extended forwards rather than lifted. This helps to maintain streamlining. The advantage of breathing to the side is that the swimmer will remain naturally more streamlined. If the technique of breathing to the side is adopted the swimmer is able to breathe in the trough of the bow wave, as in frontcrawl. This means the inbreath is being taken below the natural water surface. After the inbreath has been taken the swimmer must return the head to the water quickly as the head up position will make recovery of the arms very difficult.

It is normal for the swimmer to adopt an explosive breathing technique when swimming butterfly. This is because there is only a short period of time available to take the inbreath, and more air can be breathed in if the exhalation has been performed explosively.

Breathing – Key Points

- head can be slightly lifted or turned to breathe
- inbreath takes place during up/outsweep of arms
- the head should be returned to the water as the hands recover
- explosive breathing is most beneficial

Co-ordination

The timing of the arm movements, leg movements and breathing is essential if a swimmer is to perform effective butterfly. The movements are co-ordinated in such a way that one assists the effective execution of the other. It is the element of timing which is most often performed incorrectly in butterfly.

Leg Action Timing – butterfly is normally swum with a two beat leg action. Many teachers/coaches use the term *"kick your hands in, kick your hands out"* when teaching/coaching butterfly. This teaching/coaching point describes exactly the mechanics of timing the legs with the arms.

First Downbeat – this occurs during the hand entry and outsweep. The down beat is completed as the catch occurs. The legs beating down at this point cause the hips to rise. This has the effect of pushing the top of the body (head/shoulders and hands) into the water.

Second Downbeat – this occurs as the hands are sweeping up and out. The legs beating down at this point cause the hips to rise. This has the effect of lifting the hands and arms closer to the surface and making it easier for the swimmer to lift them out of the water.

Breathing Timing – As already mentioned the inbreath takes place at the end of the up/outsweep and beginning of recovery. At this point the legs have just completed the second downbeat. The most common breathing patterns used are every stroke or every second stroke. The type of breathing may depend on the competence of the swimmer and the distance to be swum. Both breathing patterns have advantages and disadvantages. Breathing every stroke allows a swimmer to obtain more regular oxygen intake, but has a detrimental effect on the timing. Breathing every second stroke restricts oxygen intake but maintains streamlining.

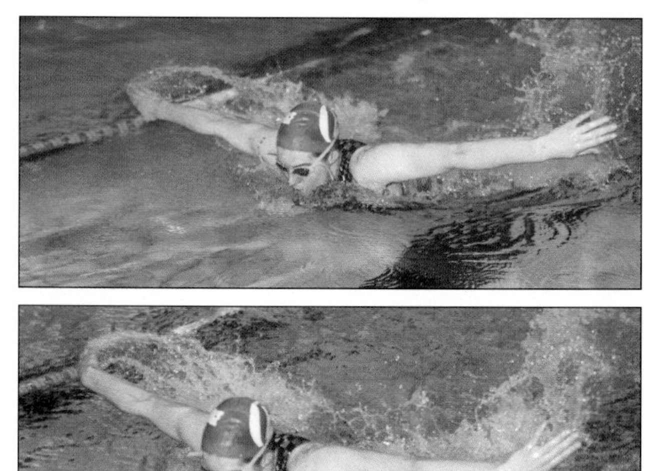

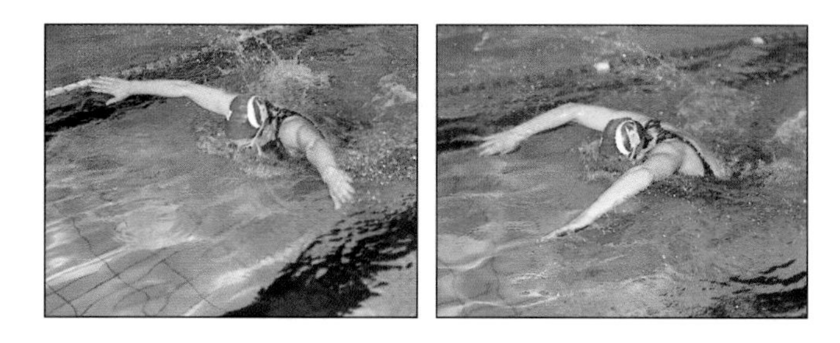

Co-ordination – Key Points

- two beat kick per arm cycle
- initial kick as the hands enter and outsweep
- second kick as the hands up/outsweep
- breathing normally occurs every one or two arm cycles

Variations in Technique

Each swimmer will adopt his own style around the sound basic principles outlined in this chapter. This means that a number of common variations are seen in the stroke. Some of these have already been described, breathing every one or two strokes, breathing to the front or to the side. This section of the chapter details some of the other more common variations.

Major/minor kick – some swimmers have adopted the technique of two kicks per arm cycle but in doing this have varied the strengths of the kick placing a strong propulsive downbeat as the hands enter to help maintain forward travel, and a weaker second kick which provides only balance. This is only recommended for skilled butterfly swimmers as it requires the swimmer to be able to maintain a good body position throughout the stroke.

Even beat kicking – this technique permits the swimmer to perform kicks of even strength as hands enter and as hands exit. This is recommended when teaching the action as the strong second kick assists with the exit of hands and over water recovery of arms.

Single beat kicking – some swimmers use only a single beat action when kicking, the only kick occurring at hand entry. Although this may be an easier action to learn it is not to be recommended as it does not assist in maintaining the body in a streamlined position.

V Pull – the long key hole shaped propulsive phase can often be difficult for a swimmer lacking in flexibility or with weak arm and shoulder strength. A simpler "V" action can be adopted. In the case of the swimmer lacking in flexibility this enables a wider hand entry position. In the case of the swimmer lacking in upper body strength this shortens the propulsive phase. The "V" pull is not as effective as the key hole shaped pull but may be useful in the initial teaching/coaching of the stroke.

Technique Development

There are a number of recognised practices/drills which develop the desired technique in all aspects of butterfly. The teacher/coach should use these practices/drills progressively at an appropriate level to suit the needs of the pupil. Examples of the most common practices/drills follow:

Common Butterfly Practices/Drills

Body Position

Push and glide and undulate in prone position

Leg Action

Push and glide, add leg action in prone position
Push and glide, add leg action in supine position
Push and glide underwater, add leg action on side
Underwater leg action, rolling from front, to back, to side
Butterfly leg action, in prone position with arms extended

Arm Action

Butterfly arm action, standing
Butterfly arm action, walking
Butterfly single arm action, arm extended
Frontcrawl arm action, with pull buoy
Push and glide, add one or two arm strokes

Breathing

Standing in water, arm action, breathe to front
Full stroke breath holding
Full stroke, add one breath
Full stroke, add breath on alternate strokes
Full stroke, add breath every stroke

This list is intended to be a guide to the teacher/coach and should not be considered to be the only practices available. The teacher/coach should observe others teaching/coaching in order to broaden his knowledge of practices/drills available.

Many of the practices/drills listed in this chapter can be found in greater detail in *'An Introduction to Teaching and Coaching'* supported by photographs and teaching points.

Faults, Causes and Corrections

It is essential that the teacher/coach can identify faults, determine the cause and apply the appropriate correction. There is not always a simple answer as there may be a number of causes related to the same fault.

Fault – Excessive knee bend

Fault – Arms not simultaneous

The information which follows identifies many of the more common faults in butterfly, provides possible causes and suggests the area and type of practices which may help in correcting the fault. Specific practices/drills are not listed for each fault. The teacher/coach needs to identify the type of practices/drills to be used and select the specific practice which is most appropriate for the pupil.

Fault – Shoulders not level

When the teacher/coach uses the practices/drills listed in a corrective manner he should always give teaching/coaching points, relating to the fault, which provide a focus for the swimmer.

Fault – Excessive undulation

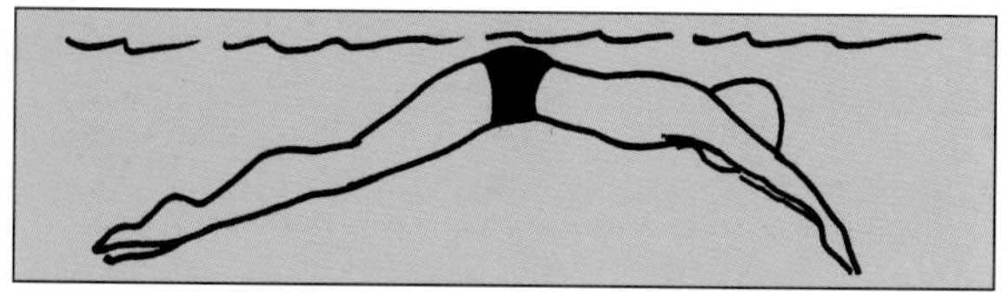

Fault – Arms not clearing water

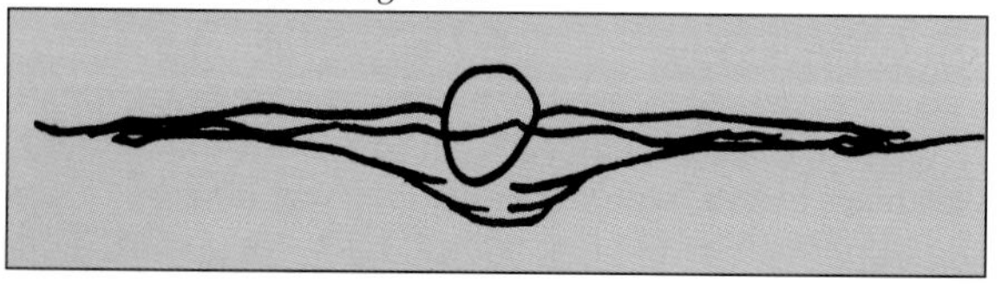

Fault	Cause	Corrective Practices
Head high, hips low	Weak leg action	Early leg action practices
	Fear of putting face in water	Early water confidence practices
	Lifting head too high to breathe	Breathing practices
Excessive undulation	Kicking from knees	Early leg action practices
	Entry close to head	Early arm action practices
	No outsweep after entry	Early arm action practices
Shoulders not level	Turning head to side	Breathing practices
	Arm action not simultaneous	Early arm action practices
Excessive knee bend	Kicking from knee	Early leg action practices
	Bending knees more than 90°	Early leg action practices
Alternating leg kick	Legs not kept together	Early leg action practices
Small shallow kicks	Little movement at hips	Early leg action practices
	Legs only bent slightly at knee	Early leg action practices
Arms not clearing water	Body not streamlined	Leg action practices
	Weak out/upsweep	Early arm action practices
Arms not simultaneous	Head turned to one side	Body position/breathing practices
	Dropped shoulder	Body position practices
Pausing after hand entry	Incorrect timing of leg beats	Timing practices
	Fatigue	Simplify practices or rest
Head up as hands enter	Incorrect timing of breathing	Breathing practices
Entry wide of shoulders	Head out of water at entry	Breathing practices
	Stiff shoulders	Flexibility practices
Lifting head too high to breathe	Not pushing chin forward	Breathing practices
	Excessive undulation	Body position practices
More than 2 kicks per arm cycle	Shallow, fast kick	Early leg practices
	Incorrect timing	Timing practices
Incorrect timing	Too many/not enough leg kicks	Timing practices
	Pausing after entry	Timing practices

CHAPTER 18

LEARNING TO DIVE

Introduction

Dives performed from springboards or highboards are a form of aerial gymnastics, a sport which combines athletic ability, body control and courage to give an aesthetically pleasing performance. The ability to enter the water from poolside by a dive is enjoyable, it is also necessary for a good racing start and it may be an introduction to an exciting and challenging sport. The initial teaching of diving should be an integral part of swimming lessons so that there is a safe and gradual progression leading to the elimination of fear.

Basic Principles

The success of any dive depends upon a good take off. At take off it is necessary to overcome inertia, and in order to do this there must be a strong push against the poolside. Frictional force is developed between the feet and the poolside which prevents the feet slipping backwards and enables the legs to extend against a fixed point. This emphasizes the importance of a good foot grip in the stance and the need to develop maximum velocity upwards and forwards. Any dive is a somersault or part of a somersault. The rotation comes from the angular momentum initiated at take off. The flight pathway, and the angle of entry into the water, are determined at take off and there is little that can be done to alter the body rotation whilst in flight. A strong extension of the legs gives power to the take off. The arm swing gives a transfer of momentum of the body weight forwards. Once the feet leave the poolside the centre of gravity of the diver will follow a pre determined path in flight. The body enters the water in a streamlined position continuing the line of flight under the water. The entry may be near vertical or at a shallow angle.

Safety Factors

Diving must always be carefully supervised and the teacher/coach should impress on the class the safety factors involved so that the chances of accidents can be reduced as much as possible.

Water depth – the teacher/coach should check that there is an adequate depth of water for all underwater activities, even pushing and gliding underwater can be dangerous in very shallow water. There are certain guidelines:

- head first entries from early starting positions should be into water which is at least 1.8 metres deep. When pupils are learning to dive they do not automatically make a shallow entry; they are unpredictable and it is unsafe to take diving practices into shallow water.
- plunge or racing dives, which have approximately a 45° angle of entry, can be performed into 1 metre of water by a proficient diver. The learning stages, however, are safer in at least a depth of 1.8 metres.
- starting blocks give an elevation of 500mm to 700mm above the water level which, if used by an unskilled person, risks a steep entry into shallow water. Diving from blocks should only be introduced into a depth of at least 2.0 metres.
- the height and weight of a diver must be considered because height and weight increase the velocity of travel through the water. The taller and/or heavier the diver the deeper the water needed for safety.

Pool Space for Diving

Care must be taken to ensure there is no danger of a diver hitting anyone in the water. This can be avoided by using an agreed diving code for the use of water space.

- a diver must always check that the entry area is clear before starting a dive. The teacher/coach should consequently remind pupils to do this.
- on resurfacing from a dive the diver should swim straight to the poolside to avoid crossing the path of another diver.
- there should be no free swimming in the diving area. A rope, with coloured buoys can be used to delineate the diving area.

Class organisation and discipline

The aim throughout is to encourage pupils to take responsibility for their own actions. The teacher/coach should also explain why certain rules are being enforced.

- all diving activities in the water, or from the poolside, should be planned to enable each pupil to have a safe working space. For shallow end activities check that all pupil are safely away from the walls of the pool and are well spaced.

- entries from the poolside must be carefully organised with the divers understanding the procedure. The organisation adopted by the teacher/coach will depend upon the availability of deep water, the width of the pool, the number of divers and the activity to be performed. Examples of how the available deep water can be organised in a safe and efficient manner follow:

Plan A
Enter, swim across the pool and climb out. This is a safe organisation, particularly when teaching a plunge or racing dive. The position of the teacher/coach gives a good sideways view of the flight and entry.

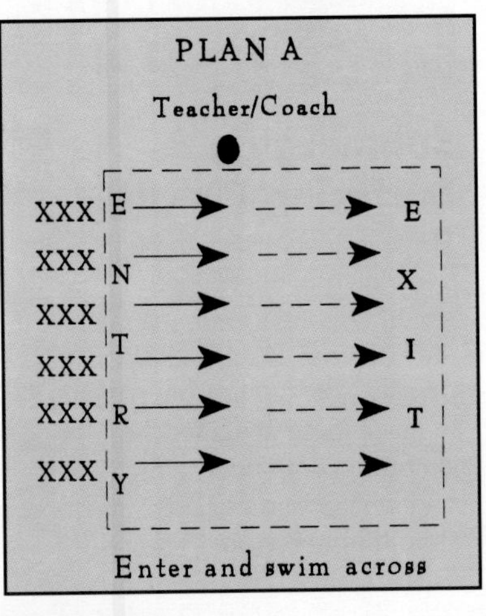

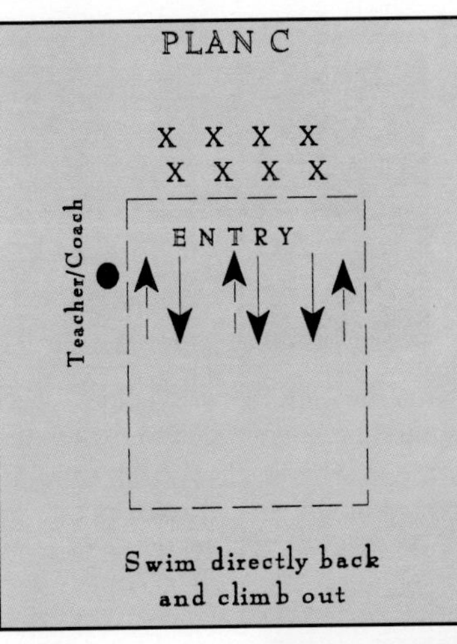

Plan C
The same planning as plan B, but may be used where there is a more limited area of deep water. By changing positions the teacher/coach has a closer view of, and communication with, the whole group.

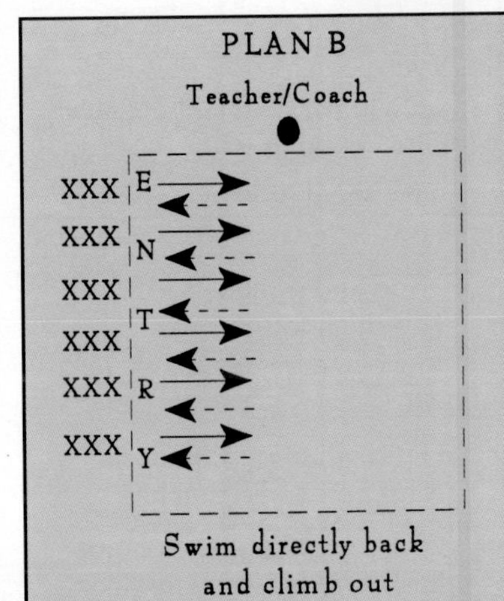

Plan B
Enter and swim directly back to the side. The next diver does not go until the diver in front has touched the poolside. The teacher/coach can observe down the line and, if necessary, control the take off for a whole line.

Plan D
This may be adopted in a wide pool where there is no danger of divers colliding in the centre of the pool. It is a suitable plan for practices involving vertical entries, assuming, of course, the depth is appropriate.

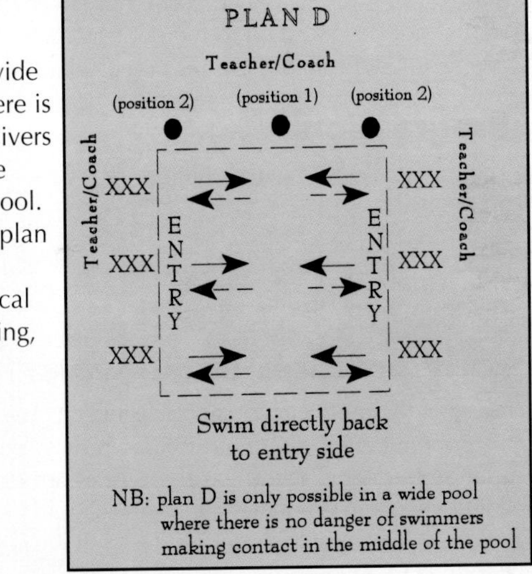

General Safety Points

- divers with long hair should wear caps
- goggles should not be worn
- toes should curl over the poolside
- dives should be performed from a stationary position
- for a safe entry the arms should be extended beyond the head with the hands clasped together

Starting to Dive

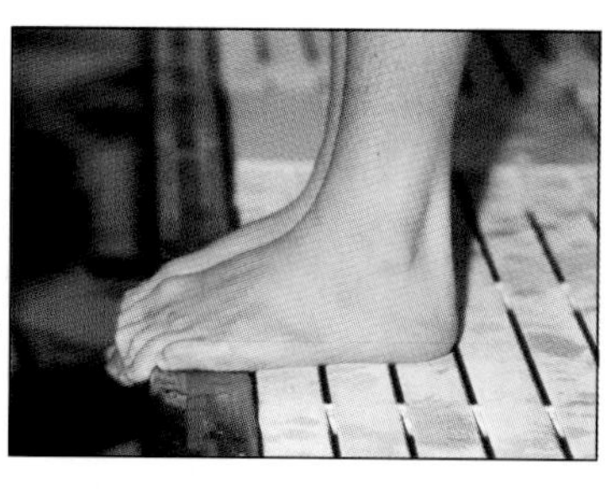

The initial stages in diving are introduced alongside early swimming practices and are combined in a watermanship programme. Throughout the learning process the pupils should know why they are performing certain tasks, what they are trying to achieve and, within safety limits, they should be encouraged to experiment and to progress at their own rate. The teacher/coach should monitor carefully the progress being made by each pupil, particularly checking that one stage is confidently performed before progressing further. The more adventurous and able pupil may dive easily, requiring few lead up stages. Whilst the more timid pupil will need constant help at each stage and should not be forced on to the poolside before confidence has been gained through activities practised in the water.

Progressions

The progressions toward a plunge dive can be divided into three clear steps:

- in the water practices
- from the poolside – feet first
- from the poolside – head first

Early practices in the water

Many of the practices in chapter 6 which are used to develop water confidence can be utilised as early water activities in relation to diving. These basic practices are essential to give confidence and enjoyment and they should be fully mastered before proceeding to the poolside. In the water practices are designed to develop.

- confidence in being under water with the eyes open
- breath control
- familiarity with the inverted position
- an awareness of body line and body tension
- the ability to rotate the body
- vertical thrust through the legs
- the ability to resurface

The practices given are only a selection and can be supplemented by the teacher/coach. Practices should be selected according to the needs of the class and of individual pupils.

Submerging & Surfacing Practices

These practices should be performed in chest depth water, although some may be repeated out of the swimmer's depth as confidence increases. In all of these activities the eyes should be open underwater and goggles should not be worn.

Practice	Teaching/Coaching Points
Face in the Water (See Chapter 6)	Eyes open Let the water run off the face Blow bubbles in the water
Which part of the body can you touch underwater?	Take small breaths Look at the part you are touching
Underwater movement in variety of ways (Through or under apparatus, retrieving objects)	Head and shoulders low Hips high to submerge Move underwater in different ways
Push and glide from pool wall to floor	Hips high to push from side Arms and body stretched
As above touch pool floor and push to surface	Curl body to put feet on floor Push hard against pool floor

Submerge to sit on pool floor	Spring up, lift arms high Exhale gradually blowing bubbles Scull, palms upwards to stay down
As above, put feet on floor and push to surface	Eyes open Strong push up with feet flat on floor
Porpoise dives through hoops on the surface	Strong push from floor to lift hips Head down between arms Keep going until hand touches floor

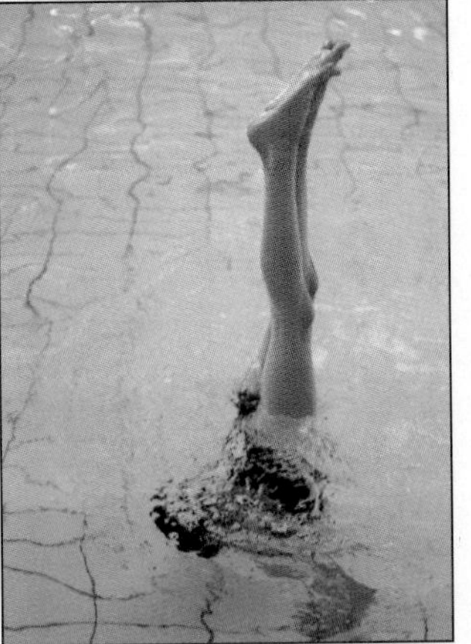

Body awareness, body shape and rotation practices

Within a dive it is necessary to maintain a body tension and shape during the flight and entry. These practices will develop the pupils' awareness of the body.

Practice	Teaching/Coaching Points
Push and glide on front, back and side	Knees bent at wall for strong push Long thin body shape
As above with rotation	Hands clasped one on top of other Head between arms
Changing positions during glide	Tight tuck position, arms round legs Star float shape Pike at waist
Rotating around horizontal and vertical axis	Scull hands to assist rotation Somersault back and forward Tread water and rotate 360 degrees
Push and glide into somersault – front and back	Hold body tension in each part Feet close to seat on somersault Sculling with hands to assist rotation
Push and glide and handstand	Strong bend at hips after push Head down, pull down with arms Legs straight on lift
Handstand, tuck and regain standing	Hold body tension in handstand Keep head still to control handstand Tuck up tight

Springing practices

The main purpose of this group of practices is to encourage the pupils to use their legs to gain maximum height and to develop a spring into the inverted position. Practices should be performed in shallow water – waist depth to shoulder depth.

Practice	Teaching/Coaching Points
Springing high off pool floor	Bend knees Push hard through legs and hips Let legs absorb landing
Spring high and streamline	Hands clasped together Head between arms, body stretched
Springing high to show different shapes	Show shape clearly Make long thin shapes Make tight tucked shapes
Springing to straight and rotating around long axis	Use head and bring arm across body Keep the body streamlined Spring high
Springing and bringing shoulders to meet water	High spring, bring hips up Twist or rotate to bring shoulders down
Springing high and placing hands on pool floor	Lift hips up, heels to seat Hands to replace feet Head down, eyes open
Spring into somersault, forwards or backwards	Arms in "Y" position to start Spring hips up, tuck body tightly Finish in standing position
Springing over or through apparatus (Hoop, stick, float)	Spring into handstand Somersault or shallow glide Lift hips during spring

These early practices may be introduced as contrasting activities in swimming lessons. They should be repeated to give ample time for the pupils to become really confident underwater and able to control their bodies and develop good thrust. Practices should be selected to suit individual abilities. Before moving on to the next stage, all pupils should be confident out of their depth, and able to perform a handstand with ease and control in shallow water.

Feet First Entries and Surface Dives in Deep Water

Once a degree of competence has been achieved with the early practices pupils can then progress to activities from the poolside (water depth 1.8m minimum) and in deep water (water depth 1.5 – 2.0m minimum).

Practices	Teaching/Coaching Points
Feet First Entries	
Stepping to enter the water in stretched position	Toes over the edge Small step forward Body straight for entry, arms by side
Springing from two feet to show shapes in flight:	
a) Long and thin, hands stretched above head	Head in line with body Eyes look slightly up Arms lift forwards and upwards at take off
b) Tucked position in flight	Body extended on take off (as "A") Knees brought up to chest Body outstretched for entry
c)High spring into a twist	Swing the arm across body to twist Keep body straight Head in line but turning with twist

Surface Dive

Push and glide from side underwater and resurface	Feet high on wall to give strong push Head tightly between arms Hold the glide throughout movement
As above but push to surface from pool floor	Strong pike at hips to surface dive Strong downward pull with arms Stretch arms out into streamlined position Curl up and push hard against pool floor
Surface dive to retrieve objects from pool floor	Head pressed down onto chest Straight leg lift to inverted position Streamlined body in descent Push hard against pool floor

Head First Entries

Some pupils may need further guided practices before attempting the plunge dive because they are still fearful of entering the water head first from the poolside. When electing starting positions for diving practices it is preferable to use those from which it is easy to overbalance.

As the following practices are to lead to a plunge dive the angle of entry will be 14° – 20° to the water. This is also necessary for safety purposes where the water is only 1.8 metres in depth.

All of the practices which follow should be executed in a minimum of 1.8m.

Sitting Position

Providing the early confidence practices have been mastered, including a surface dive, it is not generally necessary e.g. to use a sitting dive. But some pupils, particularly adults, find this a comfortable and stable starting position. However, the design of the pool might make the starting position difficult to achieve. For a head first entry it is necessary to lift the body weight from the very stable sitting position; some people achieve this by standing on the trough or rail, which may present a slippery base. It is very difficult to perform in a deck level pool where an astride position is preferable.

The pupils sit on the edge of the pool with their feet resting on the rail or trough. The feet and knees may be together or slightly apart. The arms are raised above the head with the hands gripped tightly. The pupil bends forwards and raises the hips to over-balance into the water. The feet should remain in contact with the rail until the body is submerging. It is a roll into the water. The head should be kept down between the arms to avoid an entry where the pupil may hit the front of their body on the water.

Sitting Position – Key Points

- sit on the edge of the pool
- feet rest on the rail or trough
- arms point forwards and downwards
- head between arms
- bend forwards, raise hips
- overbalance into water

Kneeling Position

The same roll into the water may be taken from a kneeling position. Many people find this an uncomfortable starting position, particularly where the poolside is rough. A lunge dive is probably a more comfortable option. A kneeling position is taken up with one knee close to the pool edge and the toes of the front foot firmly gripping the edge. The toes of the rear foot are curled under to give a base from which to push. With the arms stretched above the head the body rolls forwards to touch the forward knee. As the body overbalances there is a push from the feet and the body stretches out into a glide position underwater.

Kneeling Position – Key Points

- one knee close to edge of pool
- toes of front foot grip edge of pool
- toes of rear foot curled under foot
- kneeling leg alongside of front foot
- arms stretched above head
- body rolls forward

Crouch Position

This position leads easily into the plunge dive and the amount of crouch adopted by the pupil can be gradually reduced as the pupil gains confidence. Crouching on the poolside with the feet together and the knees slightly apart, the toes gripping the edge. The arms are extended above the head with the hands clasped. As the body overbalances there is a push/spring from the feet, the hips are lifted and the body stretches out into a glide position underwater.

Crouch Position – Key Points

- toes grip the edge
- lift hips
- head in
- arms stretched beyond the head pointing forwards
- hands clasped

Lunge Position

Some pupils find this a more comfortable starting position than the kneeling dive. It can also be used as a progression from the kneeling dive as the feet remain in a similar position. One foot is placed at the edge of the pool with toes gripping the edge. The other foot is stretched behind with the toes just touching the floor. The knees are slightly bent and the pupil stretches the arms above the head with the hands clasped. The hands should be pointing forwards. As the body overbalances the rear leg lifts. The pupil pushes against the pool side with the front foot and brings the front leg up to meet the rear leg.

Lunge Position – Key Points

- toes (front foot) grip edge
- lift back leg
- arms stretched beyond the head pointing forwards
- fall into the water
- stretch to entry

The Plunge Dive

This dive is similar to a racing dive required as a start for any prone stroke, and it is a useful shallow dive entry for recreational swimmers. When learning this dive it should be performed into at least 1.8m of water.

Stance – the feet are placed approximately hip width apart with the toes curled over the edge to give a good grip. The knees are bent to give stability and to prepare for the spring. The back is curved with the neck following the curve of the back and the chin lowered slightly to the chest. The eyes look towards the point of entry. The arms hang down loosely from the shoulder. The diver should feel balanced and relaxed.

Take off – the body weight is transferred forward by action/reaction as the arms swing back slightly. As the body overbalances the arms swing forwards strongly giving impetus to the forward movement. There is a vigorous thrust from the feet and legs and extension of the hips, knees, ankles and

toes. The feet drive back against the poolside to give forward and upward momentum.

Flight – after an initial hip lift to give some height to the dive the body extends to a streamlined position. The arms are fully extended beyond the head, which is squeezed between the arms, and is in line with the body. The hands should be clasped together. The line of flight is upwards and outwards. There should be a feeling of stretch from the finger tips to the pointed toes.

Entry – a shallow clean entry should be made. The hands lead into the water followed by the whole body which remains in the extended position until completely submerged. The hands must remain together for the entry, the head between the arms, the legs and feet together and stretched. There should not be any slapping of the water. The streamlined glide should be held after entry. The resurfacing should not be rushed as this can cause a sudden hollowing of the back which may give pain and strain. Full advantage should be taken of the glide to move smoothly into a swimming stroke.

Faults, Causes and Corrections

Many faults in diving arise from lack of confidence. This usually implies that the diver has progressed too quickly to the poolside and needs time to work at shallow water practices, surface dives and jumps. Faults during flight or entry can in most cases be traced to an incorrect take-off. The flight of the dive is determined by the power and angle of the take-off.

Faults	Causes	Corrective Practices
Unbalanced stance	Standing on toes	Check position of feet
	Toes not gripping pool edge	Check position of feet
Lack of power on take-off	Falling too far before thrusting	Practice take-off
	No push against wall	Practice jumps
	Weak or mis-timed arm swing	Re-teach arm swing
	Not bending knees	Practice jumps
Lack of height in initial flight	Falling too far forwards	Practice take-off
	Aiming down instead of up & out	Practice jumps
	Lack of leg thrust	Practice jumps
	Lack of hip lift	Practice surface dives
Lack of body tension in flight	Poor body awareness	Body awareness and body shape practices
	Anxiety about the new skill	Early diving practices
Flat entry	Falling into the water	Springing practices
	Lifting the head	Submerging and surfacing practices
	Lack of spring	Springing practices
Hands apart on entry	Lack of confidence	Early diving practices
Slapping the water on entry	Trying to swim too quickly	Submerging and surfacing practices
	Entry too shallow	Submerging and surfacing practices
Surfacing too quickly	Lifting head and hands too early	Body awareness and body shape practices

CHAPTER 19

STARTS AND TURNS

Introduction

Starts and turns are part of most competitive swimming race. Turns are also necessary when carrying out any kind of swimming activity which involves one or more laps of the pool, e.g. lane swimming, swimming lessons. Effective starting and turning places the swimmer's body in the correct position to commence a swimming stroke. It also means that the swimmer's initial speed from the block or wall is greater than that of swimming, consequently the swimmer is in the fortunate position of decreasing momentum before swimming, rather than trying to increase momentum whilst swimming.

The needs and the aims of the individual must be considered when teaching/coaching a start or a turn. In competitive terms it is all important that a swimmer has both good technique and good speed. Too often a race is lost due to poor start or turn, occasionally a combination of both. In recreational swimming or lessons a good technique is important whereas the speed may be only a minor consideration.

Starts and turns can be developed during swimming lessons or club sessions in a similar way to the development of strokes. Progressive practices at the appropriate level will ensure the skills are developed well. Later, this chapter will give several series of progressions for teaching/coaching starts and turns. The teacher/coach may think that the teaching/coaching of starts and turns is an activity confined to advanced swimming lessons only. More advanced lessons may be the place were the final product is developed, but a large proportion of the introductory work can be done at lessons prior to the advanced level.

A.S.A. Laws

Starts and turns within a swimming race swum under ASA law must be performed in accordance with the current A.S.A. Laws. The teacher/coach and those intending to use the turns in a race situation should ensure they are familiar with the up to date laws.

Competitive Starts

There are a number of key stages involved in introducing a swimmer to a successful competitive start. These stages reflect not only the importance of ensuring the swimmer is safe whilst developing an effective competitive start, but the need for progressive developmental stages:

- successful plunge dive into deep water
- competitive start into deep water
- from a starting block into deep* water
- from side of pool into shallow water*
- from a starting block into shallow water*
- 'Competitive Start' award

*see current ASA Competitive Start Award for appropriate water depth.

ASA Competitive Start Awards

A swimmer performing a competitive start in a race could potentially be diving into the shallow end of a swimming pool. The ASA along with many other bodies concerned with water safety believe that swimmers should demonstrate shallow racing dive competence before being permitted to dive into shallow water from the side or a standard starting block. The ASA's guidance is that such competence should be demonstrated by achieving the standard of the ASA Competitive Start Awards. The teacher/coach should be aware of the content of these awards if they are to become involved in teaching/coaching the Competitive Start Award.

Forward Starts

Butterfly, Breaststroke and Frontcrawl races normally start with a dive from a starting block or poolside. This Chapter will describe:

- the Grab Start
- the Track Start
- the Wind Up Start

Prior to the introduction of the grab start the wind up start was most commonly used. Once the grab start was introduced the simpler mechanics which it employs made it a firm favourite. However, the wind up start has still remained in use, primarily for relay take-overs. On a relay take-over, unlike a normal race start, a swimmer is permitted to move providing the feet are still on the block when the incoming swimmer touches. The wind up start allows the swimmer to take advantage of the arm swing to improve take off velocity.

Stance – the position on the block.

Take Off – the angle of take off will affect the height of flight and consequently the depth of entry. Modern diving technique advocates a high angle of take off to allow a better transfer of momentum from downwards to forwards to occur. When teaching/coaching racing starts the teacher/coach must be constantly aware of the water depth in relation to the swimmer's ability. Reference should be made to the ASA pamphlet *'It's Your Neck'* and the *'ASA Competitive Start Awards'*.

Flight – the movements which are observed in the air.

Entry – the path the body follows into the water.

Transition to Stroke – how a swimmer changes from streamlining to a specific stroke.

Grab Start

Stance – Toes grip the front edge of the starting block or poolside by curling the ends of the toes around the edge.

Feet should be approximately shoulder width apart in a position which the swimmer finds stable and comfortable.

Knees are flexed approximately 30-40°. The swimmer's back is curved and the head is down and looking at the water just beyond the starting block. These three points of technique ensure that the centre of gravity is correctly positioned.

Hands grip the block either inside or outside the swimmer's feet. The position of the hands is usually the choice of the swimmer.

Take Off – The swimmer pulls upwards on the starting block.

This action causes the elbows and knees to flex.

Feet drive the body outward and upward.

Arms extend upwards and forwards and the finger tips point to the water. Finger tips continue to point to the water throughout flight.

As the swimmer is in the initial fall the head is lifted and the eyes look up.

Head drops, eyes look at water just prior to the leg drive being completed.

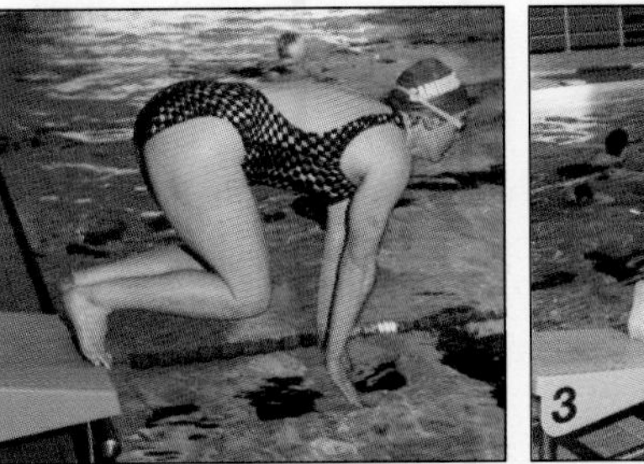

Track Start

Stance – This position resembles that of an athlete on the track.

One foot is on the front edge of the block whilst the other foot is approximately 20-25 cm (8-10") behind.

Knees are flexed, the centre of gravity is slightly further back than in the grab start and the swimmer's weight should be over the front foot. The hands hold the front of the block approximately shoulder width apart.

Head is down and looking at the water just past the starting block.

Take Off – The swimmer pulls upwards on the starting block. This action causes the elbows and knees to flex.

Feet drive the body outwards and upwards. This drive comes mainly from the front foot.

Arms extend upwards and forwards and the finger tips point to the water. Finger tips continue to point to the water throughout flight.

As the swimmer is in the initial fall the head is lifted and the eyes look up.

Head drops, eyes look at water just prior to the leg drive being completed. As the leg drive is completed the front leg is lifted to meet the rear leg.

Wind Up Start

Stance – Toes grip the front edge of the starting block or poolside by circling the ends of the toes around the edge.

Feet should be approximately shoulder width apart in a position which the swimmer finds stable and comfortable.

Knees are flexed approximately 30-40°. The swimmer bends at the waist and the head is tucked between the arms with the eyes looking at the water just beyond the starting block.

The arms are held in front of the swimmer with the fingertips pointing to the water approximately two feet in front of the block.

Take Off – Arms circle backwards in a long arc from their starting point. The arms remain straight and the head is lifted. The legs flex until the knees are bent to approximately 90°. The circular movement is continued round past the hips and ends with the finger tips pointing to the water.

Feet drive the body outwards and upwards as the arm swing is completed.

As the swimmer is in the initial fall the head is lifted and the eyes look up.

Head drops, eyes look at water just prior to the leg drive being completed.

It is clear to see that the stance and take off in each of these dives differ considerably, whilst the flight and entry which are to be described next are very similar.

Flight – The flight forms an arc through the air. Once a swimmer has completed the take off the body will be moving in an upwards and outwards direction with the hands pointing to the water.

As the swimmer reaches the peak of the arc the body then rotates in either a piked or tucked position and the direction of the flight is mainly downwards. The pike is achieved by lowering the head and lifting the hips. The hands should be closer to the water than the feet.

Entry – The entry in to the water should be achieved with as little turbulence as possible in order to minimise drag and ensure the momentum gained during take off and flight is not wasted.

Hands enter first with the remainder of the body following through the same hole.

As the hips enter the swimmer's back is arched and hands lifted towards the surface. This will ensure the transfer of momentum from downwards to forwards. The point at which the swimmer arches the back is very important. If it happens too early the swimmer's feet will hit the water behind the point at which the hands entered, too late and the swimmer will be too deep. The amount of back arch and hand lift is also dependant on which stroke is being swum, and consequently which transition is being used.

Backcrawl Start

Although the Backcrawl start can still be defined as a dive the start or stance position is in the water and restricts the height a swimmer is able to gain during flight.

Stance – The feet should be placed on the wall with the toes below the surface. The feet can be placed at the same level or slightly staggered.

The knees are bent to approximately 70° and the back is rounded with the head tucked into the chest.

The hands hold the starting block in a position which allows the swimmer to keep the knees bent and the back rounded. The elbows should be slightly bent.

Take Off – At the starting signal the elbows flex to pull the swimmer closer to the starting block. This action causes the knee bend to be increased so the seat is closer to the heels. At this point most of the body will be lifted out of the water.

Hands release the block and the head is forced back and slightly up. The push from the feet is in an upwards and outwards direction.

Back is arched and the arms thrown over the water. The throw can be in a straight arc from the starting block to the point of entry or in a semi circular swing around the side of the body keeping hands and arms close to the water surface.

The legs extend and the swimmer leaves the wall with legs extended and ankles extended.

Flight – As in a forward dive the body travels over the water in an arc. After the take off the swimmer will be travelling in an upwards and outwards direction with the whole body streamlined.

The direction of travel is changed as the swimmer arches the back and throws the head back to look at the other end of the pool.

Ideally, the whole of the swimmer should be out of the water at this point.

Entry – The entry is made with the hands first. The hands are together and the head between the arms.

As the hands enter the hips are lifted and as the hips enter the feet are lifted.

On entry the back is straightened and the fingers pointed to the surface in order to transfer momentum into a forwards direction.

Transition to Stroke

After entry the swimmer will take up a streamlined position and allow the body to move through the water as a result of the momentum gained earlier in the start. The speed of the swimmer at this point will probably be greater than race pace.

A successful transition relies on the swimmer changing from dive/start to stroke at precisely the right moment. This is when dive/start speed is reduced to swim speed.

Butterfly – From the streamlined position the swimmer begins to kick in a dolphin action to the surface. As the swimmer approaches the surface the hands and arms move through the propulsive key hole phase of the butterfly arm action. This assists the swimmer in reaching the surface.

The swimmer should break the surface of the water just as the arms are ready to leave the water.

Breaststroke – The swimmer needs to be deeper than on any other stroke to allow for the underwater arm and leg actions which are permitted under A.S.A. Law. As the swimmer reaches race speed the arms pull in a keyhole pattern down to the hips. Once this action is complete the legs kick and the body takes up a streamlined position ready to surface. As the body surfaces the hands may begin the outsweep of the first arm action of the stroke.

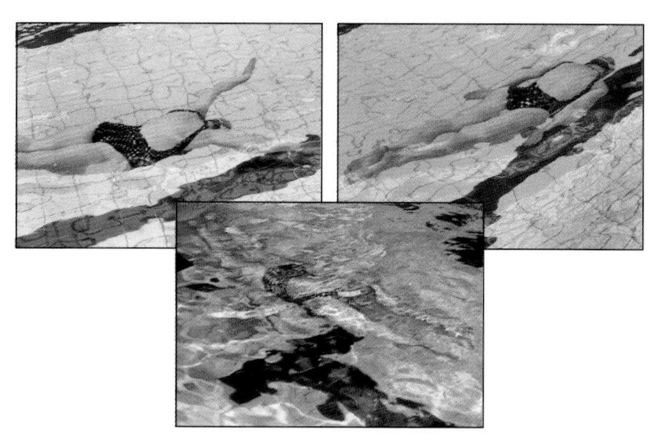

Frontcrawl – This is the shortest of all transitions because the stroke to be swum is the fastest competitive stroke and swimming speed is reached very quickly. From the streamlined position the swimmer begins to kick the legs in either a frontcrawl or butterfly action. As the swimmer nears the surface the propulsive phase of the arm action begins. The swimmer should break the surface as the propelling arm reaches the water surface.

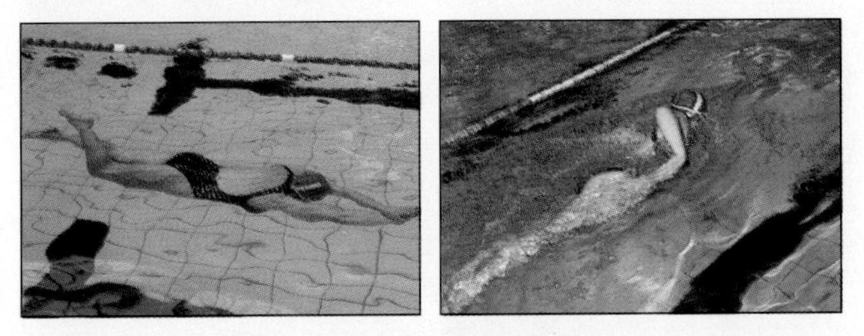

Backcrawl – From the streamlined position the swimmer begins to kick using either a backcrawl leg or dolphin action. As the swimmer nears the surface the propulsive phase of the arm action begins. The transition is complete as the swimmer breaks the surface with the propelling arm ready to begin recovery.

Turns

This section of the chapter will describe the recognised competitive turns for the four competitive strokes. The turns described are, at present, the fastest methods of approaching and leaving the wall within the A.S.A. Laws. All teachers/coaches must remember that these turns are not the only correct methods of turning. There are many other ways which may be simpler than those described i.e. the touch turn on frontcrawl, but are certainly not as efficient.

When describing a turn it is broken down into four sections:

Approach
Touch/Turn
Push Off
Transition to stroke

The transition to stroke has already been explained in detail under the section of this chapter dealing with starts, so this information will not be repeated.

Frontcrawl Turn

Approach – The swimmer approaches the wall at normal swimming speed. As the last over water arm recovery is made prior to turning the head drops and the chin rests on the chest.

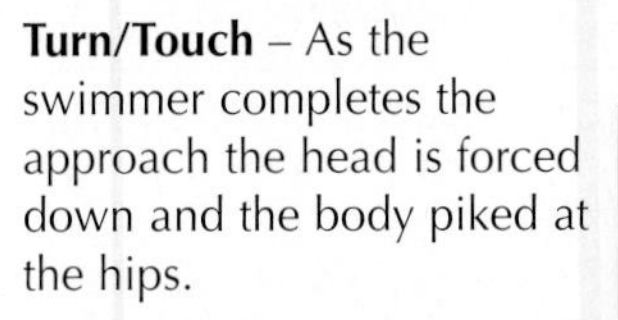

Turn/Touch – As the swimmer completes the approach the head is forced down and the body piked at the hips.

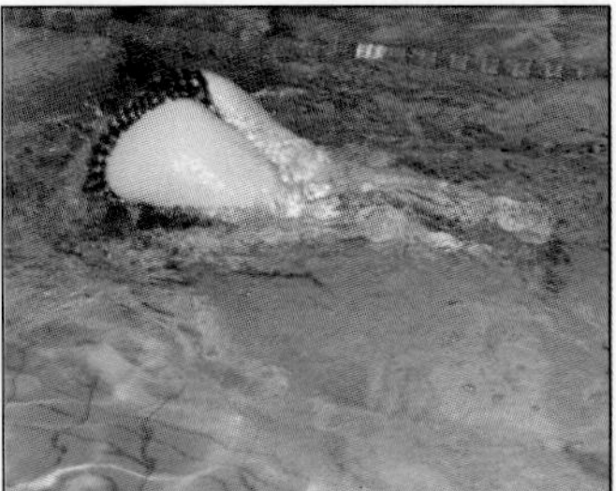

The leading arm pulls down to the hip to assist the rotation and the trailing arm also remains at the swimmer's side.

The legs are tucked into the body to assist with rotation.

Push Off – The feet are planted firmly on the wall with the toes pointing upwards. The swimmer is on the back. The knees should be bent to an angle of approximately 90°.

The hands and arms are extended into a streamlined position above the head.

The swimmer extends the legs into a streamlined position by thrusting powerfully against the wall. The swimmer rotates onto the side or front during this movement.

The swimmer is now in a streamlined position ready to begin the transition to stroke.

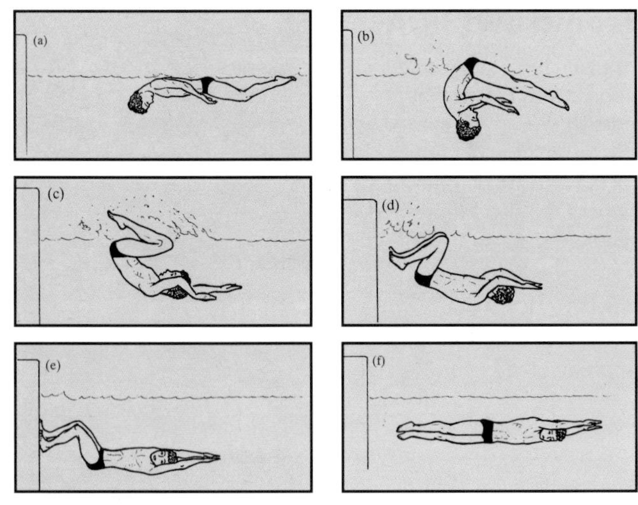

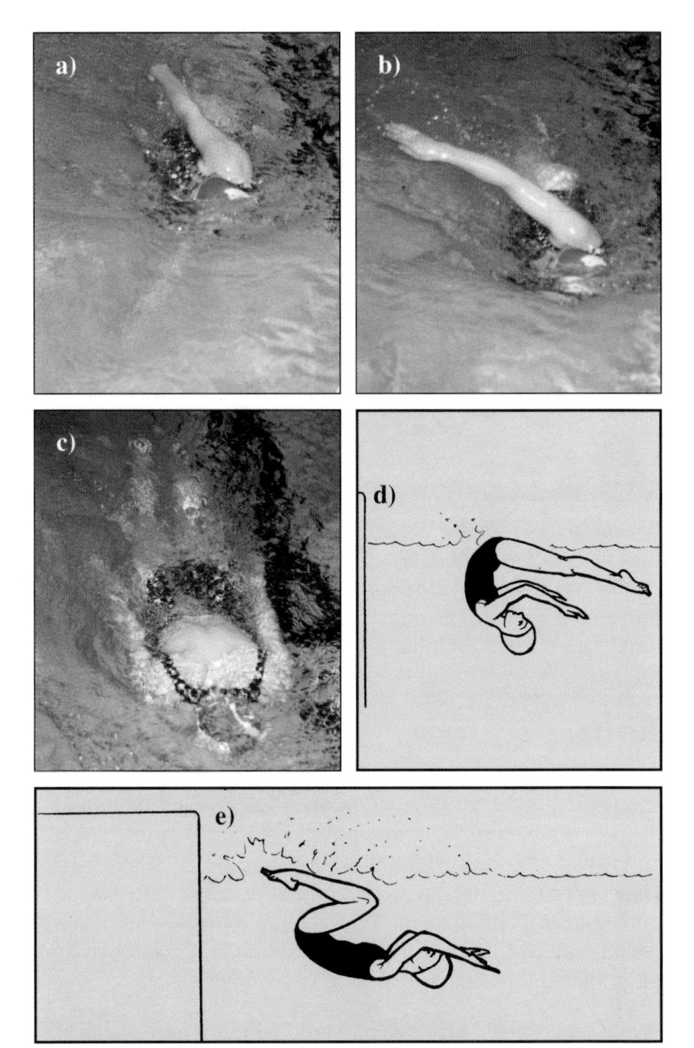

Backcrawl Turn

Approach – The swimmer approaches the wall on the back at normal swimming speed.

On the last full stroke the swimmer crosses the recovering arm over the body and enters it in line with the opposite shoulder. As the arm crosses over the body the swimmer rolls on to the front. The other arm remains at the swimmer's side.

Turn/Touch – From the position on the front the swimmer drops the head and rests the chin on the chest.

The body is piked at the hips and begins a front somersault assisted by the leading hand. The somersault can be executed with the legs in a piked or tucked position.

Push Off – The feet are planted firmly on the wall with the toes pointing upwards. The legs should be bent to an angle of approximately 90°.

The leading arm is extended in front of the head and the other arm moves from the side to meet it.

The swimmer extends the legs into a streamlined position by thrusting powerfully against the wall.
The body leaves the wall with the swimmer in a streamlined position ready to begin the transition.

Breaststroke/Butterfly Turn

Approach – The swimmer approaches the wall at normal swimming speed making adjustments to stroke length on approach in order to make the touch with arms almost at full stretch. The shoulders remain level during the approach.

Touch/Turn – The touch is made with both hands simultaneously. The hands need to make a firm contact with the wall.

As the touch is made the knees bend and the body continues to move towards the wall due to the forward momentum gained during swimming. This causes the elbows to bend.

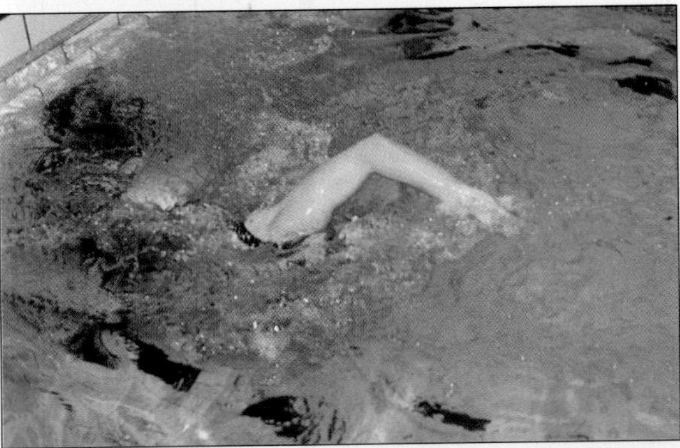

As soon as the touch has been made the swimmer releases one hand from the wall and pulls the elbow back. The head is turned to the same side.
The feet are drawn up under the body and move towards the wall and the other hand is released from the wall and thrown over the water.

During the turning action the swimmer does not turn to face the course. It is a pivoting action.

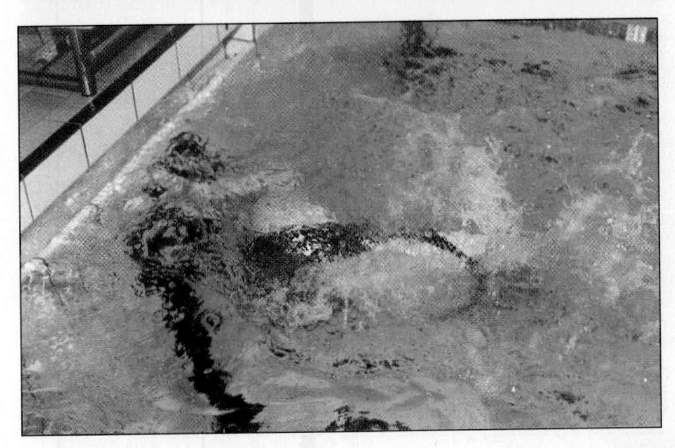

Push Off – The feet are planted firmly on the wall with the toes pointing sideways and downwards.

The body drops below the water surface and the swimmer's hands meet in an extended position above the head.

The swimmer extends the legs into a streamlined position by thrusting powerfully against the wall. As the swimmer leaves the wall the body is rotated on to the front.

The body leaves the wall with the swimmer on the breast ready to begin the transition to stroke.

Practices to Develop Starts and Turns

When developing any skill it is important for the teacher/coach to understand the progressive stages involved in developing the completed technique. Starts and turns are complex skills incorporating a number of different movement patterns in a specific order. For this reason, the teacher/coach should be aware of the possible progressions which can be used to develop the whole skill. The tables which follow give a number of practices which will help to develop starts and turns effectively. Through experience the teacher/coach should be able to add his own progressions to those listed.

Forward Start

Practice	Area to be developed
Poolside practice away from edge of pool	Stance
Poolside practice on edge of pool or starting block	Stance
Jumps from poolside, spring up and out	Take Off
Jumps from starting block over a stick	Take Off
Dive and pike in the air	Flight
Dive and pike and straighten in the air	Flight
Dive through a hoop in deep water	Entry
Push and glide and streamline	Transition
Push and glide into transition specific to stroke	Transition

Backcrawl Start

Practice	Area to be developed
Push and glide ready position	Stance
Push and glide on back over water	Take Off
Push and glide on back over water throwing arms	Take Off
Push and glide over water holding body tense	Flight
Push and glide and arch body	Flight
Push and glide under water	Transition
Push and glide and kick	Transition
Push and glide and kick and pull	Transition

Frontcrawl Turn

Practice	Area to be developed
Swim to wall counting strokes	Approach
Forward somersaults from standing	Turn
Forward somersaults from swimming	Turn
Forward somersaults at wall from swimming	Touch/Turn
Push and glide on back underwater	Push Off
Push and glide on back and rotate to front	Push Off
Push and glide and kick underwater on front	Transition
Push and glide, kick and pull with one arm only	Transition

Backcrawl Turn

Practice	Area to be developed
Swim to wall counting strokes from flags	Approach
Swim and lateral roll every six strokes	Approach
Forward somersaults from standing	Turn
Forward somersaults from swimming	Turn
Forward somersaults at wall from swimming	Touch/Turn
Push and glide on back underwater	Push Off
Push and glide and kick underwater	Transition
Push and glide, kick and pull with one arm only	Transition

Breaststroke Turn

Practice	Area to be developed
Swim to wall, two handed touch	Approach/Touch
Swim to wall, touch with straight arms	Approach/Touch
At wall, pivoting and tucking from stretched position	Turn
At wall, from pivot, arm over water and submerge	Turn
Swim to wall, pivot and tuck from stretched position	Touch/Turn
Swim to wall, pivot and tuck and submerge	Touch/Turn
Push and glide on side underwater	Push Off
Push and glide and pull to hips	Transition
Push and glide, pull to hips and kick	Transition
Push and glide, pull to hips, kick and streamline	Transition

Butterfly Turn

Practice	Area to be developed
Swim to wall, two handed touch	Approach/Touch
Swim to wall, touch with straight arms	Approach/Touch
At wall, pivoting and tucking from stretched position	Turn
At wall, from pivot, arm over water and submerge	Turn
Swim to wall, pivot and tuck from stretched position	Touch/Turn
Swim to wall, pivot and tuck and submerge	Touch/Turn
Push and glide on side underwater	Push Off
Push and glide and kick underwater	Transition
Push and glide, kick and begin propulsive arm stroke	Transition
Push and glide, kick, arm stroke and surface	Transition

Faults, Causes and Corrections

It is essential that the teacher/coach can identify faults, determine the cause and apply the appropriate correction. There is not always a simple answer as there may be a number of causes related to the same fault.

The information which follows identifies many of the more common faults in starts and turns provides possible causes and suggests the area and type of practices which may help in correcting the fault. Specific practices/drills are not listed for each fault. The teacher/coach needs to identify the type of practices/drills to be used and select the specific practice which is most appropriate for the pupil.

When the teacher/coach uses the practices/drills listed in a corrective manner he should always give teaching/ coaching points, relating to the fault, which provide a focus for the swimmer.

Forward Start

Fault	Cause	Corrective Practices
Hands and feet enter at same time	Hips and feet not lifted in flight	Flight practices
Head up as hands enter	Head not dropped after take off	Take off practices
Swimmer enters water flat	No upwards push off	Take off practices

Backcrawl Start

Fault	Cause	Corrective Practices
Pushing off on surface of water	Low stance position in water	Stance practices
	Pushing with legs before throwing arms over water	Take off practices
Feet slip down wall on take off	Feet too low on the wall	Stance practices
Going too deep after entry	Head thrown back too far in flight	Flight practices
Arms pulled to sides after entry	Incorrect order of movements in transition	Transition practices

Frontcrawl Turn

Fault	Cause	Corrective Practices
Turning too far away from wall	Not able to judge distance from wall	Approach practices
	Fear of hitting feet on wall	Approach practices
Turning too close to wall	Not able to judge distance from wall	Turn practices
Lifting head on approach	Looking for the wall prior to turning	Approach practices
Feet not planted evenly on wall	Swimmer opening up during somersault	Turn practices
	Disorientation during somersault	Turn practices
Arms by side on push off	Arms kept at sides during somersault	Turn/Push off practices
Both arms pulled to sides immediately after push off	Incorrect order to movements in transition	Push Off/Transition practices

Backcrawl Turn

Fault	Cause	Corrective Practices
Turning too far away from wall	Miscounting strokes from flags	Approach practices
	Fear of hitting feet on wall	Approach practices
Turning too close to wall	Miscounting strokes from flags	Turn practices
Lifting head on approach	Looking for the wall prior to turning	Approach practices
Kicking or pulling whilst on front	Not a continuous turning action	Approach/Turn practices
Feet not planted evenly on wall	Swimmer opening up during somersault	Turn practices
	Disorientation during somersault	Turn practices
Arms by side on push off	Arms kept at sides during somersault	Turn/Push off practices
Both arms pulled to sides immediately after push off	Incorrect order of movements in transition	Push Off/Transition practices

Breaststroke Turn

Fault	Cause	Corrective Practices
One handed touch	Beginning turning movement too early	Approach/Touch practices
Pivoting 180° in turn to face the direction of swimming	Not pivoting onto side in turn	Turn practices
Throwing arm over head before pushing off	Incorrect order of movements in turning action	Turn practices
Pushing off too close to surface	Not allowing body to submerge during turning motion	Turn/Push off practices
Pushing off too deep	Incorrect position of feet on wall	Turn/Push off practices
Too many arm/leg actions during transition	Too deep on push off	Transition practices
	Incorrect order of movements during transition	Transition practices

Butterfly Turn

Fault	Cause	Corrective Practices
One handed touch	Beginning turning movement too early	Approach/Touch practices
Pivoting 180° in turn to face the direction of swimming	Not pivoting onto side in turn	Turn practices
Throwing arm over head before pushing off	Incorrect order of movements in turning action	Turn practices
Beginning underwater arm pull immediately after push off	Unaware of importance of streamlining	Push Off/Transition practices

CHAPTER 20

PRINCIPLES OF TRAINING

Introduction

In the initial stages of swimming teaching/coaching and stroke development the teacher/coach spends the larger part of each lesson developing techniques and skills in order to achieve a level of proficiency which allows the swimmer to perform each skill repeatedly with the minimum amount of deterioration. The focus during the progressions has been almost wholly on the techniques used.

Throughout this period of development the swimmer has also begun to develop physical conditioning to enable the continuation of skill development. As the swimmer progresses to the next stage of participation in the sport of swimming it is now important that the physical conditioning is an integral part of their programme. This chapter focuses on the organisation of such sessions, the underpinning principles involved in physical development and the structuring of sessions which permit physical development to occur.

The Participant

Individuals may choose to undertake physical conditioning training for a varied number of reasons, the main ones are probably:

- to participate in competition
- to improve or maintain fitness
- to permit participation in other water sports
- to complement their training in another sport

The participant may be a child or an adult of either sex. Regardless of their reason for participating the same considerations should be made when planning a programme of work.

This chapter focuses particularly on those in the early stages of competition and those wishing to improve their basic fitness level.

Organisation of Sessions

As in any teaching/coaching situation there is no one right way to organise a training session, many ways are acceptable and successful, however there are some basic guidelines which the teacher/coach should follow:

- each swimmer requires enough space to swim reasonably continuously without interruption. The most common method of achieving this is by using lengthways lanes in the pool.
  The swimmers can be organised in a chain formation with appropriate intervals (usually 5 secs) between. If a number of lanes are swimming using this method it is normal to organise them in a clockwise, anti-clockwise rotation to maintain safety.
- each swimmer needs to be able to measure defined rest intervals and work periods. This is normally achieved by using a pace clock located around the pool.
- each swimmer needs to be able to carry out the appropriate starts and turns for the stroke they are swimming. The inclusion of equipment such as starting blocks and backstroke flags permit the swimmer to achieve this.
- each swimmer should be placed in a lane with swimmers of similar training ability. This is often achieved through a series of time trials which permit assessment of swimmers' standards. It is normal for the weakest swimmers to be placed in the outside lanes and the strongest in the centre lanes.

The underpinning Principles of Development

A number of basic principles underpin the development of physical conditioning. If sessions are planned with an understanding of these principles then improvement should follow. An understanding of these principles along with some basic information about the swimmer should permit the teacher/coach to write a useful session plan.

Training Principles

These principles are common to all sports, all aspects of physical fitness and all categories of person. A variety of publications have defined a number of training principles adding and subtracting items from the list from time to time.

This list includes the main principles but others can be found if required:

Progressive overload
Adaptation
Specificity
Reversibility
Underload

Progressive Overload
Subjecting a swimmer to a workload to which the body is not accustomed
In order for steady improvement to take place over a prolonged period it is necessary to subject a swimmer to progressive overload. Progressive overload can be implemented in three ways:

- frequency – Number of sessions attended per week
- duration – How long each session lasts
- intensity – The level at which the work is undertaken

Adaptation
To adapt to an increased stress
The human body is an amazing machine capable of adapting to new stresses placed upon it quite quickly. It is important for the teacher/coach to recognise when adaptation has taken place, in order to overload progressively on a continuous basis. It is also essential that the teacher/coach looks for signs of failing adaptation. This can occur if the overload is too much, too soon. Some of the more common signs of failing adaptation are:

Injuries
Stroke Breakdown
Illness
Demotivation

If any of these signs are spotted, the teacher/coach should adjust the workload accordingly to permit the swimmer recovery and allow progressive overload again.

Specificity
To be specific with regard to the energy systems to be trained or the muscle groups to be used

Later this chapter will look in more detail at physical conditioning for endurance (training the aerobic energy system) and speed (training the anaerobic energy systems). If a teacher/coach wishes to improve their swimmer's ability to swim a long distance on frontcrawl the swimmer must do some specific work in both of these areas, as well as the general fitness and stroke development programme. The higher the level reached, the more important this becomes.

Reversibility
"Use it or lose it"
Just in the same way the body adapts to a greater workload it also adapts to a lesser workload. The teacher/coach may have personal experience of being involved in exercise on a regular basis and finding that his fitness levels had decreased after a period of inactivity.

Underload
A workload which is below that to which the body is accustomed
Sometimes it is important to deliberately underload swimmers in order that a more specific focus can be given to other areas e.g. stroke mechanics and skills, or to permit swimmers to warm up and recover.

Early Competition

The principles already mentioned in this chapter underpin all of the training requirements of a swimmer. The teacher/coach should have a good understanding of these principles before attempting to understand the other areas involved in the teaching/coaching of swimmers of early competitive level and above.

Developing Technique

The development of swimming technique begins at a very early stage, shortly after the swimmer is able to achieve front and back paddle. Technique development should continue from this point onwards until such time as the swimmer decides not to be involved in an organised teaching/coaching environment. The teacher/coach may believe that once the basic technique is established no further focus on this is required and all the swimmer's efforts can be concentrated on developing physical conditioning. This is not the case, any high level competitive swimmer will be able to recall spending time on the development of technique throughout competitive training.

Prior to the early competition stage, activities used to develop technique are referred to as practices. At the early competition stage there is a tendency for these activities to be called drills. This is because they combine technique work and conditioning as opposed to the emphasis being on technique only.

The teacher/coach will find that he is mainly concerned with perfecting a technique and adapting to suit the individual swimmer's needs and desires to swim quickly. Technique also deteriorates with fatigue so consequently it must be carefully monitored whilst the swimmer is performing physical conditioning work.

Stroke Length and Stroke Rate

The other aspect which needs to be considered at this stage is the Stroke Length and Stroke Rate of the swimmer as these provide a measure of the swimmer's efficiency.

Stroke Length – distance the swimmer travels with each propulsive arm movement

To calculate the stroke length the number of strokes should be counted for a length. The length of the pool should then be divided by the number of strokes:
The swimmer takes 16 strokes for 25m
25 divided by 16 = 1.5625m

The swimmer travels 1.5625m with every stroke

Stroke Rate – number of strokes performed in a minute

To calculate the stroke rate sixty seconds (1 minute) is divided by the time taken for the strokes and multiplied by the number of strokes.

The swimmer takes 16 strokes in 20 secs

60 secs divided by 20 secs = 3 secs

16 strokes x 3 secs = 48 strokes per min.

Repeated measuring of stroke length and stroke rate allows the teacher/coach to identify improvement in efficiency. Activities such as stroke counting can be used to help to improve stroke rate, and swimmers seem to find this particular activity enjoyable.

Endurance/Speed Continuum

Swimming pool events in competition may range from a 25m swim in a relay race to a 1500m freestyle event. Clearly the length of time taken for these events differs enormously. After reading Chapter 9 the teacher/coach will appreciate that all of the energy systems will need to be trained to assist a swimmer to compete effectively as they are all used at various times in the different events available to the swimmer.

When considering how to plan a number of training sessions the teacher/coach needs to understand the Endurance/Speed Continuum. The continuum is like a ruler, with speed at one end and endurance at the other, the points in between being a combination of both, with a greater or lesser degree of speed and endurance, dependent on where they fall on the ruler. The competitive swimming events could be plotted onto this ruler as indicated below:

Clearly a swimmer who wished to specialise in 1500m events would need to do a large percentage of their training at the endurance end of the continuum. The early competitive level swimmer needs to experience a combination of different types of training along the continuum to assist their development in all areas.

Developing Speed

The ability to swim at speed whilst maintaining a good technique.

There are two main types of work to develop speed:

Sprinting (ATP-CP Energy System) – Distances up to 25m
Speed Endurance (Lactic Acid System) – Distances between 25m – 200m

There are certain features which should be adhered to when planning a set of work to develop speed in these two areas. Learning the features of each type of work will not only permit the teacher/coach to prepare work of this nature but will also mean that he will be able to identify this type of work in a swimming schedule.

Sprint Training

- maximum distance of swim 25m
- 95% – 100% effort
- rest interval between 20 secs – 1 min
- length of sprint set – maximum 15 mins
- Pulse rate – not relevant

Speed Endurance

- swim distance between 25m – 200m
- 85% – 95% effort
- rest interval between 30 secs – 3 mins
- length of speed endurance set – maximum 20 mins
- pulse rate 170 – maximum

Developing Endurance

The ability to swim a long distance whilst maintaining a good technique

Endurance work trains the aerobic energy system. Within one training session it could be at a range of different intensities, dependent on whether the teacher/coach wants:

- to improve the swimmers endurance
- to maintain current endurance levels
- to allow the swimmer to prepare for a swim (warm up)
- to allow the swimmer to recover from a swim (cool down)

The amount of effort to be used by the swimmer will determine what benefit is achieved from the swim. As for the development of speed, endurance swimming training displays certain features:

- swim distance between 25m – 2000m
- 70% – 85% effort
- rest interval of between 5 – 30 secs
- minimum length of endurance set – 30 mins
- pulse rate – 100 – 180

Preparing a Session

When the swimming teacher/coach begins to prepare a session, or a series of sessions, for a group of early competitive level swimmers it is useful for a test swim to be carried out. This will permit the teacher/coach to set training distances and intensities of work to the swimmer's capabilities. There are a number of recognised test swims to assess the endurance capability of swimmers. This chapter gives details of the two main swims used. Further types of testing can be found in *'ASA Teaching and Coaching – Level 2'*.

Time/Distance Swim

This is normally referred to as a "T Swim". It can cover any time from 5 minutes upwards but for competition swimmers a T20 or T30 is most common.

A swimmer will swim for a specified period of time at approximately 80% effort. The swimmer should be able to maintain an even pace throughout the time period. The number of lengths achieved is recorded.

From this information the teacher/coach can work out the velocity of the swimmer and utilise this information to plan swims accordingly.

Distance/Time Swim

A set distance is swum and the time recorded for this distance. As with the time/distance swim, it permits the teacher/coach to assess the velocity of the swimmer and plan

sessions as appropriate.
Once an assessment of the swimmer's capabilities has been made the teacher/coach is almost ready to prepare the session. The only additional information that is needed at this stage is the aim of the session, i.e., to improve endurance, and the length of the session.

DIRT

When the teacher/coach begins to plan a session for an early competitive swimmer there are a series of variables which assist the teacher to produce a meaningful session. These variables can be easily remembered by using the numonic "DIRT":

D –	Distance	– Distance covered on each swim
I –	Interval	– Interval of rest taken between each swim
R –	Repetition	– The number of times the swim is repeated
T –	Target	– The target intensity for each swim

Adjusting these variables allow the teacher/coach to change the emphasis of the session from speed to endurance:

Speed	4 x 50m	Frontcrawl	Rest: 1 min	Target: 95% effort
Endurance	12 x 50m	Frontcrawl	Rest: 10 secs	Target: 75% effort

The variables also allow the teacher/coach to progressively overload the swimmer, this is done by changing a number of the variables to increase the overload:

Speed	4 x 50m	Frontcrawl	Rest: 45 secs	Target: 95% effort
Endurance	16 x 50m	Frontcrawl	Rest: 10 secs	Target: 75% effort

Finally, the variables also allow the teacher/coach to add variety to the sessions whilst still achieving the aim

Endurance	8 x 25m	Frontcrawl	Rest: 5 secs	Target: 75% effort
	4 x 50m	Frontcrawl	Rest: 10 secs	Target: 80% effort
	8 x 25m	Frontcrawl	Rest: 15 secs	Target: 85% effort

Target Times

It is desirable and beneficial for swimmers to be set target times during training sessions. This not only gives them a goal to work towards but also allows the teacher/coach and swimmer to monitor that the intensity of work matches the intended level.

The simplest way of setting a target time is to calculate it, using the swimmers personal best time and the percentage effort to be used:

Personal Best	=	*90 seconds for 100m*
Percentage of Effort	=	*75%*

This is 25% slower than the maximum effort used to achieve the personal best.

25% of 90 seconds	=	*22.5 secs*

Personal Best + 25%	=	*Target Time*
90 secs + 22.5 secs	=	*112.5 secs = 1.52.5*

Turnaround Times

If every individual swimmer in a lane was to be given a varying target time and all swimmers were allocated the same rest interval the teacher/coach would soon find that the lane discipline deteriorated rapidly, as all swimmers would be starting and finishing swims at different times.

The common way the teacher/coach overcomes this is to set a turnaround time. This time is equal to the swim time and rest time added together. The advantage of the teacher/coach using a swim and rest time is that it permits all swimmers in the lane to start each swim at the same time (allowing for the five seconds intervals between swimmers). The disadvantage is that the swimmer at the front of the lane will, inevitably, receive more rest than the swimmer at the back of the lane.

A Training Schedule

This is normally broken down into sections in a similar way to a session plan:

Example breakdown for 1 hour session

Warm Up –	10/15 mins –	Easy swim to prepare swimmers muscles for

remainder of session.

Main Set – 20/30 mins – The main focus for this part of the session may be one of the following:
* to develop technique
* to develop endurance
* to develop speed

Sub Set – 15/20 mins – This part of the programme should complement the work done in the main set. In addition to using this section for technique, speed or endurance it can be used for sectional work (kicking and pulling) or start and turn development.

A sample training schedule is included in this chapter to assist the teacher/coach in understanding the layout and content.

Summary

In reality, working with swimmers at the early stages of competitive swimming is very similar to the basic teaching/coaching of swimmers with a swimming lesson environment. The teacher/coach needs to understand the principles underpinning physical conditioning and the training methods used to achieve the varying physical requirements of the body. This information, coupled with a knowledge of the swimmers, should permit any teacher/coach to produce a simple, effective schedule with reasonable ease.

Training Schedule – Early Club Level Swimmers

Aerobic Work – Back, Breast, Frontcrawl
Technique Work – Frontcrawl
Skill Work – Frontcrawl Tumble Turn

Warm Up

6 x 25m	Frontcrawl	R.10 secs	
2 x 50m	Choice Kick	R.15 secs	
200m	Choice		(450)

Main Set

7 x 100m
1) 75m Breaststroke, 25m Frontcrawl
2) 50m Breaststroke, 50m Frontcrawl
3) 25m Breaststroke, 75m Frontcrawl
4) 100m Frontcrawl
5) 25m Backcrawl, 75m Frontcrawl
6) 50m Backcrawl, 50m Frontcrawl
7) 75m Backcrawl, 25m Frontcrawl

Rest 5 seconds after breaststroke, 30 seconds after frontcrawl

(1250)

Sub Set

16 x 25m Frontcrawl drills
4) single arm
4) catch up
4) breath every 4
4) fists closed, fists open

6 x 25m Frontcrawl
3) distance per stroke
3) sprint

(1800)

Skills

Frontcrawl tumble turns, focusing on the approach and turning movement.

NOTES

NOTES